Bad Guys, Bullets, and Boat Chases

UNIVERSITY PRESS OF FLORIDA

Florida A&M University, Tallahassee
Florida Atlantic University, Boca Raton
Florida Gulf Coast University, Ft. Myers
Florida International University, Miami
Florida State University, Tallahassee
New College of Florida, Sarasota
University of Central Florida, Orlando
University of Florida, Gainesville
University of North Florida, Jacksonville
University of South Florida, Tampa
University of West Florida, Pensacola

BAD GUYS, BULLETS, AND BOAT CHASES

TRUE STORIES OF FLORIDA GAME WARDENS

BOB H. LEE

University Press of Florida
Gainesville · Tallahassee · Tampa · Boca Raton
Pensacola · Orlando · Miami · Jacksonville · Ft. Myers · Sarasota

Photographs have been reproduced by permission of John Delzell (page 43); Lance Ham
(page 73); Donnie Hudson (pages 59, 77, 81, 85, 87, and 88); Gray Leonhard (page 2); Curtis
Lucas (page 112); Dwain Mobley (page 188); Jon Proctor (page 4); Vann Streety (page 230);
and Mike Thomas (pages 97 and 108).

This book may be available in an electronic edition.

22 21 20 19 18 17   6 5 4 3 2 1

Library of Congress Control Number: 2016948258
ISBN 978-0-8130-6244-0

The University Press of Florida is the scholarly publishing agency for the State University
System of Florida, comprising Florida A&M University, Florida Atlantic University, Florida
Gulf Coast University, Florida International University, Florida State University, New College
of Florida, University of Central Florida, University of Florida, University of North Florida,
University of South Florida, and University of West Florida.

University Press of Florida
15 Northwest 15th Street
Gainesville, FL 32611-2079
http://upress.ufl.edu

To all Florida game wardens, before, now, and after

CONTENTS

AUTHOR'S NOTE

Many years ago, a young hippie gal sidled up to me in a convenience store. Clad in an ankle-length cotton skirt, barefoot, with a disheveled mop of waist-length blond hair, she fixed me with a glazed stare and asked, "Who do you kill?"

I thought I'd have a little fun with her and replied in my best deadpan, "We don't kill anyone unless they need killing."

"But, why," she said, clearly not seeing the gallows humor in my remark, "would you need to kill anyone if all you do is check fishing licenses?"

Indeed.

There are times when a job description cannot be summed up in a fifteen-second sound bite. In this book, I aim to dispel the notion that game wardens are mere license checkers. Too many times in my thirty-year career as a conservation lawman have I been approached by folks who ask what it is that we do. Rarely would a city cop, sheriff's deputy, or state trooper be on the receiving end of that kind of question.

After an adrenaline-fueled, high-speed nighttime boat chase on the St. Johns River, I first came to realize why what we do is often not grasped by the general populace. It was during the fall of 1978, my first full year as a rookie game warden in northeast Florida. I was alone, without backup, stuck with a clunker radio whose dependability relied more on whimsy than sound construction.

The bad guys were running blacked-out and took it to another level of danger when they set a suicide course dead center into an unlit channel marker. With only a few feet to spare, they whipped around the rusty steel I-beam support and quickly swung back onto their original course. It was a trick, a setup, to sucker me into crashing. You see, my headlamp bulb had blown, and for the moment I was running with only the faint glow of starlight to guide me. I did take comfort, however, in the guttural roar emitted by my 200 HP Johnson. It held a distinct speed advantage over the 90 HP Mercury strapped to the transom of the fleeing boat. Not being able to see where I was going was my main problem of the moment.

The race continued across a shallow sandbar and into a narrow gap between two islands. I stood up and finally managed to wrestle a flashlight from the storage compartment beneath my seat. I accelerated, hopped over their trailing wake, and brought my patrol boat alongside. I thought we'd both had enough fun for one night and decided to end the chase. I began crowding them, gunwale to gunwale, fiberglass crunching on fiberglass, gradually forcing them toward shore. In the bottom of their boat lay a pile of dead raccoons they'd taken illegally with a gun and light, my initial reason to attempt a stop.

The fleeing vessel was a sixteen-foot commercial fishing skiff occupied by a driver and a passenger who was seated amidships. Over the high-pitched whine of raging outboards, I shouted for the passenger to place his hands on top of his head. He complied, briefly. Then he reached for a 12-gauge pump shotgun lying next to him on a flat-board wooden seat. At the same time, I warily kept track of another gun, a shiny, big-barreled revolver sliding around on the blood-splattered deck near the driver's feet.

I was in a real pickle. I had to steer the boat with one hand and hold a flashlight in the other. I desperately needed a third hand to hold my service revolver.

Necessity, as they say, is the mother of invention.

I dropped my left elbow down onto the narrow rim of the steering wheel, using the soft indentation of my funny bone to guide it, while precariously holding the flashlight in my left hand. I drew my .357

Magnum Smith & Wesson with my right hand and placed the barrel right behind the passenger's head as the two boats flew through the night. I shouted a stream of blue-black expletives that ended with his brains being blown out if he didn't comply.

Ignoring my commands, he dropped his hands toward the gun.

I began to take up slack on the trigger.

At two o'clock in the morning, moisture in the form of dew coats every conceivable surface on the interior of a vessel. My left elbow's purchase on the steering wheel was already tenuous when it slipped, casting the flashlight beam into the sky for just a millisecond, before I could illuminate the suspect again.

In that brief moment, he'd managed to knock the gun into the drink. It was close. The closest I have ever come to shooting someone. But once I got them stopped, and secured the handgun and offenders, I took a moment to look around. There was no one there, just the twinkling of distant house lights from across the river at Brown's Landing Boat Ramp, three miles south of Palatka. No newspaper reporters, television crews, or documentary filmmakers were present to witness the event. And that tends to be the way it is with a lot of game and fish cases: just you and the suspects alone in the dark, in the middle of nowhere, with some who would cheerfully kill you if they thought they could get away with it.

In the seventeen chapters chronicled in this book, I pull the curtain back to give a behind-the-scenes look at the often misunderstood world of conservation law enforcement. Four of the stories involve me, but the majority of the chapters are told in the third person and are based on dozens of recorded interviews with game wardens, as well as the examination of criminal case files that include written statements, digital recordings, videotaped interviews, video surveillance tapes, and newspaper articles. Whenever possible, I tried to visit the scene to get a feel for the terrain.

In order to enliven the manuscript and engage the reader, I employed the techniques of creative nonfiction writing. I've made minor adjustments to timelines, geographic locations, and condensed storylines to provide a better narrative flow. Most of the poachers' names are fictitious, and I've altered their physical descriptions. In a few cases, I've taken the liberty of using composite characters. In the more serious stories (for example, the attempted murder of a law enforcement officer), I use the actual defendants' names. Dialogue and scenes are often re-created from memories and thus may not depict exactly how things transpired. Any mistakes are solely my own.

The stories span the full breadth of peninsular Florida. From Live Oak, twenty-two miles south of the Georgia line; south to the Everglades; over to the enormous cattle ranches west of Lake Okeechobee; and then on to the rich inshore fishing grounds in the Big Pine Island region of southwest Florida's Gulf Coast. In between, we visit the upper Kissimmee River marsh, Lake Apopka, Brevard County, Volusia County, Lake Ashby, Marion County, St. Augustine, Dixie County, and finally my home turf in Putnam County. The chapters are presented in roughly chronological order from 1972 to 2011.

Be prepared, too, for dramatic and sudden theme shifts from one chapter to the next. Variety, after all, is the spice of life, and that's what I kept foremost in mind when selecting the stories to research and write for this book.

Lastly, all fish and wildlife officers are referred to as "game wardens." This form of address is widely recognized throughout the United States and internationally as the accepted generic name for conservation law enforcement officers.

FLORIDA'S CONSERVATION LAW ENFORCEMENT AGENCIES

Understanding the complete history of Florida's conservation law enforcement agencies can be like untangling a ball of knotted twine. To spare the reader, I offer this brief summary.

The Game and Fresh Water Fish Commission (GFC)—the agency I originally began with in 1977—had constitutional authority to pass laws for the protection of freshwater fish and wildlife, overseen by a five-member commission or policy-forming board. This process was efficient and worked well for the protection of species under consideration. Best of all, it required no review or approval from the Florida Legislature.

Concurrently, the Florida Marine Patrol—under the Florida Marine Commission—was in charge of protecting coastal areas and marine species (saltwater fish, sea turtles, and manatees). They had no constitutional authority to pass laws. Instead, they had to go through the arduous procedure of submitting new laws to the legislature for final approval and passage. This process was open to influence by special-interest groups like the commercial fishing lobby and proved to be an inefficient and unwieldy system.

On July 1, 1999, the two agencies merged under the constitutional umbrella of the GFC to form the Florida Fish and Wildlife Conservation Commission (FWC). Overnight, this brand-new supersized conservation agency led the nation in the number of conservation law enforcement officers employed by any one state—more than eight hundred today. All have full police powers and statewide jurisdiction.

(The agency as a whole has 2,100-plus full-time employees; the rest work in different divisions responsible for research and management of Florida's diverse wildlife and public wildlife management areas.)

FWC officers and investigators enforce boating safety laws and protect fish, wildlife, and the environment, as well as Florida's residents and visitors. The investigations unit can target hard-core commercial violators by conducting long-term undercover (covert) operations. They are also responsible for inspecting personal and commercial native and exotic wildlife facilities as well as investigating hunting and boating accidents and environmental crimes.

The FWC is a complex agency with many tentacles. Those who wish to learn more may go to the website myfwc.com.

1

FLIGHT 401

On the clear moonless night of December 29, 1972, a young rookie game warden sat behind the steering wheel of a light-green 1969 Plymouth four-door sedan with a blue "gumball" emergency light mounted on the rooftop. His foot pressed lightly against the accelerator pedal as he inched down the L28 levee with the headlights out. Loose chunks of lime rock cracked and popped under the tires as he crawled ahead.

From his vantage point atop the levee, Gray Leonhard had a commanding view across thousands of square miles of darkened marsh. An elevation of only eight feet felt like being on a hilltop in the Everglades. The night was a balmy 72 degrees, the mosquitoes surprisingly sparse. The lack of biting insects allowed him to roll the driver's window down to better hear a shot fired from a poacher's gun.

Gray moved the shifter into park, cut the motor, and stepped out. Standing by the open door, he carefully scanned the unbroken horizon with a pair of wide-lensed binoculars.

The young warden felt a sense of mission as he looked out into the black swamp, the mystique of a job where cunning and stealth often determine the winner. The high-stakes game of cat and mouse played with real-life backwoods characters is a seductive one.

Warden Gray Leonhard sits atop his patrol airboat in the Everglades, 1972.

That notion was first instilled in him by a chance encounter with two game wardens five years before. He happened upon them one day, quite by accident, while they were hidden in the woods on stakeout next to a highway in northeast Florida. Gray was curious and asked who they were after. The wardens took the measure of the quizzical nineteen-year-old, saw a potential convert, and decided to confide in him. "We're waiting for a refrigerated box truck to come by with a load of bootlegged speckled perch," one of them explained. Gray thought that was "pretty neat." The memory had stuck, and now here he was. On stakeout, alone, without backup, in a wild-ass place where a lawman stood just as good a chance of stumbling into a South American dope drop or finding a bullet-riddled body as he did of catching a wildlife crook.

Gray noted nothing of interest. No flicker from an air boater's headlamp. No roar of unmuffled high-horsepower engines. No gunshots. Only silence—broken by the intermittent croaking of bullfrogs and the occasional rustle of tall reeds as an unseen creature passed through them. The hint of a pale glow lightened the sky above Miami more than forty miles away. Everything else was a blank slate.

The rookie warden climbed back in the Plymouth and idled on south, nosing the low-slung sedan into the inky black—unaware that his night had only just begun.

Meanwhile, 1,100 miles to the north, an Eastern Airlines jumbo jet lifted off in bitter cold from New York's John F. Kennedy International Airport. The time was 9:20 p.m. Flight 401, as it was operationally known, was on a short-haul flight to Miami.

Stewardess Beverly Raposa, twenty-five, recalled nothing unusual about the flight as it passed high over the Atlantic Ocean en route to Miami International Airport (MIA). The petite brunette stood just five-feet-one-and-a-half inches tall. She had been turned down by TWA Airlines for a job because she was a half inch under the five-two minimum height required for all stewardesses. But Eastern had overlooked the half inch, whether by design or error she didn't know. But to play it safe, she always wore an add-on hairpiece, teased up into a bouffant, to make her look taller.

Beverly smiled cheerfully while she collected empty drink cups and dishes from the passengers. The only thing she looked forward to on arrival in Miami was going to bed. She was whipped.

Sometime in midflight, passenger Ron Infantino switched seats with his wife, Lilly, after she returned from the bathroom. They were seated on the right side of the middle section—designed for four-abreast seating—near the trailing edge of the right wing. They'd been married only twenty days and were returning from their honeymoon. They were both twenty-six years old. At the time, the innocent decision to change seats carried no meaning.

The captain, and his first and second officer, had every reason to feel good and confident about flying this particular ship. The plane was virtually brand-spanking-new, having been put into service only three months before.

The Lockheed L-1011 Tristar 1 was the "next generation" design in the wide-body class of commercial airliner. The outer fuselage was attractively trimmed with Eastern Airlines' signature blue and purple band against a background of white that ran around the nose and down both sides of the fuselage. On the tarmac it stood five stories high. If the massive jet could have been parked sideways on a football

A rare photograph of the Eastern Airlines Lockheed L–1011 Tristar 1 jumbo jet a few months before it crashed in the Florida Everglades on December 29, 1972. At the time, it was the worst disaster in U.S. civil aviation history.

field, the wingtips would overlap the distance between the goal line and the stripe at midfield. Customers quickly fell in love with the state-of-the-art features offered in this new class of twin-aisle jetliner that was designed for luxurious seat comfort, extra legroom, and a superquiet "whisper" ride.

After three hours aloft, Flight 401 had so far been uneventful. A trio of newly minted Rolls-Royce turbofan jet engines barely made a rumble to the 163 passengers and thirteen crew members seated inside the spacious cabin and reconfigured cockpit.

Ten minutes out from MIA, the plane began to descend from cruising altitude and entered into its final landing approach. Beverly sat in seat R4, located in the tail section, at the very back and right side of the plane. The seatbelt sign flashed on, so she buckled into her four-point seatbelt harness, with a strap crossing over each shoulder. Almost directly across from her sat stewardess Stephanie Stanich. They were best friends. A cheerful voice boomed over the cabin's loudspeaker address system: "Welcome to sunny Miami," the captain announced. "The temperature's in the low seventies, and it's beautiful out there tonight."

Ron and Lilly were exhausted from having celebrated Christmas with his parents in New York. They both looked forward to some rest and then a big New Year's celebration with her Cuban parents in Miami and the traditional whole roast pig cooked over an open fire pit.

Ron closed his eyes, arms crossed comfortably across his chest, and let the gentle engine thrum lull him into a light sleep. Lilly leaned back in her seat, resting quietly.

At 11:32 p.m., Capt. Robert A. Loft, fifty-five years old, with thirty years' experience and 29,500 flight hours under his belt, gave the order for the nose landing gear to be lowered. Following deployment, the nose wheel-well light failed to illuminate green—confirmation that the nose landing gear was fully extended and locked in the down position.

Two minutes later Flight 401 called the MIA tower: "Ah, tower; this is Eastern, ah, four zero one, it looks like we're gonna have to circle. We don't have a light on our nose gear yet."

"Eastern four oh one," the tower advised, " . . . roger, pull up, climb straight ahead to two thousand . . ."

The captain climbed to two thousand feet and locked the autopilot to "on." The plane traveled on a rectangular go-around loop that would take it west of MIA and then south over the pitch-black savannah of water and grass that was the Everglades. Left behind was the mosaic of colored lights flickering from high-rise condominiums, beach hotels, convention centers, and the lamp-lit streets of a tropical resort city populated by a half-million people.

Flight 401 streaked above a primordial swampland filled with poisonous snakes and alligators crawling through razor-sharp saw grass and open-water sloughs, sparsely dotted with small tree islands. At twice the landmass of Rhode Island, the largest subtropical wilderness in the United States is one of the most formidable terrains on earth. It cannot be traversed by foot, car, or truck. The ubiquitous south Florida airboat—a gigantic, cage-like desk-fan mounted on a small aluminum boat hull, powered by an aircraft engine—has been the standard form of backcountry transportation in these parts since the 1930s.

Had the cockpit crew craned their necks to look below, they would have seen nothing but a black void. The lack of even a single light on the ground made it difficult to visually detect a subtle decrease in altitude. The captain hoped the circling delay would give them time to fix what seemed to be a minor problem.

★

By now Gray's eyes had become night-sensitive to the low-light conditions of ambient starlight. He peered through the front windshield at a limitless horizon, where the black silhouette of an indistinct line of saw grass melded into a gray-black, star-speckled sky. He was looking for a "working light," the glow from an airboater's headlamp beam sweeping above the marsh. If he saw a light, he'd shut the patrol car off to listen.

The manner in which an airboat operator drove his boat was a vital clue in determining whether or not a game law was being violated. Outlaws often cut their engine at regular intervals to listen for a game warden slipping up behind them in a "blacked-out" airboat. Rather than take the risk of carrying a gun to unlawfully shoot a deer at night, many of them would flush a deer up and then run over it with their airboat, again and again and again, in tight, skidding circles, until it couldn't move anymore. The deer was left flailing in the water and nearly pounded to death from blunt-force trauma, with the coup de grace delivered by stopping the airboat on top of the deer and mashing the animal down into the muck until it drowned. Thus, a game warden's success or failure in this shallow-water no-man's land was often determined by how well, from a distance, he could judge the operator's intent by engine sound patterns that indicated abrupt course changes. If Gray saw or heard a suspicious airboat, he'd find where the operator had launched and wait nearby, hidden in the bushes, until the bad guy returned for his truck and trailer.

Gray had the credentials that the Game and Fresh Water Fish Commission (GFC) valued in a game warden. During a preemployment interview before a board of veteran GFC brass, he was grilled about his childhood. "I told them I had grown up in Volusia County, Florida," Gray recalled later, "a rural area where pretty much all we did for recreation was hunt, fish, camp, and track animals. I even night-hunted from horseback for deer, which was about one of the worst game laws you could break back then. And I told the board that. But like I explained to them, 'I was raised by my grandparents, and we were poor. I had to put food on the table.'"

Then a major asked Gray if he carried a pocketknife. Gray dug into his pants pocket and pulled out a Case folder and handed it to him. The major pulled out the trapper blade, touched it lightly with his thumb, and then ran it down the top of his forearm. The hair shaved right off. He folded it up and handed it back to Gray. Then he smiled and said, 'I think you'll do just fine.'"

One week later Gray was hired. Indeed, times were simpler back then.

At a lanky five eleven, with a trim waist and fine blond hair brushed straight back from his forehead, the twenty-four-year-old warden filled out the GFC's green and tan uniform like it had been a tailor fit. He was one of the few conservation lawmen diligent enough to put a spit-shine on a pair of Vietnam jungle boots. Back then most wardens gave their rough duty boots a thin lick of polish every six months or so, if that.

Inside the plane's cockpit, the crew's attention was diverted by trying to slide in a replacement bulb, a roughly two-inch-square all-in-one light assembly unit covered by a translucent green plastic lens (valued at twelve dollars). But it kept jamming, and all the finagling in the world wouldn't make it go back into place. At some point the captain inadvertently bumped the control wheel, knocking the autopilot partially off—a technical glitch that some Eastern Airlines pilots were aware of, but not Captain Loft. The jumbo jet was no longer locked at two thousand feet but would fly steadily at whatever level the pilots selected through pressure applied on their control wheels. The unintentional jar had apparently caused the plane's nose to tilt down a few degrees.

The altimeter showed a decrease in altitude, but none of the crew noticed. The plane was subtly dropping from the sky at a rate of two hundred feet each minute. Then an alarm chimed in the background—signaling a 250-foot drop.

The crew, however, was narrowly focused, like a carriage horse wearing blinders. Finding a solution to the vexing problem of the wheel-light indicator had consumed all their mental energy. And now, no one was flying the plane.

At 11:42 p.m., the first officer said, "We did something to the altitude."

"What?" asked the captain.

"We're still at two thousand, right?" the first officer asked.

"Hey, what's happening here?" the captain immediately exclaimed.

★

Beverly sensed a different tone in the engines. It didn't sound like they were in midair anymore. The engines sounded like they did when approaching the ground just before touchdown. She looked over at Stephanie, "Man, those engines don't sound right."

"Oh, yes they do," Stephanie replied.

"No, they don't, and I'd hate to be sitting back here in the tail if anything went wrong. Boy, you'd get it in a minute." These would be the last words she would ever speak to Stephanie.

Ron's eyes blinked open upon hearing the engines roar to full power. Startled, and now fully awake, he wondered, "What's going on here?" A former crew chief on a B-52 in Vietnam, he had a keener sense than most passengers would have when a plane was in trouble. Then a sudden jolt rattled the aircraft. His last complete thought before losing consciousness was, "This is going to be one hell of a rough landing."

At an altitude of 101 feet the plane's attitude was adjusted to a level similar to a glide slope for landing. At the last moment the captain, or one of the crew, became aware of the impending tragedy and attempted to correct it. Then the first of six radio altimeter warning "beep" sounds began—signaling an impending crash.

Too late.

The left wing tip banked into the marsh at 227 miles per hour.[1] Huge gouts of mud and aquatic vegetation shot high into the air as 250 tons of screeching metal ripped into the muck and grass. A fireball rushed through the fuselage as the plane began pinwheeling like a giant Ferris wheel spun loose from its mount. Passengers were violently whipsawed back and forth. Some took a hellish roller-coaster ride while seat-belted to crumbling metal. Others were flung free of the wreckage, only to find themselves coated in caustic jet fuel. Some passengers were left with shredded garments, skin hanging in strips from their appendages like ghoulish zombies in a B-grade horror film. Others were shoved down into the mud, trapped beneath ragged chunks of the aircraft's superstructure.

To those who survived, the scene must have had an eerie, end-of-the-earth feel, with wisps of gray mist swirling, a baby crying, the wails and groans from the injured and the dying. Night sounds of unknown critters moving through the water lent a disturbing backdrop to the cacophony of misery.

Beverly Raposa stumbled out of the nightmarish apocalypse, hurt, disheveled, and covered in clumps of dripping swamp grasses. She choked on the acrid fumes from 6,300 gallons of spilled aviation gas and screamed, "No one light a match!"

Flight 401 had just become the first jumbo jet to crash, and up to that time, the worst disaster in U.S. civil aviation history.

Gray happened to be looking southeast across the glades. "An orange glow suddenly lit up out in the marsh toward Miami," he recalled. "It looked like someone had poured gasoline on a campfire, and poof, up it went. After a few seconds it died out. I knew there was no way for anyone to make a campfire in the glades. Therefore, something had to

---

1 The jumbo jet's wreckage was located 18.7 miles west-northwest of MIA. National Transportation Safety Board investigators measured the cone-like debris field as 1,600 feet in length by 300 feet in width.

have fallen from the sky, probably an airplane. I thought a small commuter plane had crashed." Curiously, Gray never heard the impact. He was more than twenty-five miles away.

In those days, the GFC did not provide 24/7 radio dispatchers for the wardens. Instead, dispatchers went home at five o'clock. Gray's patrol car radio could only be used for car-to-car transmissions after hours. If no other wardens happened to be out and someone on solo patrol became involved in, say, a shootout, or their airboat broke down (which frequently happened), or they just plain needed help, they were slap out of luck until eight the next morning.

Gray turned around on the narrow dead-end levee and sped north toward Alligator Alley. Ten minutes later his patrol radio crackled.

"A jumbo jet just crashed in the Everglades north of the Tamiami Trail," said Sgt. Jimmy Sistrunk, Gray's supervisor. "Pick your airboat up and meet me at the Twenty Mile Boat Ramp. We'll launch from there."

Gray hit the gas as he toggled on the blue light and siren. He had to make an around-the-elbow-type detour of some fifty miles before he would arrive at the boat ramp on the north side of the Tamiami Trail. The big sedan's back end fishtailed in a controlled skid as Gray turned east onto the Alley. He straightened her up, gripping the steering wheel at ten and two while the big block V-8 rocketed through the night doing 120. Telephone poles whipping past every second reminded him of his youth, when he used to drag-race a souped-up Camaro down the rural back roads of Volusia County.

By one in the morning, Gray had launched his airboat. Riding with him were two Federal Aviation Administration (FAA) officials. "The area I was about to go in was uncharted territory for me," Gray said. "We were in Dade County, and my patrol zone was Broward County to the north."

One thing that concerned Gray was not knowing where any airboat trails were or the location of open-water sloughs where he could avoid the thick grass and drive in relative ease and safety to the crash site. "When I found out I had to carry two guys from the FAA in the boat with me," Gray said, "it put more pressure on me because I didn't want them to be injured, and I didn't want them to think I was an idiot. After all, I had only been on the job two months, and that's not a lot of time to get used to driving something as squirrely as an airboat."

Gray was literally running "by the seat of his pants," to borrow a term from the parlance of early aviation, when pilots had few navigation aids and often had to make decisions on the fly.

The warden fired up the 6-cylinder Continental aircraft engine, grabbed the rudder stick, and nosed into the marsh. "The saw grass was twelve feet high," Gray said, "and thickly interwoven, so dense I couldn't see beyond the grass rake of the airboat." Bolted to the bow, the grass rake is a homemade four-foot-long extension fashioned from metal conduit pipes separated every eight inches and angling upward at about thirty degrees. While under way, it presses the grass down and forward ahead of the airboat to lessen resistance.

Another thing weighing on Gray's mind that night was an important lesson drilled into him during in-the-field airboat trainings. Senior wardens had told him, "Never stop, or slow an airboat down in rank grass, because you may not be able to power out of it. Once you become stuck in the glades, you could be there for a long, long time."

Gray donned ear protection and then put on a plastic hardhat with an aircraft landing lamp strapped to it. The 110,000-candlepower incandescent bulb cast a brilliant spotlight, an intense, cone-like beam that can illuminate hazards up to a hundred yards out. Gray shined his light into the green jungle ahead and mashed the foot throttle. The engine roared, spinning the aircraft propeller up to three thousand revolutions per minute, repeatedly cracking the sound barrier into a blur of thunderous *clapppssss.* The aluminum hull vibrated like an out-of-balance cement truck. The backward air blast slowly pushed the little fourteen-foot boat forward, straining against a dense wall of water-anchored grass.

"The only visual reference we had for the crash site," Gray recalled, "was the spotlight from a Coast Guard helicopter hovering eight miles away. At that distance it looked like a bright star circling in the sky. I kept the bow pointed in that direction."

Thirty minutes later, Gray and his passengers suddenly burst out of the grass. The hull slingshoted forward as it dropped a couple of feet down into an open-water slough. The brief change in elevation felt like the sudden lurch of an elevator starting down.

Ten feet in front of them was what looked like two mannequins to Gray—a partially clothed woman lying faceup in the mud and a naked man lying facedown. She wore panty hose and looked like she'd been scalped with a razor. He was left wearing nothing but a necktie and belt pushed up under his armpits. The FAA guy sitting closest to Gray yelled, "Holy shit!"

"An airboat doesn't have brakes," Gray explained. "And before I had time to even let off the throttle or do anything else, I ran over those two people, which I knew were both dead. But we idled back around to double-check on them just in case. That was how our night started, and it went downhill from there."

Though Gray was only a rookie, the sight of death was not unfamiliar to him. Two tours with Uncle Sam in Southeast Asia had hardened him. "I was ready to put all that behind me," Gray said. "But the scope of this civilian disaster, and suddenly having to work it, was an eye-opening experience. I never dreamed I'd be doing this when I signed up to work for the game commission. I thought all I'd be doing was chasing poachers."

Gray shut the engine down so they could listen. The *whop, whop, whop* of whirling helicopter blades shattered the night as the aircraft wheeled overhead, preparing to hoist up the injured and fly them to hospitals in Miami. When the rescue helicopter departed and the racket subsided, the empty void was filled with the keening and wails and moans of the survivors. Filtering through it all came the faint tune of a Christmas carol. Gray doesn't remember which one. Only that later, a Coast Guardsman told him they'd found a determined stewardess standing alone atop a large section of cabin wreckage, leading a half dozen of the fortunate in song.

The last thing Beverly remembered before she was knocked out was a waterfall of colors. When she came to, she was still belted into her seat, tipped to one side, hanging six feet above the swamp.[2] The No. 2 engine and tail section had broken away from the main fuselage, coming to rest on its side, in a remote area far away from the main crash site.

The sudden silence was unnerving, compared to the horrendous ear-splitting roar of the crash moments before. She screamed for help, but no one answered, and she wondered, "Am I the only one left alive?"

Beverly popped the release buckle and fell into the marsh, landing on her hands and knees. Her face burned from the jet fuel. She dug down into the black muck, cupped a double handful to her face, and smeared it all over the affected places. It seemed to help. (Doctors would later say this simple action saved her from receiving serious burns.)

She looked into the distance, saw the dim lights of Miami framed against a coal-black horizon, and thought, "It's so far away." She was very scared, especially for someone who had never been in the Everglades. With an injured back and a cut foot, she slogged through sucking muck and shredded saw grass, honed even sharper by flying plane wreckage. The stiff-limbed reeds cut into her legs and arms with each unsteady step. She found a piece of the cabin floor with a stewardess still strapped into her seat-belt harness. Mercy Ruiz was badly injured, with a broken pelvis and a severe head injury.

Beverly did not have any blankets. She had no first-aid kit. She had nothing. But the passengers were her people, her responsibility, and it was still her job to help them. Serving coffee and tea and soda pop was all very nice, but this was what counted. With a determination born of her immigrant Portuguese grandparents and of having worked on a 160-acre dairy farm as a young girl growing up in Rhode Island, the former Girl Scout troop leader shouted out into the night, "I'm a stewardess. If you hear my voice, come toward me. Follow my voice." Within minutes, six to eight passengers crawled

---

2 An emergency chute had deployed inward—instead of outward—cushioning her head and neck from four hundred pounds of debris stacked above her, much like an airbag would do in a car wreck. Aviation investigators later said this had kept her from being killed.

out of the dark and were seated on the scrap of flooring, shivering, afraid, and in shock. In a weak voice one of them asked, "What about the alligators?"

Beverly didn't hesitate: "We made such a loud noise when we hit. I'm sure they all ran away." She had spit the words out quickly, doing her best to sound convincing. Ever the good Catholic, she crossed herself in the dark and silently prayed, "Oh, God, please let that be true."

A Coast Guard helicopter flew toward them with a bright searchlight sweeping the marsh, and then it swung away. Beverly's survivors became upset and worried. "They're not going to find us," an anxious passenger whispered.

"Yes, they are," Beverly assured them. "The rescuers are picking people up from the nose section of the plane first. They'll find us eventually."

Beverly had the survivors scoot together, sitting back to back so they could stay warm. In a calm, soothing voice, she said, "Now close your eyes and pretend you have a cup of hot coffee, or chocolate, or tea in your hands. Picture that in your mind. That's what you're going to get when we get out of here. Now take a sip. Feel the warmth going down."

The hours clicked off, and still no rescuers had arrived. Beverly was struggling for ideas to keep her group occupied. "Why don't we sing to help warm ourselves up?" she suggested.

"What songs will we sing?" one passenger asked.

"Let's sing Christmas carols," Beverly replied. "How about we start with 'Rudolf the Red-Nosed Reindeer?'"

Ron Infantino woke up to a cold chill. Heart pounding. Breath erratic. At all points of the compass around him there was nothing but dead silence and incredible darkness. A cloak of black like he'd never seen before was made all the more intense by the surreal stillness. My God," he wondered, "what do I do now? Am I the only one left alive?"

Buried up to his neck in freezing water and muck, completely naked—except for the spandex rims of his socks—severely injured, shivering, and in shock, Ron feebly called out into the night, "Lilly, where are you? Help. Lilly, where are you?

Quiet.

Then a big, bold female voice reverberated somewhere out of the gloom, "Don't anyone light a match!" Then a few minutes later, "If you can hear my voice, come to me! Follow my voice!"

But Ron couldn't follow the voice. He was trapped beneath the water. Unable to move and weak from severe loss of blood, his body hung suspended in the watery muck, still bent in the sitting position. His left arm rested on the right armrest of the seat he had been sitting in, which was now submerged by his side.

Now that his left arm was accounted for, Ron desperately wanted to find his right arm. But he couldn't locate it. He kept asking himself, "Why is my right arm so far away from my body?"

He finally found it, three-quarters severed and barely attached by tendons and skin and strings of muscles. When he grabbed it with his left hand, his fingers sunk all the way into the bicep. "This can't be good," he told himself. His left knee was broken too—wrenched sideways at a vicious right angle.

Oddly, he felt no pain. Shock had taken over.

An hour or so later, a Christmas carol floated out of the night, reassuring Ron he was not alone.

A young man walked up to him, a vague silhouette. Ron looked up. "Please don't leave me," he whispered, so weak he could barely utter the words. "Stay here. Please. They will never find me."

"That's all right," the survivor said, mouthing the words in a misty daze, as if Ron wasn't even there. "Don't worry about it. I'm just taking a little walk." And off he went, erratically slogging into the night.

A couple of hours later, a lady heard Ron moaning and came over to him. She was looking for her family. "Please help me," Ron said. "I'm so cold." She took off her sweater and dropped it to him. It landed in front of his face in a soggy clump. His head jerked back, his nostrils assailed by the harsh stench of JP-4 jet fuel. Pure kerosene. The garment was supersaturated in it. Ron had a choice: risk death by hypothermia or become ill from breathing in the potent fumes. He chose the sweater and put it over his bare chest, which was still exposed to the cool water. It helped to staunch the loss of valuable body heat.

Ron begged the woman not to leave him.

"I'm sorry," she said, "but I have to look for my family. I'll tell rescue you're in this area."

Time passed in agonizingly slow increments for Ron. Early stages of hypothermia and loss of blood were gradually sapping his strength. He could barely keep his head upright. He began to nod off, then jerk awake. He worried that if he fell asleep, his face would tip forward into the water and he would drown.

Five hours after the crash came the welcome sounds of voices, legs sloshing through water, labored breathing, and flashlight beams probing the dark. They were heading his way. "Please don't leave me!" Ron yelled. "Please don't leave me!"

A Miami-Dade fireman shined his light on Ron, panting from the exertion of wearing full bunker gear while breaking a trail through the densely vegetated swamp. "Sir, don't worry," he said. "We're not going to leave you."

Lilly would be found two days later, trapped beneath one of the wings. Sadly, she did not survive.

★

The young warden played his headlamp beam across a massive cone-shaped opening carved out by the plane when it ripped across the marsh. "This was one of those moments," Gray said, "when there aren't enough words in the dictionary to describe the devastation. Dead bodies hung, lay, and floated everywhere I looked. And they were in every conceivable position you could imagine. But we knew our job was to rescue the survivors first. There would be plenty of time for body recovery."

By now, four GFC airboats were on the scene. They streaked back and forth, shuttling survivors to a spur levee that jutted north from the Tamiami Trail. Only a half mile from the crash site, the water-control structure now served double duty as a crucial staging area for emergency rescue workers who waited for new batches of survivors to arrive.

The airboat Gray operated had a covered aluminum deck. It offered no place for the injured to lay or sit. "So what we did," Gray said, "was to place two or three of them lying crossways on the grass rake. It was the only way to make it work. The airboats we patrolled in forty years ago weren't designed for rescue. Their function was to transport one or two of us from point A to point B in an unforgiving environment."

Gray worked through the night, often changing partners, sometimes working alone. "We spent a lot of the time out of the boat wading in knee- to thigh-deep muck and water with every kind of crud in it you could imagine," Gray said. "Wreckage was everywhere, and we were worried about our airboat propellers kicking up debris and maybe blowing it into one of the rescue workers, or a victim. You had to be extremely cautious about how you turned an airboat, or when you gave it power. Generally, it was just safer for everyone to be on foot, unless we had survivors to transport."

Scattered haphazardly about the crash scene, like so many apocalyptic lawn ornaments, were the personal effects of those who had ridden the plane down: purses turned inside out, torn wallets, and broken suitcases. Their contents shook free like confetti, becoming swamp flotsam swirling about the rescuers' legs: pants, jackets, skirts, and undergarments; cash money in all denominations; credit cards; driver's licenses; passports; personal photographs of families and friends, wives and husbands; and, perhaps most poignant, a tattered baby doll.

As the men sorted through the petrol-soaked water, playing their flashlight beams into broken sections of the plane's fuselage and into miles of tangled wires, sometimes finding a survivor and sometimes a victim, one thing became crystal clear to them. It was simply "luck of the draw" as to who lived or who died.

By 2:00 a.m., hundreds of rescue workers had descended on the scene. The Tamiami Trail and the spur levee had become a stream of flashing red and blue emergency lights, the air rent with blasting sirens. Grainy 16mm films taken at the crash site show game wardens, police officers, sheriff's deputies, U.S. Coast Guardsmen, firefighters, emergency medical technicians, aviation officials, and civilians working shoulder to shoulder as they sloshed through the marsh, hurriedly rushing victims onto waiting airboats or into wire baskets to be cable-hoisted up to helicopters hovering overhead.

★

By 3:30 a.m., Beverly's flock of survivors had all been rescued. Now it was her turn. Col. Frank Borman, her boss, a former astronaut, and vice president of Eastern Airlines—now turned first responder—came to escort her into a helicopter hovering at ground level a short distance away. He put his arm around her, and they began slogging through knee-deep muck and water. Suddenly, he stopped, "Wait a minute," he said. "I lost my boot."

"Well," Beverly said, "I'll help you find it."

"No, I'm supposed to be helping you."

"That's okay," Beverly laughed. "I'm a tough Portuguese girl from Rhode Island."

★

Around 4:00 a.m., Gray waded up to a willow head, a thick tangle of weepy trees with limbs draping into the water. The copse of brittle cover was an acre or so in size. Gray had discovered a hole in the bushes, roughly circular in shape, and a little larger than the mouth of a culvert pipe. He probed it with his flashlight beam, sweeping it all around the edges. Branches had been freshly snapped off all the way around the opening—all pointing inward.

Curious, Gray rubbed his hand across the splintered base of one sapling, a good three to four inches in diameter. "I called out to a Coast Guardsman who was working nearby to come and help me out," Gray said. "It looked like a piece of the wreckage, or something, had been propelled on a near horizontal trajectory, traveling just a foot or two above the water's surface and rocketed into the willows with tremendous force."

Bent at the waist, the two men waded into the hole, following a ragged debris trail of damaged vegetation. They crawled over broken limbs and ducked beneath hanging branches. Fresh willow leaves knocked loose from the impact lay sprinkled in the water, shining a lush light green in the men's flashlight beams. "We worked deeper and deeper into this hole," Gray said, "until we'd gone about fifty yards. Incredibly, we found a man sitting alone on a small tussock. He was in the fetal position, head on his knees, hands covering his face, leaning against the trunk of a willow tree. He was conscious and moaning. We were able to communicate with him a little bit, and he started to come around. He had a broken arm and some cuts and scrapes, but no other visible wounds.

"This guy had been hurled from the plane like a human cannonball. After all these years, I can still picture him in my mind's eye like it was yesterday. I wouldn't be a bit surprised if the speed he'd been traveling was well over a hundred miles an hour."

What the two rescuers didn't know was the extent, if any, of any internal crushing wounds the man might have had. "We knew already," Gray said, "from looking at a good many of the victims that they had died without any obvious injuries, so we decided to move this guy in a hurry. Luckily for us, he only weighed about 170.

"But it was still a nightmare getting him out. It took eight of us carrying a stretcher filled with his dead weight in a kind of bizarre relay. We had to work as a team, where those in the back had to continually rotate up to the front. What made it so hard was trying to manhandle this guy in the stretcher, up and over the broken willows. It probably took an hour to get him out. We had him in an ambulance by five thirty in the morning. I don't know this for sure, but I seem to remember he was the last survivor to be rescued."

Daylight found Gray sitting on the largest piece of the airplane's superstructure. A massive chunk of what had once been the cabin stood about eight feet above the swamp. The outer walls and ceiling of the upper fuselage had been peeled away, leaving only the floor and seats. A Coast Guard helicopter lowered down breakfasts of coffee and biscuits to Gray and his fellow rescue personnel.

"As the sun came up," Gray said, "the horror of what had happened became even more obvious to everyone. Aviation investigators asked us to leave the bodies. And now all of the dead were visible in the harsh morning light."

A ten-by-ten-foot scrap of the cabin floor lay fifty feet away from Gray. A young couple sat, still belted into their seats.

Gray sipped his coffee while contemplating the lives of this man and woman. "She was slumped into his shoulder," he said. "He leaning over her. It seemed to be an act of love. Maybe, in the few seconds it took for the plane to break apart, they realized this was their final moment together. It was a sobering experience."

Also sobering was the grisly work of body recovery. Wardens back then didn't have chest waders, or any protective biohazard gear to wear while wading through what would now be considered an extreme health hazard. The only item handed out to aid them was a roll of orange survey tape.

"We had to flag all the bodies," Gray said. "Since there were no stakes, we cut willow branches, stripping the smaller limbs away, or even used a part from the plane if we could find one four or five feet long. Most of the work was done by slowly wading through the water in a grid-like pattern across the visual path of destruction left by the plane. I'd bump into something with my foot. Then nudge it. If it felt like a body, I'd sink down into the muck, sometimes up to my chest, reach up underneath and carefully shake it loose from the grass. Then the body would lay suspended a few inches under the water."

By the night of day three, the wardens were finished and could finally go home and to bed. Many of them had gone seventy-two hours straight with little, if any, sleep.

If the script for this story had been crafted by Hollywood screenwriters, Gray Leonhard would have certainly rescued Beverly Raposa and Ron Infantino, wrapping it all up in a neatly tied bow. But real life does not follow Hollywood scripts, and neither did Flight 401. Haphazard, chaotic, confused, disorienting, and senseless are but a few descriptors that apply to this epic disaster. And in that light, it makes perfectly good sense that Gray, Beverly, and Ron never connected during the rescue operation. Except for one tenuous bond that drew them together in spirit: a distant Christmas carol drifting through the night.

Postscript

Ron Infantino

Ron's injuries were grave. Mud had caked the arm wound, preventing an even greater loss of blood, but it came with a price. An infection set in from bacteria, causing gas gangrene. Ron was flown in a Learjet to the Pensacola Naval Air Station in the Florida panhandle, where he underwent ten days (six to eight hours a day) of treatment inside a hyperbaric chamber to force pure oxygen into the wound. Surgery, debridement, and cleansing of the wound were done without anesthesia. A two-hundred-pound male nurse had to hold him down by the shoulders to keep him from coming off the table. Though hellishly painful, this course of treatment did prevent amputation of the arm. Later, his left knee would be rotated a full ninety degrees and surgically put back into place.

Even though Ron is sixty-eight now, he will tell you that Flight 401 shaped his life forever. He doesn't measure life's problems like a lot of folks who have never experienced what it feels like to be on the precipice of death or to lose the love of their life in the blink of an eye.

"I number things from 1 to 10 in life," Ron told me during a telephone interview. "If I'm stuck in a traffic jam, or backed up at the checkout line in a grocery store because someone writes a check they can't get approved, I pause for a moment and say to myself, 'Okay, Ron, what number is this?' It certainly is not a 10.

"The crew on Flight 401 was so preoccupied with a fifty-cent lightbulb that nobody was flying the plane. People concentrate so much of their energies on minor problems that sometimes they miss the big picture."

Beverly Raposa

Beverly spent her twenty-sixth birthday recovering at Mercy Hospital in Miami. She still suffers from two disintegrating vertebra in her spine and one in her neck as a result of the crash.

Beverly shared these thoughts with me on the aftermath of Flight 401: "After you stare death straight in the face, you never take people for granted. Tell people you love them, do the things that you want to do, because tomorrow is not a guarantee—enjoy today. When you see someone without a smile, please give them one of yours."

Gray Leonhard

"It's hard to know what the takeaway might be for a disaster such as this," Gray told me, "except it seemed to bring out the best in people: rescuers and survivors alike. We had a job that needed to be done, and we did it." Gray would go on to participate in hundreds of search-and-rescues throughout his twenty-five-year career in conservation law enforcement. But nothing would ever compare to Flight 401.

Author's Note

The full scope of this tragedy was too great to tell in a single book chapter, other than from the point of view of a young rookie game warden, a stewardess, and one passenger. In no way do I intend to diminish or ignore the valiant work performed by hundreds of good-hearted civil servants and civilians, or the crew and survivors who found the courage to help each other on that terrible night forty-two years ago.

Of the 176 passengers and crew aboard Flight 401, seventy-seven survived the initial crash; of those, two later died; leaving seventy-five survivors and 101 fatalities. (Captain Loft was one of those who later died at the scene.)

As a result of Flight 401, cockpit awareness has greatly improved. To reduce the human factor (read, tunnel vision) in flying commercial airliners, a program called Crew Resource Management (CRM) was developed. Before CRM, the captain was regarded as God, and anything he said went. Now the cockpit responsibilities are more evenly distributed among crew members and allow for the first or second officer to voice a concern if they become aware of a potential problem. In the case of an impending crash, cockpit alarms emit extremely loud warnings coupled with voice commands such as, "Pull up! Pull up!" Other measures—too numerous to include in this brief summary—have also been put into place to increase airline safety.

For those who would like more information on Flight 401, you can find movies, documentaries, reenactments, newspaper stories, and books that provide detailed background, including a memorial website dedicated to the victims, survivors, and first responders.

A LANDMARK CASE

Tucked away in the Big Bend region of Florida's upper Gulf Coast, Dixie County today feels like a place trapped in a time warp, always thirty years behind the times and never quite escaping the state's rearview mirror. That quirkiness, though, lends a quaint appeal to the tiny coastal fishing village of Horseshoe Beach, which has become synonymous with family-friendly summer vacations spent snorkeling for scallops in the Gulf of Mexico's gin-clear waters.

But beneath the bucolic surface of wholesome fun lies a dark history, the classic struggle of an off-kilter justice system seeking to right itself.

Flip the calendar back to the 1970s, and one would find a very different Dixie County. At that time, it was lawless, frontier-like, a virtual no-man's land. Families were clannish. No one cared what their neighbors did, and most kept their mouths shut—if they were smart—about any criminal shenanigans. During the full moon, tightly wrapped bales of marijuana were transported up tidal creeks in small, unlit skiffs. Moonshine was cooked in the deep, dark woods. A lone gunshot ringing out on a hot summer's night was, well, ordinary. It was a poacher's paradise, the kind of place a man could depend on kinfolk, friends, and coworkers to watch his back. It was predictable and expected. An unspoken code of the backwoods to be adhered to come hell or high water.

Back then a by-the-book game warden assigned to Dixie County ran into a stiff headwind each day he strapped on a gun. Something as simple as finding a place to rent in Cross City—the county seat and about the only habitable area in that sparsely populated county of roughly seven thousand—could be an almost insurmountable hurdle.

Warden Paul Hoover found out the hard way. "They weren't even nice about it," he recalled, when in 1974, he began work in a county previously described as a "hellhole" by other officers.

"I'd knock on a landlord's door," Paul said, "and as soon as I had the words out of my mouth, 'I'm interested in renting this apartment or that mobile home,' they'd look me dead in the eye and shout, 'No!' And all I'd see was a wall of wood coming at me as the door slammed shut. Gun-toters wearing green and tan uniforms were not well thought of back then."

Paul's posting to Dixie County was more by default than grand design. His hiring interview board consisted of a one-on-one with the director of Law Enforcement, Col. Brantley Goodson. "The colonel liked my background," Paul said, "and the fact I'd grown up trapping and hunting small game in the Ohio wilderness. He liked my four-year degree from Ohio State University in natural resources and wildlife management and that I was already working for the Game and Fresh Water Fish Commission as a game manager. But what he didn't like was that my left eye is 20/200 uncorrected. The minimum standard at the time was 20/40 uncorrected."

Even though Goodson had a problem with Paul's eyesight, he had an even greater problem finding someone to work in Dixie County. No one wanted the job. Desperate to fill the slot, the colonel came up with a solution, a compromise of sorts: an arrangement absolving the GFC of blame if Paul got hurt on the job. So he floated a question to him, "If you were out in the woods and got into a fight, and your good eye was injured, could you see to drive home?'

Without hesitation, Paul answered, "Yes."

In an interesting twist of coincidence, Jeff Hahr, the warden assigned just south in Levy County, had a background similar to Paul's. He grew up on a hundred-acre dairy farm in New Jersey. By the age of ten he was running his own commercial trap line for raccoon, opossum, and fox. He also subsistence hunted for deer. While working toward a degree in wildlife ecology at the University of Florida, he entered into a work-study program with GFC. He liked it so much that he up and quit in his junior year, deciding right then and there he wanted to be a game warden.

His hiring interview board didn't care for that decision. "They raked me over the coals," Jeff recalled. "Finally, I got aggravated with them and said, 'Look, I'm wasting your time and you're wasting mine if you think I'm going back to college just to make you folks happy. I'm sorry, I want to be a game warden, and I'll do you a hell of a job at it. There're boys waiting outside for an interview right now. Why don't you give one of them a position?"

When Jeff left the room, the next candidate in line was waiting in the hallway. He asked Jeff how he did. "Well, there's one opening I know of for sure," he replied, resigned to the fact his interview had ended in a train wreck.

One week later Jeff was thrilled and a little baffled when he received the news he'd been hired.

"Back in 1973, they took the blind and the infirm, too," Jeff said, with a chuckle. "You see, I've been blind in one eye since birth. Maybe that's why Paul and I ended up working together so much. It took the two of us to make one good set of eyes. Seriously though, there were a lot of times we needed to partner together for backup, or to puzzle out how to catch a particular poacher."

Both men were in their twenties, the prime of life, and about to become involved in a game case with historic consequences. Not that anyone in the world would raise an eyebrow, or even care. After all, wildlife crimes rarely got mentioned on the six o'clock evening news. But for the big bosses in the GFC, one young prosecutor, a GFC biologist, and a brand-new judge, it would become a landmark case.

★

Most folks would sniff disparagingly at the idea of spending their workday hunkered down in the bottom of a shallow stump hole. A climate-controlled, glass-enclosed office it was not. But for Paul Hoover and Jeff Hahr, it kind of felt like home, maybe not La-Z-Boy-recliner-in-the-den type of home, but it would do.

The hole was no more than a sandy divot, a three-foot-deep dimple gouged out of an unremarkable landscape. It was created two years earlier when a timber company harvested three hundred acres of planted pines inside the Steinhatchee Wildlife Management Area.

The public hunting ground was desolate country comprising 425,000 acres of open clear-cuts and reforested areas, dense, native pine scrub intermixed with cypress strands, gum swamps, and narrow creeks streaming dark-brown water into vast saltwater marshes bordering the Gulf of Mexico.

Since the land had been timbered, a patchy mix of weeds and brambles had grown up to about knee height. The wardens needed more concealment than that to conduct a stakeout, hence, their adoption of the empty stump hole for a hideout.

The lawmen were after a forty-year-old serial turkey poacher. Randall Comer stood a little over six feet, with a pronounced bald spot and a sagging paunch. He was a Dixie County native who scraped out a marginal living with his hands. He worked off and on as a carpenter, logger, and a crew member on a gill-net boat.

Paul and Jeff knew about Comer's illegal bait-site of cracked corn scattered near a makeshift hunting blind constructed of cut gallberry branches and palmetto fans inside an oak hammock. They'd memorized his foot tracks and the tire-tread patterns of the green and white International Scout he drove. And they also knew where he liked to park. They knew all of these things because of a tip called into Paul a couple of days before. The information came from a renowned poacher who had finally seen the light. He firmly believed that if the rampant slaughter of deer and turkey continued, there would be nothing left for his kids to enjoy.

Third Saturday in March 1978, 5:00 a.m.

It was the opening day of spring gobbler season, when wild turkey, North America's premier big-game bird, can be hunted. Only gobblers, or birds with beards, a hairy appendage hanging beneath the neck, can lawfully be taken.

A light veil of fog lay suspended at ground level, dimly illuminated by the pale rays of a setting moon. It lent the morning an ethereal, almost surreal quality as the young wardens sat beneath the thin layer of mist on the bare dirt in the bottom of the hole. They clutched camouflaged jackets tightly to ward off the chill and patiently waited.

An hour later the *wha . wha . . wha . . . wha. . . . wha. . . . . wha* of decelerating off-road tires broke the morning stillness. The sound was unmistakable: thick-lugged rubber slapping against hard asphalt. A truck was turning off the Horseshoe Mainline, the eighteen-mile connecting artery between Horseshoe Beach and Cross City.

The wardens scrambled to their feet. Paul turned to Jeff. "Think that's our boy?"

"I sure hope so," Jeff said. "It would be nice to have someone show up when they're supposed to. We seem to spend a lot more time waiting than we do catching."

The wardens usually worked three to four days a week on stakeout, either alone or together. They scheduled their own shifts, working the best eight out of twenty-four. Whether it was day or night, or part day and part night depended on what species of fur, fish, or fowl was in season.

Beyond the hole and across the half-mile-wide clear-cut headlight beams bounced and wavered. The truck's four-wheel-drive suspension slowly negotiated an uneven track marred by washouts and dotted with overgrown bushes.

"He's coming down the tram road," Jeff observed, following the vehicle's progress along a hastily built two-rut road for onetime log extraction.

Paul peered through 7-power binoculars and fingered the focus dial, zeroing in on the truck. The landscape had begun to take on a faint glow as the predawn gray gave way to an unseen sun creeping toward the eastern horizon. The vehicle's distinct, box-like profile helped with identification. "It's a green and white Scout," Paul said, with a smile. "That will be Randall."

"Good deal," Jeff said, hands stuffed in his pockets, calmly waiting to see what happened next.

The Scout came to a stop 150 yards from the wardens' hideout. The engine shut off. A truck door slammed. Paul and Jeff crouched, peering through a row of palmetto fronds they'd carefully stuck around the rim of the hole earlier that morning. The poacher walked down the tram road and past the wardens. He wore dark clothing. Maybe an olive-green Vietnam-style military jacket, blue jeans, and some sort of ball cap. It was hard to make out details in the dim light.

But there was no doubt about the dark barrel of the long gun slung over his shoulder. Back then, most hunters in Dixie County depended on one type of firearm to fill the pot, a 12-gauge, single-shot shotgun with a thirty-inch barrel colloquially known as a "Long Tom." Soon he was out of sight, lost in the low brush that grew along the road shoulder. His bait site was about three hundred yards from where the wardens were hiding.

The clock ticked on as the sun crested the horizon, throwing sharp, golden-hued rays across the landscape. Then, from the bait site, came the sounds Paul and Jeff had been waiting for: *yelp, yelp, yelp, yelp, yelp.* Pause. *Yelp, yelp, yelp, yelp, yelp.*

"Sounds like a wooden box call," Jeff said. "He's doing a pretty fair job of imitating a hen."

"He only needs to be good enough to attract a lovesick gobbler close enough to kill it," Paul said. "I wouldn't want to take a bait case to court in this county without a dead bird to go along with it."

"Agreed."

One thing that worried the lawmen was that they'd heard no gobbler respond. Usually, if one is anywhere in the vicinity, it will call back to a hen. It could mean another day on stakeout if Comer didn't kill a bird, so they settled in.

Fifteen minutes later.

Boom!

Jeff glanced at his watch. Then he took out a small, wire-bound pocket notepad and in precise block lettering wrote, "One shot, 12-gauge, from direction of bait site, 7:15 a.m."

"Things are looking up," Jeff said, as he slipped the notepad into his shirt pocket and buttoned the flap.

"You would think we would have heard a gobbler call before he shot," Paul said.

"Well, maybe he came in silent. Sometimes they'll do that."

"You're probably right."

A few minutes later Comer hurried past the wardens and toward the Scout. Paul tracked him through the binoculars. Jeff watched him through a narrow split in the palmetto fans. The wardens had a problem. Comer had walked by empty-handed. No gun. No turkey. Nothing.

Paul and Jeff quietly talked it over. They came up with more questions than answers: What exactly did Comer kill? Did he kill something too big to bring out, like a deer? Where might he have put what he shot? Is he going to stay around his truck? Is he going to walk or drive back to the blind? Will he leave in the Scout and come back later?

The wardens' patrol truck was hidden more than a mile away. They would have to figure out a way to catch Comer on foot or risk losing the case. Timing would be key, the ability to pick out that one sweet spot, the perfect window of opportunity when an unsuspecting poacher could be surprised and overwhelmed.

Unexpectedly, the Scout drove right by the warden's belowground hideout heading toward the bait site. Discussion time was over. Both men leapt from the hole and sprinted for the tram road. Twenty yards. Four to five seconds. The men braked to a stop. Paul cautiously poked his head out of a wax myrtle bush anchored into the road shoulder and looked right, in the direction the truck had gone. "He's got no side mirrors, Jeff. Let's chance it."

Paul ran down the left rut and Jeff took the right, pounding along after the Scout as fast as they could. It seemed like they'd only been running for a minute or two when the brake lights suddenly blinked on. Paul broke left, diving headfirst into the bushes. Jeff went right.

Paul crept back to the hump of the road shoulder where a tangle of briars and vines and low cover grew. Using the brush as a shield, he eased up above the dense vegetation until only his binoculars showed. The Scout was parked in the middle of the road, two hundred yards away, with the driver's door open. Comer stood on the floorboard, peering out across the truck's cab. His head swiveled like an owl; worry etched his face.

Paul could feel the adrenaline building. Comer had killed something illegal.

Comer jumped off the running board and disappeared into a ditch. Three seconds later he returned with the gun, reached in through the driver's side and stuck it muzzle down on the passenger floorboard. He walked out into the middle of the overgrown tram road and stopped. He cupped both hands behind his ears, slowly turning his head from side to side while he looked and listened for anything out of place.

Jeff was still hidden, squatted down in the brush on the opposite side of the road from Paul, waiting for his cue.

Suddenly, Comer darted into the ditch and returned seconds later with a scrap of rolled-up carpet, about three feet long by eighteen inches wide. He stuffed it behind the passenger seat, jumped in behind the steering wheel, and slammed the door.

Paul made eye contact with Jeff. "We got to go!" he mouthed the words, gesturing wildly toward the Scout.

The wardens leapt out into the road and hauled ass. Jeff's singular thought at that moment was to try and grab onto something, anything, a bumper, a door handle, or a part of Comer. Just find some way to stop that damn truck.

Comer spun the starter a few times before the worn-out engine caught, allowing the wardens a few precious seconds more to close the gap. Then the truck jerked and began to roll forward. It was a hundred yards away, the length of a football field. Maybe fifteen to twenty seconds for an Olympic sprinter running on uneven ground. Double or triple that time for Paul and Jeff, who were not world-class athletes and laden down by the additional burden of heavy gun belts and thick leather boots. Although between the two, Paul was more the runner, head erect, chest out, elbows swinging freely on a lean frame. He loped along with long, easy strides while Jeff struggled mightily to keep up.

The gears ground noisily. Comer tried desperately to force the stick into second. It stubbornly refused. The Scout continued to stutter and jerk, heaving back and forth. Jeff said a silent prayer: "Lord, just give me the strength to let your will be done. Please, please let me catch him."

If Comer had checked his rearview mirror right about then, he would have seen two men in disheveled green and tan uniforms bobbing up and down as they negotiated washouts and rocks and dodged small saplings growing in the middle of the seldom-used logging trail. And if he'd looked real hard, he might have detected a hungry glint in their eyes. If hunting another man is the ultimate challenge, the ultimate prize is catching one.

Before either lawman realized what had happened, they'd closed the gap. The two men ran abreast, directly behind the Scout's rusty back bumper. Neither spoke a word. Instinctively, knowing what must be done.

Both the driver's and passenger's side windows were rolled down.

Paul, running in the left rut, dropped back a bit, allowing Jeff, in the right rut, to take the lead.

"I knew if Jeff got to him first," Paul recalled, "it would divert Comer's attention away from me. What I needed to do to get the truck stopped was tricky."

Jeff sprinted beside the passenger door, grabbed the sill with both hands and heaved himself through the open window, legs dangling out. He was close enough to count the twisted stubble sprouting from the poacher's chin.

"Shut the truck off now!" Jeff shouted. "Shut it off! Shut it off!"

Comer's eyes left the road to stare at the warden in shocked disbelief. He paused in midchew, cheeks swollen, filled with masticated tobacco leaves.

At that instant Paul propelled his head and upper torso through the driver's window to land on the turkey poacher's lap. His left hand stretched out, grabbed the keys, and twisted hard. The engine shut off, bringing the truck to an abrupt halt while hurtling all into a tangled mess.

Startled, Comer sucked the gigantic chaw of tobacco deep into his lungs. Then he coughed in an explosive exhale, spraying rotten tobacco juice mixed with saliva and bits and pieces of sticky, dark-brown leaves all over Paul's uniform shirt and the back of his head. The sickly sweet, pungent smell of overly gummed tobacco juice filled the cab.

"What the hell?" Comer gagged. "You nasty sons-of-bitches, get off of me."

Paul wiggled back out of the window, yanked the door open, and grabbed a double fistful of Comer. He dragged him out of the Scout and dumped him onto the dirt.

Jeff opened the passenger door, grabbed the shotgun, and unloaded it. The rolled-up carpet was still lying behind the seat. Paul couldn't see anything sticking out of it. From Jeff's vantage point he couldn't see anything, either. The two wardens exchanged a worried look. In that brief moment they both thought the same thing: "Did we mess up? Is the turkey back in the blind?"

Jeff picked the bundle of carpet up and walked around the truck until he stood directly in front of Comer. "So what's in the rolled-up carpet?" Jeff asked, silently praying for something dead and illegal to be stashed inside.

Comer shrugged.

Jeff held one edge of the flooring material and let it unravel. Without ceremony, a hen turkey plopped onto the ground.

"You're under arrest," Paul said.

"For what?" Comer sputtered, seated on the ground with his legs crossed.

"Taking turkey over bait and taking a hen turkey during the closed season."[1]

"You two are just plain full of shit," Comer spat, his eyes seething with resentment. He jabbed one quivering finger at the deceased bird. "Neither one of you got enough sense to tell the difference between a gobbler and a hen, or to know a wild turkey from a domestic bird."

---

1 Hunting turkey over bait is a second-degree misdemeanor punishable by up to sixty days in jail and a five-hundred-dollar fine. The killing of a hen turkey in closed season carries the elevated penalty of a first-degree misdemeanor, punishable by up to one year in jail and a one-thousand-dollar fine.

"Oh, we know the difference," Paul said.

"Well, we'll just have to see about that," Comer huffed, crossing his arms.

Jeff smiled and then calmly told Comer, "I can't believe you'd be foolish enough to take this to court based on those arguments."

But this was Dixie County, and in 1978, game violations were rarely prosecuted; in fact, no jury had ever convicted a county resident of a wildlife crime.

Two Months Later, Cross City

The only courtroom within the Dixie County Courthouse was packed. The trial of Randall Comer was about to begin. The faint odor of fresh furniture polish lingered in the air as spectators sat shoulder to shoulder on stout oak benches. They bent their heads to talk in excited whispers about the prospects of a win versus a loss. All bets were on the home team, led by public defender Don Saunders. Wide around the center, thick across the chest, with big arms and legs, he reminded some of a bear standing upright on his two hind legs. His gruff voice belied a brilliant mind. Hostile witnesses cowered before him. Rookie attorneys on opposing council were butchered. He didn't just walk into a courtroom, he burst into it.

Batting for the state was Richard Rossi, a thirty-year-old assistant state attorney who traveled a four-county rural circuit prosecuting misdemeanor cases and juvenile offenses. He hailed from Lake City, an hour's drive north, where his dad owned and operated a local hardware store. Rossi spent three years practicing business law in Clearwater before he was stricken by the "Perry Mason Syndrome." He'd grown up watching episodes of the 1960s fictional television courtroom drama where Perry Mason, a gifted defense attorney, always gained a reluctant confession from the real murderer through relentless grilling. "Because of that show," Rossi recalled, "I always felt like I couldn't be a real attorney unless I had tried a criminal case in court."

In many ways Rossi was the polar opposite of Saunders, quiet, reserved, matter-of-fact, a man whose lean frame perfectly filled out a tailored suit. Rossi was not given to exaggerated theatrical displays. Instead, his approach was smooth and straightforward when presenting the facts of a case. Interestingly, the two men got along quite well.

The GFC pushed hard to go the distance with this case and to make an example of Comer. Rossi was committed to the task—even though he didn't think he stood a chance of winning. Why should he? The cards had always been stacked against the state when it came to game cases in Dixie County. But Rossi clung to a slim glimmer of hope. There was a new judge in town.

In 1978, County Judge Marshall M. Clements had been in office for a little over a year when the turkey case landed on his docket. He was forty-five years old and one of only a handful of nonlawyer judges still practicing in the state. He slipped in under the wire, because in 1978, legislative changes required all county judges to be a member of the bar. Judge Clements took this to be a fortuitous sign because come reelection time the only person that could run against him would be another attorney. At that time there were only two lawyers in all of Dixie County, which greatly enhanced his long-term odds of retaining a seat on the bench.

The judge wore glasses and had a thick head of salt-and-pepper hair. Physically, he was not an imposing person, but he carried an air of confidence when he walked into a courtroom that drew people to him. His natural charisma to captivate and motivate folks was first noted, perhaps, in 1951, when he was voted senior-class president at tiny Dixie County High School. He spent the next twenty-five years working in the electrical-power generation industry. The judge's family on his mama's side went back seven generations in Dixie County, to the 1840s. He knew everyone. He made it a point to.

Before his election, Clements noticed a disturbing trend in his home county. It took longer and longer to find a fresh deer track to put his hunting dogs on. Sometimes his hunting party wouldn't locate one until ten in the morning. The deer were being slaughtered, their population all but decimated.

The game wardens were catching the poachers, but for whatever reason the county judge was turning these Dixie County residents loose as fast as they showed up in court. It was a lot like catch-and-release bass fishing, where the caught fish is returned to the water unharmed so it can grow up to become a bigger fish. In the case of the poachers, they became bolder and bolder with each free pass. Wantonly killing deer and turkey and illegally netting fish had become the biggest sport in the county.

Unbelievably, blood kin to some of the hardened outlaws had finally begun to grumble.

It was time for a change. Judge Clements officially took office on January 3, 1977. Sometime after his inauguration, the judge told Paul Hoover that he would one day like to see deer grazing on the Dixie County Courthouse lawns.

The Trial

As one might imagine, jury selection in Dixie County tended to benefit the defense more than the prosecution. Richard Rossi had the sheriff standing nearby to confer with, since he knew the exact lineage of every single person born and raised in Dixie County going back several generations. Rossi's goal was to find folks who were less sympathetic to the outlaws and didn't have close familial ties to the defendant.

Jury selection lasted all morning. It was almost noon when the sheriff leaned close to Rossi. With a fatalistic shrug, he said, "Richard, this is the best that you can do."

Rossi looked up at the judge. "Your honor, I accept the jury."

Paul Hoover testified first. He pulled a freshly thawed hen turkey out of a cooler and laid it on a plastic tarp covering a small wooden table in front of the witness stand. He recounted the facts of the case in bare-bones fashion. His testimony laid the foundation for the debate on two key issues that the state had to prove: (1) the hen turkey was indeed a hen, and (2) it was not a domestic bird.

Paul and Jeff were certainly well acquainted with the differences between hens and gobblers, and they could tell wild turkeys from domestic birds. Neither of them, however, held a degree in that particular field. Thus, they lacked the necessary qualifications to be considered an expert witness.

Then Rossi brought out the big gun, Steve Stafford, the GFC northeast regional biologist. Rossi took Stafford through the preliminaries of his background and various fields of expertise. Then he turned him over to Saunders for cross-examination.

The defense wasted no time. "Mr. Stafford, you can't tell me this is a wild turkey," Saunders stated, while gesturing toward the deceased bird lying on the table. The subtle implication to the jury was that a turkey was a turkey.

But Stafford knew otherwise. He could talk turkey with the best of them. He could yelp turkey, gobble turkey, and make the nuanced purr of a big tom in love. But more important, the graduate from the University of Tennessee with a master's degree in wildlife ecology could identify any species of turkey that happened to be put front of him. And that's exactly what Saunders did. Without any warning he dropped the hen turkey right in the biologist's lap, where it landed with a feathery plop.

Stafford remained unruffled.

The jurors leaned forward in rapt attention.

The prosecutor looked up from his notes, his pen stopped dead in its tracks. The hint of a smile creased his face as he leaned back to watch the show.

Stafford had dissected the carcasses of so many bears, deer, and wild turkeys for scientific research that another dead critter meant nothing to him. He knew the physical traits of tame birds and wild ones were distinct and arguably different.

"Can you definitively say Mr. Comer didn't kill this bird somewhere else?" Saunders asked. "This bird could be a domestic turkey. Why isn't it?"

"I have no idea where the bird was shot, but I can tell you it's a wild turkey," Stafford said.

"How do you know that?"

Stafford pulled up a wing from the evidence bird to use as a visual aid. "The wing feathers in a domestic bird will have a lot of broken lines," he explained, "whereas a wild turkey will always have black and white bars on the primary wing feathers." He turned the wing so the jury could see and pointed to the markings. "The distinct barring is very typical of the Eastern and Osceola turkeys; both subspecies are found in north Florida." The biologist glanced at the jurors' faces and felt encouraged by their reaction. The distinct barring on a wild bird was one important key, and they seemed to have bought into that.

Another key point Stafford hit on was how the tarsal (lower leg bone) of a domestic bird is shorter, thicker, and stockier when compared to the more flattened, tapered leg bone of a wild bird.

Saunders ignored Stafford's testimony and smoothly moved on. He was in a bit of a bind because he had no expert witness of his own to counter with. In all likelihood he would not have found one, either. What Stafford had testified to was established methodology for the identification of wild turkeys.

"Is the bird you're holding a hen or a gobbler?" Saunders asked.

"It's a hen," Stafford said.

"How do you know that?"

"By distinct markings on the breast feathers of the bird, and on the metatarsal (ankle), you see no spur, maybe just a bump. This is a hen turkey."

"Are you 100 percent sure this is a hen turkey?" Saunders asked.

"Yes," Stafford said.

"Can you be more specific?"

"There are many different ways to distinguish this bird as a hen. But the best and most obvious way is by examination of the breast feathers. On a hen, the breast feathers are buff-tipped. On a gobbler, the breast feathers are tipped with a black metallic bar." Stafford reached into a paper bag and pulled out samples of each for the jury to see. Next he yanked a breast feather from the bird in his lap and held it up for a side-by-side comparison to a known gobbler feather. Then he moved on to the legs. "On the back side of the turkey anklebone, a spur will grow out on a gobbler. The length is determined by age. Generally, the longer it is, the older the bird. On the anklebone of a hen, the most you'll see is a bump." Stafford pulled up one foot from the bird in his lap and pointed to a thumbtack-sized raised area.

"That doesn't sound very conclusive," Saunders said, and left it at that.

Randall Comer sat quietly at a rectangular wooden table assigned to the defense, hands clasped in front of him, while he tried to keep a confident smirk from becoming larger. The case was winding down. He anticipated a favorable outcome because of certain friends on the jury. He knew they would not let him down.

Saunders put on a few character witnesses—family members and close friends—to testify on Comer's behalf and then rested his case.

The case went to the jury late in the afternoon. By seven o'clock a soft knock sounded on the jury-room door—a verdict had been reached. They trooped back into the courtroom, single-file, until the men and women were seated. The foreman handed over a slip of paper to the bailiff, who passed it over to Judge Clements.

The court clerk read the verdict: guilty on all counts.

Comer sat stunned. Bewildered. He looked as if he'd been sucker-punched. How did this happen? He couldn't understand how his own people could turn against him.

Memories fade. No one can remember exactly what fines or type of sentence Comer received. But one person has a very good recollection of what happened immediately after the trial let out.

"It was twilight," Rossi recalled, "when I climbed into my car for the hour's drive back to my home in Lake City. Within two blocks, a couple of dark pickups pulled in behind me. I recognized them as being friends of the defendant. They hung back about three to four car lengths and stayed there. In those days, we had citizens band radios, our badge, and a weapon. I did not have my weapon with me. I didn't carry it unless it was unusual circumstances. I began to regret that decision as I looked into my rearview mirror and realized I was experiencing the unusual now.

"I called the Dixie County Sheriff's Office on the radio. Got hold of the supervisor and explained what was happening. He told me, 'A marked patrol unit will be waiting for you at the intersection of 351A and Highway 19. He'll escort you home.'"

As the young prosecutor passed the intersection, a sheriff's green-and-white pulled into traffic behind him and the suspicious trucks peeled off. The squelch broke on Rossi's radio. It was the sheriff's office supervisor sending him a parting farewell: "Richard, smooth sailing to Lake City."

Rossi turned on his AM radio and rested his arm on the car door as warm evening air swirled through the open window. It might not have been a big-time murder trial or kidnapping case, but he had just broken a new trail in wildlife law enforcement in Dixie County—the first conviction of a *resident* for a game offense. Honest hunters throughout the county owed Judge Marshall Clements a vote of thanks for dealing the entrenched, good-old-boys cabal a serious setback and ushering in a new era of real justice.

Author's Note

Don Saunders is a pseudonym. The defense attorney did not agree with the storyline and asked that his name be changed. I re-created scenes and dialogue for this chapter based on recorded telephone interviews with Paul Hoover, Jeff Hahr, Richard Rossi, Steve Stafford, and a telephone conversation with Judge Clements.

MURPHY'S LAW

A rookie game warden learns two valuable lessons: be prepared for the unexpected, and keep your guard up at all times.

And who, might you ask, was the lucky recipient of this hard-earned wisdom? Well, of course, that would be me.

A solid-steel trailer ball mounted to the bumper of a Dodge Ram Charger makes for a decent enough anvil. I swung a ball peen hammer over my head and brought it down with a precise blow. *Clang*! Again. *Clang*! Again. *Clang*! Mopping the sweat from my brow, I paused to examine a blade from the stainless-steel high-performance propeller of my patrol boat. I turned it in my hands so the natural sunlight revealed the dings and bumps and twists in the metal.

My once-a-week ritual of pounding the blades back into their original shape by eye had its limits. Eventually, a point is reached where no matter how much beating one does, a propeller remains misshapen. Rubbing my fingers across the uneven surface of the burnished metal convinced me the prop had become unserviceable. The time had come to send it off to be reconditioned, again.

I grabbed a spare cast aluminum power prop from a storage compartment in my patrol boat and mounted it to the engine's foot. It made for a weak substitute. I worried about the softer metal, as one good strike against any hard object would shred it apart. A game warden patrolling with an inferior propeller was like a carpenter trying to build a house with a rubber hammer—not the best way to do the job.

Two Days Later

On a hot and muggy evening in the summer of 1978, I set out for patrol up the Ocklawaha River. The Creek, as the locals like to call it, is fed primarily by Silver Springs, fifty miles upstream and east of the city of Ocala. The river and all of its meandering side creeks flow through a vast swamp that has changed little since the early 1900s, when paddle-wheelers first ferried well-to-do northerners on alligator sightseeing tours. This setting, with the moss-draped trees, delicate wild orchids, and birds of fine plumage often reminded me of a jungle backdrop for a Tarzan film. In fact, fisherman occasionally report seeing escaped monkeys from the Silver Springs Zoo swinging through the trees. The only impediment to navigation was Rodman Dam, located ten miles upstream from the Ocklawaha's confluence with the St. Johns River in northeast Florida. This section of the river, which remained relatively pristine and untouched by man, was the area I had chosen to work.

My patrol boat was an eighteen-foot fiberglass Old Timer with a 200 HP Johnson bolted to the transom. The vessel was utilitarian and open, and originally made for the convenience of commercial fishermen who ran hoop nets: giant, webbing-sheathed catfish traps that were emptied by rolling them over the vessel's low gunwales and into the boat. A high-pointed bow rose abruptly and was designed to ram through heavy lake chop. In profile, it resembled a slimmed-down version of a Viking warship.

I piloted the vessel from a starboard-side console. Upon entering a curve, I would roll the boat up sharply on its side so a thin film of water splashed over the gunwale and against the deck, which remained near vertical during this maneuver. The overflowing water made a satisfying swish. In a righthand turn I could stick my hand out like a slalom water-skier and feel the cool water sluice through my fingers.

The author steers an eighteen-foot Old Timer patrol boat around a sharp curve in the Ocklawaha River, 1981.

The sun had set, and the gloom of twilight had deepened the shadows on the dark water. I eased the throttle back, letting the boat settle fully in the water before shutting the engine down. I listened, turning my head from side to side while cupping my hands behind both ears, straining to catch the faintest noise. I was hoping to hear the steady thrum of a big outboard engine idling along in one of a maze of side creeks that ran parallel to the main river. Outlaw commercial fishermen would often hide out in these less-traveled watercourses while they illegally electrocuted catfish.

The device of choice for generating an electric shock was homemade and constructed from a small electric motor that drove a magneto removed from an antique telephone. Mounted to a wooden board, the whole contraption was about the size of a loaf of bread. Two wires from the magneto, their ends stripped down to bare copper, were dangled into water from the bow and the stern. The sting of the electric current flowing between them drove fish crazy. To escape, they shot straight to the surface where they zigzagged and rolled while fishermen wielding long-handled dip nets frantically scooped them up. A skilled two-man crew could catch up to six hundred pounds of catfish in four hours.

Every half mile or so, I stopped to listen, then gently nudged the boat up on a plane and motored ahead. As I came under the Highway 19 Bridge, faint bubbles from an outboard began to appear. Dark stains, six inches high, showed against the base of trees growing along the bank where the wake from a passing vessel had recently washed against them. I paused to listen.

Silence.

Continuing upriver, I came into a shallow curve. Ahead lay an intersection where two creeks joined the Ocklawaha. A cloud of blue-black smoke hung motionless in the still air above the confluence of watercourses. Boils of residual turbulence remained on the water's surface. The acrid odor of burnt outboard motor fuel stung my nostrils.

I was totally switched on.

Someone had heard me coming.

I pulled the throttle back, letting the hull settle fully into the water while I looked hard into the mouth of each creek. The angled nose of a black wooden boat was barely visible, partially hidden by overhanging tree branches and deep shadows just inside the entrance to one, and about seventy-five yards away. I straightened the boat out and gunned it. I drew a mental bead on the target and set my course dead ahead. The blur of a dark object flew into the air and landed with a heavy splash next to the suspicious boat. Surprisingly, the two men sitting in the vessel didn't attempt to flee. They were trapped, blocked by a bank-to-bank logjam of epic proportions. A logger's chain saw would be the only way to cut a corridor through the tangle of fallen trees blocking their only path of escape upstream.

I careened sideways into their boat, throwing up a wall of water that washed over their port gunwale. "Turn off the engine now!" I shouted. "Shut it down! Shut it down!"

They were calm, nonplussed even. The passenger wore a dingy white T-shirt, blue jeans, and white rubber boots. He sat on a flat-board wooden seat in the middle, head bent, hands clasped patiently in his lap. His most distinguishing physical feature was unusually large ears, which tended to drape forward a little when his head tilted down.

The driver looked at me with one good eye. The other one bulged out of a red-rimmed socket, the iris colored with a milky-white film. It looked painful. Among the wardens he was, of course, known as "Pop-eye." His partner, well, we called him "Wing-nuts." Collectively, they were known as the "Telephone Twins."

Pop-eye fingered the key, hesitating for a moment before switching the outboard off.

"Hand me the key," I told him.

He stuck out a gnarled hand, scarred and calloused from skinning catfish and tying knots into the heavy webbing used to build fish traps. The key was small, made from stamped aluminum. But I proudly stuck it in my pocket and thought to myself, "You are some caught sons-of-a-bitches."

With my quarry compliantly sitting alongside and the evidence lying in only a couple of feet of tea-colored water, the rest of the evening seemed a mere formality. The old saw, "If it seems too good to be true, it probably is," did not register with me at that moment. No, I was brimming with the confidence of a nine-month rookie game warden as I pulled out a heavy-steel trap drag attached to a coil of braided nylon line. It was fashioned from an old window-sash weight and designed like a grappling hook. I tossed it into the water, trying to snag one of the loose wires connected to the electric shocking device.

"Now you two just sit there and relax," I told them over my shoulder. "When I get the machine in the boat we'll finish our business."

Business meant seizing their boat and motor and issuing them citations. There were no fish in the boat. Apparently they'd just gotten started.

"Bob, we're not going to give you any trouble," Pop-eye said. "You should know us well enough by now. It's going to be dark in a little while, and I've been having problems with my running lights. You mind if I fiddle with the wires to see if I can get them working?

"Knock yourself out," I told him.

Out of the side of my eye I saw him follow the wiring with his hands from under the steering console to where it disappeared below the lip of the engine cowling mounted to the front of a straight-stack 150 HP Mercury outboard. My attention, however, was mostly riveted on recovery of the prize. I'd inadvertently let their boat drift a few feet away from mine. Unfortunately, the bow of my boat was now rubbing against the bank, and the bow of their boat was conveniently pointed toward the open creek mouth. I glanced down at the shocking device lying on the sandy bottom, diligently working the line back and forth with one hand as I tried to guide the drag underneath a tangle of submerged wires.

Varrooommmmm!

They shot out of the creek like a rocket ship, spraying a white frothy wake against the bank and leaving me rocking in their backwash. Pop-eye raised his hand in a middle-finger salute. I was pissed beyond words. They'd pulled out a hidden key from underneath the engine cowling.

I shook my fist at them. "Come back here right now, you're under arrest!" I hollered at the receding transom of the little flat-bottom skiff. I jumped into the driver's seat and cranked the engine. But I couldn't go forward. I would have to back up first. When I jammed the throttle into reverse, the engine slammed into the trunk of a submerged swamp maple and stalled. I cranked it again, moving ahead this time, and rammed the bank, then reversed it, just a little, frantically maneuvering the gear-shift handle back and forth. Desperately trying to extricate myself from the natural entrapment resulted in a furious froth of foam and spray accompanied by the high-pitched guttural whine of an outboard being cruelly manhandled. Finally, I managed to swing the bow around until it was pointed toward open water.

I mashed the throttle. The engine screamed as the propeller blades dug in, spinning at six thousand revolutions per minute. An easy-to-follow bubble trail lay before me. Two things worried me as I felt the hull rise up on a full plane: The power prop did not have the top-end speed I was used to, and the boat was handling funky. It just wasn't responding like I had become accustomed to with the high-performance propeller.

I skidded into the first turn wide open. Ahead lay a fallen cypress tree that blocked most of the creek, leaving a narrow gap of only a few feet to one side for navigable passage. I spun the wheel, angling hard for the opening, but the boat continued to slide in the opposite direction. I became desperate as the nearly horizontal tree that extended a good ninety feet out from the opposite bank loomed closer. It was as dense and stout as a fresh-cut telephone pole and hung a full foot above the water's surface.

Decision time.

I straightened the wheel out and hit it dead on. The hull ramped up, shooting out of the water, bow arrowed toward a darkening sky. The propeller screamed as it freewheeled in waterless air. I crouched like a horse jockey on his mount, keeping a ten-and-two white-knuckle grip on the steering wheel. In my mind's eye I saw a flashback from the 1976 movie *Gator*, where Burt Reynolds plays an ex-con/moonshiner who runs circles around a waterborne posse of clumsy southern cops in the Okefenokee Swamp. Some boats crash; others perform intricate aerial maneuvers that would have made a stunt pilot proud.

Unlike the movies, though, reality can be a bitter pill to swallow. The hull slammed down stern first, before the bow smacked into the water, snapping my head and neck forward, nearly catapulting me over the console.

Twenty-five miles per hour was all I could coax out of my patrol boat now. Without even looking I knew the spare prop was shredded like spaghetti. I was done. I shut the engine off. Only one sound remained, the teasing whine of a six-cylinder outboard fading into the distance. I pounded the steering wheel with both fists, while I singed the air blue with a streak of expletives that would have made a bosun's mate blush. I knew I was behaving like a three-year-old toddler, but it felt too damn good to quit.

Murphy's Law, "Anything that can go wrong, will go wrong," had struck again.

★

The following day I met with my lieutenant. He was former military, wore his hair shaved in a severe buzz cut, and had ice-blue eyes that could bore a hole through a cinder block. He spoke in declarative sentences, often using emphatic hand gestures to punctuate salient points. He took no prisoners and hated excuses. Our conversation went something like this.

"You what!" he shouted, giving me a flinty stare that would have wilted a desert cactus. "Did you just tell me another boat got away from you?"

"Yes, sir," I sheepishly replied. A few months earlier my patrol boat had become stuck on top of a submerged tree trunk while escorting a seized boat operated by two prisoners. We were en route to the Highway 19 Boat Ramp on the Ocklawaha River. They, too, had fled but were eventually caught after a swamp manhunt that, by all accounts, everyone involved found to be great fun and excellent sport. My lieutenant, however, held a dim view of the whole operation because the money spent on spotter aircraft put his quarterly budget in the red. How in the hell did I know I would get stuck on a log?

The lieutenant came up with a simple solution to the vexing problem of my repeated failures: "In the future, you will take your pocketknife and cut the gas lines of all boats you plan to seize. Do . . . you . . . understand . . . me?"

"Yes, sir." I stood ramrod straight. In the back of my mind I couldn't help but think of the Telephone Twins. I was happy they weren't present in some sort of preternatural state to witness my dressing down. They would have laughed like hell.

Postscript

Since I knew the real names of Pop-eye and Wing-nuts, I filed the appropriate wildlife charges for their misdeeds in the County Court of Putnam County. (Back then no law existed for fleeing and attempting to elude a law enforcement officer on the water.) Memories wane after thirty-some-odd years, but I seem to remember them getting a few hundred dollars in fines. The boat and motor were never seized, the result of a legal technicality that negates forfeiture of a vessel if it is registered to an innocent party. Outlaw commercial fishermen were well aware of this legal loophole and frequently used it to their advantage by registering the vessel—or a vehicle—in a relative's or friend's name.

KISSIMMEE MARSH AIRBOAT CHASE

On a frigid moonless night in the winter of 1985, an unlit GFC airboat lay hidden behind a screen of dense reeds along the northeastern shore of Lake Hatchineha. The entire boat was painted a flat black. Although it was a game warden patrol craft, the standard yellow and green decals marking it as such had been removed. The only thing that identified it as a law enforcement vessel was a blue strobe light, and even that could be quickly detached if it looked like it might compromise the plainclothes patrol detail being conducted by Reserve Sgt. Robby Holland and Investigation Sgt. Donnie Hudson.

It was an unconventional craft, but perfect for tonight's stakeout in a region of shallow lakes and vast marshes that comprise the upper Kissimmee River Valley in south-central Florida. It takes an airboat to catch an airboat when going after poachers who frequent swampy wetlands to ply their trade.

On board, the wardens huddled around the low blue flames emitted by a one-burner Coleman stove in the cramped quarters of the forward deck. One reached down and grabbed the handle of an old aluminum coffeepot, sooty and dented but still serviceable, and filled two metal camp cups with freshly brewed black coffee. They raised the steaming beverage until it barely touched their lips, letting it linger for a moment to inhale the delightful aroma. The wardens savored every drop of that hot coffee, not so much for the caffeine buzz as for the warmth it provided on a wickedly cold night.

These conservation lawmen were a rare breed. Admired by their peers as "catch-men," the title bestowed an unofficial recognition of abilities that far exceeded those who dwelled in the unheralded ranks of mere license checkers. Noted for their tenacity and resilience, the men often relied on gut instinct and animal cunning to get the job done.

Few lawmen—or women—would willingly endure freezing wind-chill factors down into the teens while riding in a top-heavy water-craft that tended to be tippy, had no brakes, and offered zero protection from the elements.

What motivated them to do it?

In a manner of speaking, it came down to who could outwit whom. It was a rugged night, but sometimes the worst weather made the best conditions for arresting a wildlife crook. The wardens knew most poachers held a low opinion of them, often underestimating their resourcefulness and ability to withstand discomfort. They hoped some clever and calculating poacher would be brave enough to play the odds, betting no tenured civil servant would be dedicated enough to patrol on a night when actual Fahrenheit temperatures plunged below freezing.

End of Shift

Robby Holland quietly put away the cooking gear in the airboat's forward compartment and lowered the fiberglass lid, careful not to let it bang shut. He looked up at his partner, best friend, and brother-in-law, Donnie Hudson, who sat above and behind him in the driver's seat. Donnie's head and shoulders silhouetted like a black inkblot against the star-speckled sky. The top of his head stood a good seven feet above the vessel's waterline and a little higher than the carburetor atop the massive engine. Donnie peered into the gloom from his elevated perch, which offered a commanding view of a gray-black horizon, the solid nightscape broken only by a distant halo of light that was the cattle town of Kissimmee, five miles to the west.

"So, what do you think?" Robby asked, glancing at the luminous dial on his watch. "It's almost midnight, and I'm just about froze solid. Even my toes are numb."

"Let's give it five more minutes and then we'll head in," Donnie answered, conflicted by the urge to seek warmth and the even greater urge to catch someone. While both men technically held the same rank, Donnie, the warden in full-time status, had the final say. Robby, thirty-nine, had the weekend off from his day job at Verizon. He first became a reservist in 1970, paying his own way through the police academy, and was a fully certified state law enforcement officer. Working with his brother-in-law guaranteed his best shot at a little action. Among his peers, Donnie had the reputation as a hard-charger who pursued game violators with a grim determination born of sheer willpower and grit.

A couple of minutes passed before Robby cocked his head. "Hear it?" The guttural roar of an airboat engine cranking off on a still night was unmistakable.

"Yes," Donnie said. "Sounds like it's coming from over by Bullshit Hill."

The oddly named Bullshit Hill is a grassed-over spoil mound of unearthed soil and muck, the product of a canal dug through a four-mile-wide isthmus between Cypress Lake and Lake Hatchineha back in the late 1940s. As the flamingo flies, the area lies about seventeen miles south of Orlando.

The thirty-foot hump of land provides a stunning view of Lake Hatchineha in the daytime, with shorelines rimmed by a lush green marsh that gives way to lowland cow pastures dotted with pines and clumps of saw palmettos. The wilderness landmark attracts weekend airboaters who ride their gigantic propeller-driven rigs like wild stallions to the flat top of the high berm. A convivial time is had by all while they dry-land drag race, build bonfires, chug copious amounts of beer, and swap wild tales, thus the homey moniker of Bullshit Hill. The wardens were about a half mile to the east, sitting near the mouth of Dead River, a tight, twisting creek of tannin-stained water that flowed between the two lakes.

Robby and Donnie patiently waited as the airboat's engine grew louder. Occasionally the sweep from a headlamp beam would flair above masses of tangled, woody-stemmed buttonwoods, a water-anchored plant that grows in patches throughout the marsh. Navigating through the jungle of dense vegetation in an airboat made for slow progress.

"He's coming on," Donnie announced, as he put on a hardhat with an aircraft landing lamp strapped to it. Wherever he looked, the light followed, casting a brilliant white beam that could pierce the darkest of nights. When under way, it clearly illuminated the slick water of narrow airboat trails that cut through meadows of aquatic grasses and around nature's hazards like stumps and floating logs. A common household electrical wire draped from the helmet-mounted toggle switch to a 12-volt battery secured to the deck.

The airboat emerged from the buttonwoods and glided into an open glade of wet grass, puttering along at an idle speed. The operator's headlamp beam cut a clean swath through the inky black. The manner it was being swept, far out and near level with the horizon, indicated they were looking for deer or gators, which is a major game violation while in possession of a firearm. Someone hunting frogs, an innocent pastime practiced by many, would have held the light pointed down and around the boat to better spot the amphibian's pearl-sized eyes so they could impale it with a gig.

The suspicious light was worth investigating and formed the legal basis for many nighttime stops, be it on water or land.

The airboat's current course would bring it to within thirty yards of the blacked-out patrol airboat. The wardens did not have to worry about noise discipline now. No one in the other airboat could hear anything over the engine racket and thunderous claps of a six-foot-wide airplane propeller cracking the sound barrier.

"You ready?" Donnie asked.

"Yeah," Robby answered, securing a firm grip on the handrails.

"When I hit them with the light, try to get the FL numbers," he said, referring to the Florida boat registration identification required by law.

"Ten-four."

Donnie cranked the engine over. By now the wardens could make out the vague silhouettes of the operator and a passenger bundled up in heavy winter coats, dimly illuminated by the headlamp's back glow. As they passed directly in front, Donnie toggled on the blue strobe light. A second or two later he flicked on the headlamp and pressed down on the foot throttle. His left hand steadied the rudder control stick. The rattling vibrations increased until the warden's thirteen-foot fiberglass hull was set free from the wet grass beneath them and accelerated slowly ahead.

Coming alongside another vessel in an airboat requires nuanced driving and a delicate touch on the controls. Unlike a motorboat, there is no reverse, no way to slow down and readjust should the initial approach be too fast. Donnie set his speed so it was a hair faster than the other airboat and cautiously moved ahead.

The first thing Robby noted was a blank spot on the other airboat's rudder where the boat registration decal numbers should have been mounted. Nor were there any affixed to the side of the hull. "These guys are up to no good," he told himself. Sensing what was about to happen next, he curled his fingers around the handrail in an iron grip.

Donnie swung in behind the other boat. He got to within ten feet of the stern when the driver suddenly whipped his head around and flashed a searing bright light into the warden's eyes. In the next instant the unknown airboat went full throttle. The cyclic reverberations of deafening concussive waves shattered the night while a 150-mile-per-hour blast of ice-cold air hit Donnie square in the face and blew his headlamp off. He spit out a leaf and shouted, "Get my helmet! Get my helmet!"

He let the engine idle while Robby leapt to the deck and collected the hardhat-mounted light.

Donnie reached down, grabbed the helmet, and snugged it firmly back on his head. He clenched his teeth and gave it a solid slap to wedge it around his skull for extra insurance.

The fleeing airboat was almost a quarter mile away now and flying through the night up Dead River. The bright-white cone of the operator's headlight beam whipped manically back and forth, desperately searching for dangerous obstructions to avoid and a clean path by which to escape.

Donnie hammered the throttle down, and they were off. Zooming into the night while an icy blast of Arctic-like air cut into every fray and loose fiber of the wardens' insulated coveralls—"freezer suits" they liked to call them.

One thing was for sure. Whoever piloted the other airboat better have his testicles cinched up tight, because neither warden, as it turned out, was a stranger to speed. In their youth, both men had participated in unofficial drag races around the Plant City area of west-central Florida where they'd grown up. Hanging at local hamburger joints like the Dog & Suds and Strawberry Drive-in on a Friday or Saturday night was the "in" thing to do back in the 1950s and 1960s. Driving around in beefed-up hot rods often resulted in a challenge to "drag." One time, Donnie and Robby squared off in an unsanctioned head-to-head race on the tarmac of the Plant City Airport. Robby drove a 1962 red Corvette while Donnie rode a Triumph Bonneville motorcycle. "That was a bad bike," Donnie recalled later in an interview. "I hit 111 miles per hour in the quarter mile and beat him by seven to eight car lengths. But if you ask Robby, he'll probably never own up to it. Nobody wants to admit they were whupped that bad."

Robby grudgingly admitted to the loss. But he offered this in the way of a comeback: "My Corvette's little 327 cubic engine wasn't much in the quarter, but I've run it up to a 157 miles an hour on the interstate. No way could Donnie have touched that speed with his bike in an open road race with no set distance limit."

Not too surprisingly, Donnie had special work done on the Game and Fish airboat engine. If there was any way to modify it to run better or stronger or faster, he was going to make it happen. Even though he was forty-one years old, the need for speed and the need to win were still an integral part of his psyche.

The 0470 six-cylinder Continental factory engine originally pumped out 225 HP and was designed to power armored personnel carriers for the military. After an airboat mechanic friend of Donnie's added a few goodies to it—like a five-inch-high rise manifold and a Holly 500 carburetor—the horsepower shot up to nearly 300. Donnie also removed the exhaust pipes to pick up a little more speed. He always ran light, too. Each extra pound in an airboat slowed it down that much more. He only carried one 12-volt battery, no anchor, and no heavy metal grass rake. And to shave even more weight off, he never began his shift with more than three-quarters of a tank of aviation gas.

While most airboats driven on dry ground had a hard polymer shell to protect the hull's bottom from wearing out prematurely, Donnie avoided them all together. "They were just too heavy," he explained. "Whenever I saw the fiberglass rubbing thin on my boat, I'd flip the hull over and apply a couple of layers of glass to it. Back then the game commission was strapped for cash and expected us to provide the labor to maintain our equipment."

Perhaps the best weight advantage came from the wardens themselves. Both men happened to be lean and wiry, standing around five seven to five eight. Robby weighed in at no more than 145 and Donnie at about 160.

But the real trick to enhance engine performance was to put a can of Slick 50 additive in the oil reservoir. The Teflon lubrication kept the pistons from seizing up when run hard for extended periods, even on bone-dry ground. With the stripped-down hull and highly modified engine, the GFC airboat could hit a blistering 80 miles per hour under ideal conditions across ankle-deep water and a hard sand bottom.

Dead River left little room to maneuver, the creek being only about two boat widths wide. Donnie's heart sank as he pursued the distant flicker of light. The distance to make up was an enormous deficit. But that didn't dissuade the fifteen-year veteran from having a go at it. He'd never backed down from a race yet.

Somehow Donnie needed to gain an advantage or at least even the odds. He decided on a risky course of action. "The only chance we had of catching them," he explained, "was to cut across the dry oxbows and straighten the river out. Our suspects were playing it safe, taking the longer route by staying in the narrow channel and following the natural turns as they came."

Donnie reached down and grabbed Robby's shoulder. "Hold on!" he screamed.

Robby nodded.

The patrol boat skidded up the shallow slope of the first oxbow at full power. The bow smashed through waist-high reeds and willow bushes, rocking violently from side to side as it hurtled across bumpy ground. Bits and pieces of freshly flayed plants became a hailstorm of green confetti in the warden's light. Whenever the boat charged through a high-topped willow bush, the whippy branches flailed Robby's face until it was raw. Brown pond birds—colloquially known as "shit-quicks"—shocked by ground-shaking reverberations, fluttered up in front of the speeding airboat and unloaded a watery stream of white poop. Thus unencumbered, they gained sufficient altitude to narrowly escape becoming a feathered ornament plastered against the metal protective cage built around the whirling propeller blades.

Occasionally, the flat-bottomed hull hit a solid root-clump hardened by soil. The angled change in terrain became a ski ramp of sorts, launching the airboat skyward, simultaneously bouncing both men out of their seats and slamming them back down when gravity dictated the boat meet terra firma again.

On each aerial hop, Donnie kept his eyes glued straight ahead while he rigidly focused on not moving the control stick and keeping his foot hard on the gas. One inadvertent nudge to the stick or a letup on the throttle might have thrown the hull to the left or right, causing it to land cockeyed and flip ass-end-over-teakettle.

"My biggest worry," Donnie said, "was running into an eleven- to twelve-foot alligator. It would have been like hitting a foot-and-a-half-thick telephone pole laid flat on the ground. That's not something you want to have happen and could very well have caused Robby and me to be ejected. End of story."

At the time, neither warden could have predicted how long a teeth-rattling ride they were in for, but both would later admit that an airboat chase is one of the quickest ways they know of to die. "The first rule of an airboat chase," Donnie insisted, "is to end it quick." Without hesitation, Robby, who measured life's risks against his combat experience as a former Marine and armored-tank driver in Vietnam, readily agreed.

The wardens got through the first oxbow without incident. Then they powered across thirty to forty yards of roiling creek water left by the outlaw airboat before they took the next series of shortcuts, rocketing across a second oxbow, and then a third, and a fourth, and a fifth—a miraculous feat to accomplish without cracking up.

The deck was now covered in a thick green mat of mangled plant parts. Bugs of all shapes and descriptions crawled out from under the vegetative debris. Lodged in the cage mesh were the wide green leaf tips of a soft-stemmed wetlands plant called "flags." Shaped like Roman spearpoints and floppy like the elephant's-ear plant, they easily broke off when clipped by the bow of a speeding airboat.

Fast approaching a T intersection with Reedy Creek, Donnie pushed the control stick forward to shift the rudders and channel the air into a high-speed sliding right turn. Both men leaned in unison away from the direction of travel to counter the harsh tug of centrifugal forces.

Intercepting the churning boat wake and debris trail of broken lily pads left by the other airboat told the wardens they were tightening the gap. A few more turns in the creek brought them to within sight of the suspects' transom and the blur of spinning propeller blades blowing out a gale-like spray of fine water droplets. Donnie fell in behind the airboat's slipstream doing about 55. Robby's mustache instantly iced over from the foggy mist. In order to see, Donnie took his glasses off and clenched them between his teeth.

The two boats raced in tandem through the coal-black night, each throwing a dagger of bright-white light in search of a tactical advantage. They blasted out of Reedy Creek and into the broad expanse of Cypress Lake, all 4,097 acres of it.

"That's when I screwed up," Donnie admitted. "They took a left, riding along the lake's shoreline across shallow grass. I went to the inside of them instead of staying on the outside where I could control them and force them toward shore."

Sgt. Donnie Hudson powers through a radical 180-degree turn in his patrol air-boat, 1985. This is the only way to quickly stop or reverse course in a slick-bottomed watercraft with no braking mechanism.

The suspects abruptly changed course, darting out into an area of open water that varied in depth from four to seven feet.

The sudden change in path added another level of peril for the lawmen. Optimum conditions for operation of an airboat are water depths measured in inches, not feet. In deep water, the boat sinks lower, making the steering sluggish and the top-heavy hull less responsive and prone to roll over in a sharp turn. Another hazard is caused by the shallow-draft hull, which has only a few inches of free-board at the transom. A sudden stop or a following sea can cause a backwash of water to flood over the stern and sink it, quick.

A biting wind swept across the lake, throwing up a stiff chop, causing Donnie to fight the control stick to keep the hull running true. He artfully feathered the throttle so the bow didn't submarine into the next wave and cause the hull to pitch-pole over on top of itself. Sixty yards ahead, the fleeing airboat suddenly spun out, hurling up enormous curtains of white spray as it whipped around in a tight, skidding turn. Then it straightened out and charged the patrol craft, on a direct course to ram the bow. It bore down on the wardens with its white light blazing into their eyes. Huge jets of foam and froth sprayed out from underneath the bow as it bulldozed angrily across the waves toward them.

Instinctively, Donnie flared the hull, thus avoiding death, injury, or a dunking in chilly waters that would have exposed the lawmen to the threat of deadly hypothermia.

Donnie swallowed hard as he thought back to a similar incident forever etched into his memory. It happened to him as a first-year rookie. In 1970, he and another warden were on night patrol in Lake Okeechobee when their outboard engine propeller got hung up in an illegal trawl net. The transom was being dragged down, the boat in danger of capsizing. While they feverishly worked to cut the net free, a gang of outlaw commercial fishermen made repeated high-speed passes by them, which caused a wall of water to surge over the gunwale with each successive pass. The patrol boat took on more and more water until it finally sank. Donnie and his partner were left treading water at midnight, six miles offshore, in the one lake that contains more alligators than anyplace on earth. "That was not fun," Donnie recalled. "We were scared, especially when the outlaws came back hunting us. They cut back and forth across the lake all night looking to run us over. We anticipated they would do this and also anticipated the course they thought we would take to swim to shore. We took a different tack, about thirty degrees off the shortest route. It kept us away from the area they were searching for us in and probably saved our lives, because if they had found us, they would have run us over with their propellers and cut us to ribbons."

Donnie and his partner shucked their shoes. The men swam, and swam, and swam, and eventually reached the cattail-rimmed shoreline at daylight, exhausted. When they finally crawled up onto a hard soil bank, they had to endure the added insult of walking a mile and a half barefoot through thick mats of prickly sandspurs to reach the nearest fish camp. Donnie summed it up this way, "I'll be damned if I was ever going to let some son-of-a-bitch do that to me again!"

The fleeing airboat came around for a second high-speed pass. Again, it lined up true with the bow of the wardens' boat. Once again,

Donnie flared the hull and avoided a catastrophic crash. The lawman who had tried so hard never to hurt anyone while on the job—unless they deserved it—had had enough. He was going to end the chase now.

Donnie leaned down, grabbed Robby's shoulder, and screamed out at the top of his lungs, "Robby, pull your gun and shoot the driver! Shoot the driver!"

Robby nodded, but his mind was already there. The men were not only brothers-in-law but *brothers-by-law* and closer than blood.

"When Donnie told me to shoot the driver," Robby recalled, "I realized he was thinking the same thing I was thinking: *If they ram us out here in deep water we're in big trouble!*

"I had already made up my mind to pop the driver once in the chest with my .357 and dive overboard if it looked like the other boat was at a point of no return. I'm an airboat driver, too. After a while you get a sense for knowing when a crash is inevitable."

Robby drew his chrome-plated .357 Magnum service revolver and laid it across his lap. With his feet braced against a metal storage locker, he locked his thighs and shoved back, wedging his butt and upper torso firmly into the seat. Both hands were now free to wield the gun.

The unknown boat came around again.

Robby brought the gun up.

Then an odd thing happened. The outlaw rig abruptly changed course, veering off on a different track that would take them in the opposite direction, backtracking down the bank of Cypress Lake.

The immediate threat of deadly bodily harm to the wardens by ramming was gone. Then Donnie remembered he hadn't retracted his orders. "Holy shit!" he thought. "Robby still might try to shoot them."

Donnie leaned down and hollered, "Don't shoot! Don't shoot!"

Robby stuck one thumb up and nodded. He'd already holstered his gun. He was the son of a Baptist preacher and deeply religious. He wasn't about to shoot someone unless there was no alternative.

Donnie got back to the business at hand. He now had the advantage. He was on the outside as he slid up from behind toward the port (left) side of the suspects' airboat and began crowding them.

When the outlaw rig didn't budge from its current path, he nudged the control stick forward, banged into the fleeing craft's gunwale, and bounced off. He hit it again and again and again. Big crashing booms echoed out above the thunderous roar of both engines tearing through the night.

Robby held on as best he could with all four appendages splayed out in an awkward attempt to remain seated and not be ejected. That had happened to him once before. He found it to be an unsettling experience, one that left him with a permanent neck injury after bouncing across the ground like a spent cannonball at more than 50 miles per hour. Donnie had been the driver then, too.

The suspects' airboat began to drift in toward the bank. As the wardens kept pace, shoreline reeds and then wax myrtle bushes began to appear, flashing by on either side of the law enforcement craft in a hazy blur of mottled greens.

Ahead, Donnie spotted a massive patch of fresh hog rooting over an acre in size. Dark and ugly, the soft black muck was dug up a foot to two feet deep by wild pigs. The broken ground would be a hellish roller-coaster ride for any airboat. And that got Donnie to thinking.

When the suspects swung their bow to tack around it, Donnie smashed into them and then spun away from the freshly churned earth, avoiding the glutinous trap. The fleeing airboat powered down as it wallowed into it and finally ground to a halt, coming to rest tipped up on one side. The warden's boat slid to a stop fifteen to twenty yards ahead.

During the five-mile race Donnie's headlamp cord had whipped back and forth, entangling him. While he worked to free himself and keep his light trained on the driver, he shouted, "Robby get the driver! Get him off that boat! Now!"

Robby leapt out, sinking calf deep into sucking muck, and made a beeline for the other airboat. He offered no cordial "How do you do?" greeting as he climbed on board and cat-crawled up the metal support frame to where the driver and passenger were seated. Without ceremony, and driven by the pure adrenaline of the chase, Robby grabbed a double fistful of the burly thirty-something-year-old operator and flung him off the boat—all two hundred–plus pounds—and into the dank mud. Robby pounced on his back, burying the suspect's face into turbid marsh water. He pulled his .357 and jammed the barrel into that tender spot just below the ear. "You move," Robby yelled, "and I blow your brains out."

At that moment the suspect only wanted relief. He needed air.

"Let him up, Robby," Donnie said, now untangled from the helmet wire. "He can't breathe."

Robby got a handful of shaggy hair and snatched his head back. There was an audible inhalation as the prisoner sucked in a refreshingly huge gulp of the crisp night air.

"I ain't going nowhere," he coughed out, spitting up flecks of mud and grit and bits of broken sticks and decayed leaves.

"You . . . are . . . under . . . arrest," Robby panted. And then, once he caught his breath, "The charge is fleeing and attempting to elude a law enforcement officer on the water."

The passenger, having had a front-row seat to the aforementioned event, was left pale and shaken. He wisely decided surrender was the best option available and stuck both hands up in the air.

As the drama wound down, a faint background noise was all that remained: the hissing and popping of cooling red-lined engines meeting the cold night air, the signature sounds of a hard-fought airboat chase.

Beneath their heavy winter coats, the suspects wore empty leather shoulder holsters for carrying powerful big-bore revolvers. One of them eventually admitted to Robby they'd chucked the guns into the lake. At the time neither suspect would say what they might have been hunting. No explanation was given for why they ran or what their intention may have been when they tried to ram the wardens. Nor did they have outstanding warrants out for their arrest, an incentive that inspires many to run.

The ride into jail, however, can sometimes generate unexpected conversation of a revealing nature. The prisoner thinking back to that intense moment continuously relives the event in his mind, feeling the massive adrenaline dump and how good it felt. Thus, he feels compelled to talk, to have a manly recounting of the night's adventures, and what better person to talk to than the adversary who had just bested him?

The outlaw airboat operator piped up from the backseat of Donnie Hudson's state Ram Charger, his wrists securely cuffed behind his back, "I got one thing to say."

"Oh, and what's that?" Donnie asked, thinking the guy's about to pop off with a smartass comment.

"You can damn sure run an airboat!"

"Well, thank you."

"You know," Donnie continued, "you tried to put my boat down twice by ramming it. The third time you lined up and all of a sudden you changed your mind. Why?"

"Well," he chuckled, "I seen what's-his-name there," nodding toward Robby seated in the front passenger seat, "with his chrome revolver out, and I heard you hollering, 'Don't shoot until I tell you!' To tell you the damn truth, I didn't know if he heard you or not."

The benefit of time and sober reflection, however, tends to make suspects reevaluate their actions. The outlaw airboat operator met with Robby and Donnie a couple of months later and apologized for his behavior. "I did what I did, and it was stupid," he told them. "I'll never do anything like that again. I'd appreciate it if you could give me a break this one time. I've got a good job with the county, and they'll fire me if I'm convicted of a felony."

The wardens met with the prosecuting attorney, and it was mutually agreed to give the guy a break. The felony charge was reduced to a misdemeanor.

Thirty years after the event, Donnie reflected on that decision: "We were pretty well convinced they [outlaw airboat] were trying to run us over that night, but we could have been wrong. Robby and I tried to represent the GFC well and give everyone a fair shake. For some folks giving them a break doesn't mean much. But I think it meant something to this guy.

"He held good to his word and never poached again."

SKY POACHERS

Poachers are cheaters, and cheaters always seek an unfair advantage. Be it in games of chance or in methods of taking game, every crook will do whatever it takes to gain an edge.

There are countless reasons why people cheat. For some, it's illicit riches; in the case of poachers, it can be for profit too. For others, it can be the thrill to kill and a chance to beat the law—outwit, outsmart, and outplay them in a high-stakes game of catch-me-if-you-can. This is a story of the latter, of the brazen and ballsy arrogance of one south Florida businessman and his sidekick who took to the skies to illegally kill game. You would expect to find something like this in Alaska, with its wayward bush pilots, but rarely in a populous state like Florida.

The case would force the Game and Fresh Water Fish Commission to dip into a meager budget and spend an inordinate amount of time and money they could ill afford. And it would test the mettle of a Vietnam combat veteran turned GFC helicopter pilot in a daring aerial duel with a couple of sky poachers.

A Weekday in October 1987, 3:00 p.m.

The gray Dodge pickup crawled to a stop along the road shoulder of Highway 27, about a mile outside of Moore Haven, in Glades County.

By all outward appearances, the truck seemed inconspicuous enough. Plain magnetic signs that read "Johnson Survey, Inc." clung to the sides of both doors. In the bed sat a stack of orange traffic cones and a couple of beat-up lane barricades. A thin, wiry man with inquisitive hazel eyes and a thick shock of unruly dark-brown hair climbed out from the passenger side and shut the door. He wore faded blue jeans and a fluorescent orange and yellow safety vest over a sweat-stained T-shirt. Hidden beneath the loose-fitting shirt was a .357 Magnum revolver strapped to his side. The other hip carried a handheld radio.

The gray Dodge pulled away.

Cars streamed past Warden George Pottorf as he ambled along the shoulder of the busy four-lane highway. No one paid any attention to the thirty-four-year-old conservation lawman. He was just another disheveled-looking guy wearing dusty dungarees and a frayed traffic safety vest, scraping out a minimum wage living under the hot Florida sun.

Before joining the GFC in 1984, George spent thirteen years working full-time as a plumber. Pretending to be a member of a road construction crew was not a stretch for him. In fact, he felt right at home.

A five-minute hike found the warden abreast of a twelve-lot mobile home park on the north side of the highway. The park was an oasis of sorts, surrounded on all four sides by fenced pastureland except for a dirt access road. A few cabbage palms and a handful of scraggly live oaks offered scant relief to an otherwise bland landscape that stretched unbroken from horizon to horizon.

George checked out the mobile home park. His main worry was whether or not someone was watching. A handful of beater pickups were parked haphazardly in a few yards, plastic children's toys lay scattered in others, and a mud-splattered all-terrain vehicle sat under a lone cabbage palm. But no one was wandering around outside. And no curtain was pulled back with a half-hidden face peering suspiciously at him from behind a window.

"Perfect," he told himself.

George walked up to the edge of a deep drainage ditch and paused. When there was a break in traffic he slid down the bank and disappeared out of sight. He slogged through calf-deep water and thick aquatic grasses until he was hidden in the dark recess of a large metal culvert. The access road for the mobile home park crossed overhead. The diameter of the culvert was about five feet. George was five seven, so he had to bend over just a bit when he stood. His height, or to be more precise, the lack of it, was why he was selected for this particular stakeout.

The target of the surveillance was a white double-wide, indistinguishable from the other manufactured homes except for a red International Harvester tractor parked out back. The tenant was absent. Curtis Simmons had left to go hunting with a local businessman and good friend, Ken Nesbitt. They'd flown out in Nesbitt's yellow J-3 Piper Cub, a single-engine, fixed-wing, two-seat aircraft with an aftermarket gun rack installed inside the narrow fuselage. The men were due to return sometime before sunset and land right in front of the warden.

★

That same afternoon, a red and white Cessna 172 took off from the Clewiston Airport. The words "State Wildlife Officer" normally identified it as a GFC patrol aircraft. But if someone looked under the wings, they would not see those stenciled markings. They had been covered with white shoe polish.

As the plane gained altitude, the ground below gave way to a crazy-quilt pattern of sugarcane fields, pastureland dotted with tiny specks that were cattle, and, to the east, big Lake Okeechobee, bright and shimmering until its vast expanse melded into the horizon.

Investigation Lt. Donnie Hudson sat on the right side of the aircraft across from the pilot, Lt. John Thomas. They were tailing the yellow J-3 Piper Cub that had taken off ahead of them.

Donnie was the puppet master in charge of assigning more than a dozen officers and supervisors to specific roles in a massive undercover wildlife investigation that covered Hendry, Highlands, and Glades Counties in southwest Florida. Some were members of investigative units and others pulled from uniform patrol. They needed so many bodies that Donnie even had to recruit his wife, Marie, into being a lookout at the Clewiston Airport, where Nesbitt often kept his plane. She was dark-haired, petite, and lithe as a cat. Being light and limber had its advantages. A good portion of her surveillance time was spent wearing camouflage war paint while sitting eighteen feet above the ground in the top of a leafy melaleuca tree.

The investigation was enormous—in scope and assigned manpower—because Ken Nesbitt and his sidekick, Curtis Simmons, were landing and trespassing wherever they pleased and hunting whenever they liked. The total landmass of their poaching grounds exceeded that of the state of Delaware.

Complaints from the owners of big cattle ranches were the catalyst behind the detail. They reported seeing the yellow Piper loping along at treetop level while on suspected scouting missions. These were Texas-sized properties that ranged upward of one hundred thousand acres or more. The pastures were annually maintained through prescribed burning or dragging the fields with massive tractors pulling fences and huge tires to spread the cow manure evenly. The highly enriched grasses attracted a multitude of wildlife and turned the fields an emerald green. When these open areas followed the uneven contour of natural wood lines, the color contrast was so startling that from the air they resembled manicured golf courses. The attendant flatness and lack of sharp topographical features made these pastures into passable landing strips.

The J-3 Piper Cub had been modified from its original design to better adapt to bumpy backcountry landings and takeoffs. Nesbitt had installed oversized tires for soft turf, beefed up support struts, and switched out the factory-installed 65 HP engine for an 85. The plane only needed about a football-field-sized runway to zoom in and take off. In spite of the aircraft's nimbleness, the wings were all banged up and dented from scraping tree branches and hitting saplings and underbrush during the habitually dicey takeoffs and landings.

Nesbitt, thirty-four, was a heavyset guy with a big, bushy beard and thick mop of brown hair. He was a respected local businessman who owned a pool hall and a mini-warehouse in the fishing village of Clewiston. Undercover wardens followed him from the time he got up to the time he went to bed. He proved to be a creature of habit and usually began his mornings with a visit to the local coffee shop, maybe stopping in at an office supply store, doing some odd errands, and then hitting one of the cafés for lunch. By around two or three in the afternoon he'd be at the airport readying his plane.

★

The pilot of the GFC Cessna held steady at 2,500 feet, above and a little behind the Piper Cub cruising at 60 miles per hour. That position kept them in Nesbitt's blind spot and reasonably safe from detection. Nesbitt rarely flew above two hundred feet and would often hug the ground at twenty-five.

Donnie imagined the yellow Piper as a giant dragonfly lazing across the landscape below. It stood out in stark contrast to the mottled greens and browns of the natural background vegetation beneath it.

The conservation lawmen had spent the better part of three months chasing these guys. The big brass in Tallahassee headquarters and Donnie were becoming impatient and a little frustrated with the lack of progress. This was an expensive detail to run, and they needed results. They'd seen Nesbitt land on a couple of properties, documenting each one as a trespass violation. But they'd never witnessed him or Simmons kill any game.

The closest they'd come was the week before, when the pilot and Donnie watched the Piper fly over a shallow flag pond while one of the men fired a semiautomatic rifle at a running deer. A series of four- to five-foot-high geysers erupted behind the animal before it escaped unharmed into the brush. Technically the wardens had witnessed a violation. You can't shoot game from a moving vehicle. You can't herd wildlife. And you can't take game during the closed season.

The wardens needed a kill. They needed to catch them red-handed with a bloody deer or turkey carcass in their possession. Back then, the Hendry County court system had an apparent lack of fondness for game cases, particularly when it involved a respected resident of the county. An attempt-to-kill case was not something that impressed them and would often get tossed out of court.

★

Nesbitt led the wardens on an ambling course that afternoon, never flying in a straight line but following the contours of cow pastures juxtaposed against cypress heads, oak hammocks, and natural prairies as they continually scanned the ground ahead and beneath them for game.

About an hour into the flight, the Piper abruptly circled and landed alongside a drainage canal. Donnie glassed the terrain below with a pair of 7-power binoculars, holding the optics as steady as he could in the vibrating plane. Simmons ran out of the Piper with the prop still spinning, put something in a black plastic garbage bag, and jumped back inside. The wardens suspected the men had shot something. But the Piper's design—with the wing mounted atop the fuselage—prevented them from seeing the shooter stick a gun barrel out.

The Piper took off, heading straight for Simmons's home. Thirty miles one way as the buzzard flew.

George Pottorf's handheld crackled. "4446," Donnie said.

"Go ahead," Pottorf answered.

"It looks like our guys may have something. Keep an eye out for a black plastic garbage bag when they land."

"Ten-four."

By now it was sunset, and the landscape was beginning to take on a diminished glow when George heard the clattering drone of the yellow Piper. It dropped from the sky and sat down in the cow pasture, the wings tipped awkwardly from side to side as the landing wheels rolled across uneven ground dotted with thick clumps of grass. The plane pulled up alongside the highway right-of-way, about fifty yards away from George, who had a good view of the operation from inside the shady recess of the culvert.

Curtis Simmons, fifty-two, crawled out of the plane. He had a face like cracked leather and a week's worth of stubble sprouting from his chin. He wore a green and yellow John Deere ball cap, a short-sleeved camouflaged T-shirt, blue jeans, and cheap, slip-on shoes. In one hand he held a 12-gauge shotgun; the other held the black plastic bag.

He crossed the fence and strolled up to the back door of his double-wide. He dropped the bag on top of a wooden cleaning table before entering through the back door with the gun. A screened door snapped shut behind him.

The Piper Cub spun around and took off with a throaty *varoom!*

George waited. He watched, anxious to find out what was in the bag. Good dark had settled in when an outside light flipped on, an incandescent 100-watt bulb screwed into a naked socket. Moths flittered around the dull yellow light. The glow illuminated the wooden table, a built-in stainless-steel sink, and a black metal staircase descending from the rear entryway.

The back door banged open. Simmons strode straight to the cleaning table. He pulled a turkey out of the bag and began plucking. Through the wide-angle binoculars George held it looked like someone had ripped open a down feather pillow and was shaking it out.

George couldn't tell if it was a gobbler or a hen, only that it was a wild turkey. They finally had hard evidence. Well, not quite, he still had to get his hands on a piece of that bird. The investigation was in the building stages, and there were no plans to take Simmons down tonight.

One thing the wardens needed to establish was that Nesbitt and Simmons habitually landed on private properties with the intent to commit wildlife crimes. This would negate the inevitable defense of an "emergency landing" should the case ever go to court.

It took Simmons about twenty minutes to butcher the bird, wash the parts in the outside sink, and drop the cut-up pieces in a stainless pan. He ascended the metal steps and disappeared through the back door. The light snapped out. Quiet ruled the night, except for the steady *whoosh* of passing automobiles along Highway 27.

George crept out of the ditch, jogged around to the access road, and followed it to Simmons's trailer. He ducked into the backyard and snuck up to the cleaning table, paper bag in hand. He grabbed up feathers and pieces of skin and a wing, stuffing them into the bag as quickly as he could.

He encountered one minor setback when the fresh feathers stuck to the palms of his hands. George had to manually scrape them off to get them inside the bag. Time-wise, it only added another ten seconds to the mission. A trivial holdup in most circumstances—until the outside light unexpectedly turned on.

"Oh, shit!" George thought. He stood in the open, totally illuminated and vulnerable to detection at any moment. He frantically looked around. But there were no bushes, hedges, or large trees to offer concealment.

From within the mobile home came the heavy clumps of approaching footsteps.

There was only one place to hide. He scrambled underneath the tractor, crawled up behind a tire, and pulled himself into a tight ball while clutching the evidence bag in a death grip.

"I had about decided," George recalled, "that if Simmons stuck his head under that tractor, I would haul ass and pretend like I was a burglar. Crossing all of my fingers and hoping and praying like hell he wouldn't take it in his mind to shoot me for one. I only had three years on the job, and there was no way I was going to be the one to tip off Simmons he was under surveillance."

Simmons came out the back door and walked right by George, so close the warden could have reached out and grabbed his pants cuff. The poacher picked up a utensil he'd left on the cleaning table and returned to the trailer. The outside light blinked out.

George could finally breathe again. He hustled back to the culvert and then pushed the talk button on his handheld. "I'm ready for pickup."

A few minutes later headlight beams swerved out of the traffic flow. A nondescript Dodge pickup pulled over to the road shoulder. A door opened and snicked quietly shut. The truck pulled away, merged into the flow of traffic, and became lost in a steady stream of fading red taillights.

The Takedown

Thursday, November 5, 1987, began with guarded optimism as the wardens dispersed for their assignments on what would be the final day of the plane-poaching stakeout.

By three in the afternoon, Lt. Donnie Hudson thought things were

Lt. Lance Ham stands next to the Jet Bell Ranger helicopter he flew while working the Sky Poachers case, 1987.

shaping up pretty darn good. Members of the aviation surveillance team watched Simmons—who sometimes piloted the Piper—drop off Nesbitt with a shotgun in a remote pasture in the Hilliard Brothers' Ranch. A storm rolled in, forcing Simmons to flee the area and land the yellow Piper at an airport in Immokalee.

Meanwhile, Donnie was riding out the same storm inside the bubbled canopy of a GFC blue and white Jet Bell Ranger helicopter parked in an open field—five miles west from where Nesbitt had been let out to hunt. The helicopter rocked gently on its skids as the wind and rain buffeted the craft with a relentless thrumming. Conversation was limited until the worst of it abated a few minutes later. Sitting across from Donnie in the right seat was the pilot, Lt. Lance Ham. Lance had pulled off his flight helmet during the shutdown.

Donnie marveled at the pilot's hair. He wore it in a 1960s slicked-back style, a modest version of the late Conway Twitty's majestic pompadour. In spite of being tucked inside the tight-fitting helmet, not a single strand was out of place. Given Lance's natural laconic drawl, it wasn't a stretch for Donnie to imagine him on the big stage as a country music singer.

Lance may have had the look, but he didn't have the voice. He'd be the first to admit that, except for mouthing the words to a few gospel hymns, he couldn't sing a lick.

Behind them sat Lt. Ken Pickles, the local supervisor and twenty-six-year veteran of uniform patrol. Thin and lanky, he wore a short crew cut and had a chaw of tobacco crammed in one corner of his mouth. He was there for one reason. This was his patrol area, and he wanted to be part of the takedown. Even though he believed Nesbitt and Simmons were "ineffective" poachers, they still needed to be caught, if for no other reason than to send a loud, clear message to copycat poachers. Already, rumors were circulating that two more airplanes were illegally scavenging the big ranchlands for game. Enough was enough, and Pickles wanted it stopped.

The three men idly chatted while the wind diminished and the sun finally broke through the clouds. It was about time. The radio crackled: "4101," Lt. Ronnie Potts said, pilot of the tailing plane.

"Go ahead," Lance said.

"The Piper's lifting off now, heading back toward the Hilliard Ranch."

"Ten-four."

More than a mile above them circled another GFC fixed-wing flown by Lt. Jim Truitt. He would be backup should the tailing plane encounter engine problems or have to leave the area. His plane also carried a representative from the Federal Aviation Authority. Nesbitt had committed a variety of aviation violations, and Donnie wanted an expert opinion on what charges should be filed.

Thirty minutes later, the tailing plane called Lance: "The Piper's made a loop around the pickup site and moved on. Apparently Nesbitt is still hunting. Simmons is heading your way. Not sure if he suspects something or if he's just burning time. But his current flight path will take him right over you."

"We're moving now," Lance said.

He revved the turbine engine up to full power until the chopper lifted in a hover. Then he tilted the nose down and took off running in an imaginary line away from the approaching plane, trying to put as much distance between them as he could.

"In Vietnam," Lance recalled, "we did a lot of nap-of-the-earth flying. You mask with the trees and the terrain and whatever else is available. If the Piper Cub was flying at, say an altitude of one hundred feet, we couldn't fly above that altitude and remain undetected. The moment we exceeded his altitude we would have been visible on the horizon and above the tree line to him."

In addition to his military combat experience, Lance Ham spent seven years piloting a GFC crop duster, spraying for invasive aquatic weeds. He felt very comfortable with this sort of intense flying that was largely dependent on gut instinct and lightning-fast reflexes. But he also admits some people not accustomed with this technique might feel a "little bit uncomfortable."

Donnie's eyes widened into saucers as that "little bit uncomfortable" was happening to him right now. At times it felt like he was on a wild-ass roller coaster. At other times it felt like he was on an elevator that had short-circuited and couldn't figure out which way to go: Up . . . Down . . . Up . . . Down . . . as they skimmed across pastures and down old logging trails, jumping barbed-wire fences, metal panel gates, spindly pine trees, and grazing cattle. The copter came in so low and so fast the poor beasts had no time to react except to look up in white-eyed terror as the metal skids whooshed right over their heads and the rotor blast matted the fur flat to their backs.

Donnie involuntarily jerked his knees up every time Lance leaped over an obstacle.

At one point the pilot glanced at Donnie with a puzzled expression and asked, "What are you doing that for?"

"Because it makes me feel better," said Donnie, who had never objected to a fast ride before so long as *he* was the one driving.

"Skids will hit first," Lance replied, matter-of-factly, cracking a tiny smile while he focused on threading through the blur of terrain rushing toward them.

Pickles, strapped into the backseat, wore no headset, so he just gripped the sides of his seat and held on. "It was the most exciting helicopter ride of my life," he recalled. "I loved every minute of it and trusted Lance explicitly as a pilot, though I do believe he pushed safety over to one side of the plate that day."

Donnie's "E" ticket ride finally came to an end when the tailing pilot informed them the Piper had turned around and was heading back to the pickup site.

The helicopter pilot reversed course, too, and backtracked across the same terrain they'd flown only moments before. They had ten miles to go before they'd reach the drop-off site. Timing was critical. They wanted to catch the plane on the ground with Nesbitt and Simmons inside. And they would only have about a thirty-second window of opportunity to get it right. Lance adjusted his flight patterns and speed according to the information relayed to him by the tailing plane about what the Piper Cub was doing and how fast it was traveling at any given moment.

The yellow Piper was five miles ahead of the Bell Ranger, traveling at 60 miles per hour. Estimated time of arrival at the drop-off site: five minutes. Lance needed to close the gap. He cranked the helicopter up to 110 miles per hour and increased the altitude to one hundred feet. He figured it would take Nesbitt one to two minutes to load on board the Piper once it landed.

Five minutes later, the tailing pilot said, "4101."

"Go ahead," Lance said.

"The Piper's circling the landing area. He's running off a herd of cattle to clear a runway.

"Ten-four."

One minute later: "The cows are gone. He's circling back around for touchdown now."

"Ten-four."

Lance dropped his speed back and went belly to the earth, rocketing across the ground, rolling and yawing and zigzagging through narrow tunnels and gaps in the trees and openings ahead.

Donnie's knees started bouncing again.

Pickles couldn't believe he was getting paid to do this.

"Okay, Lance," Lieutenant Potts said, "Nesbitt is out in the open and running for the plane. He has a long gun in one hand. You're about a half mile and thirty seconds out."

Lance double-clicked the mic button—message received.

Lt. Donnie Hudson snapped this photo looking out through the windshield of the Game and Fresh Water Fish Commission Jet Bell Ranger helicopter, 1987. The J-3 Piper Cub is fewer than thirty feet away and on a direct collision course with the helicopter.

Nesbitt jumped in the Piper and took over the controls. He throttled up and began rolling down the grassy clearing for takeoff. The Piper pilot didn't have a worry in the world that day until the Bell Ranger overtook the taxiing aircraft and dropped down in front of him, filling up his windshield with whirling rotor blades. Simmons, seated in the front seat, instinctively crossed his hands in front of his face. Like that could somehow stop the helicopter's rotor blades from chopping his head off.

The first foolish thought that entered into Nesbitt's head was to gun it. The plane lifted off and headed straight on a collision course with the Bell Ranger. "Hold on, Donnie," Lance said, in an eerily calm voice. "He's trying to ram us."

At that exact moment Donnie snapped a photograph with a camera using a standard-sized lens. It shows the Piper Cub so close to the bubble windshield of the chopper that the spinning propeller blades fill most of the picture—a distance of fewer than thirty feet.

Nesbitt may have thought he was a shit-hot pilot, but his skills paled in comparison to his adversary flying the Bell Ranger. Lt. Lance Ham had flown a yearlong combat tour in Vietnam with the 281st Assault Helicopter Gunships. His mission was to insert U.S. Army Special Forces teams behind enemy lines for long-range reconnaissance patrols. When the teams called for pickup, they were often engaged in a firefight. The gunships together with Phantom F-4 fighter jets streaked in with machine guns and rockets blazing to break contact (annihilate the enemy) before the soldiers could be extracted. Lance was awarded two Distinguished Flying Crosses, the Bronze Star, a fistful of combat air medals (several with a *V* for valor), and the Vietnamese Cross for Gallantry with a star.

What Lance also understood better than Nesbitt were the aerodynamics of a Piper Cub. He'd flown a Piper Pawnee spray plane for years and knew he could blow the lift out from underneath the J-3 Piper with the Bell Ranger's powerful rotor wash.

In the next instant relief coursed through Donnie, while he stared dumbfounded at the scene unfolding before him. It looked like an invisible hand from the Jolly Green Giant had dropped from the sky and slowly pushed the Piper Cub straight down onto the ground. Nesbitt's plane bounced a couple of times, spun around, and tried to take off in the opposite direction.

Lance banked the helo into a steep turn, circled around, and elevator-dropped straight down in front of the Piper. The two aircraft faced off nose to nose. By now, Nesbitt realized whoever sat behind the controls of that helicopter was not going to blink first. Donnie gave a stiff flat-hand slice across his throat, the universal gesture to cut the throttle.

As soon as Donnie saw the Piper idle down, he unsnapped the four-point restraining harness, shoved the door open, and prepared to jump out. "Wait a minute, Donnie," Lance warned.

Too late. In the brief millisecond before he stepped out, Donnie couldn't understand why Lance would say that. All of these months, the time and expense invested by so many wardens and the agency to finally reach this point. This was the moment he'd been waiting for, and he would not be denied. It was only when he was in midair, with the chopper above, and the ground still a good ten feet below that he began to appreciate the pilot's caution.

Fortunately for Donnie, he had the hard, muscular physique of a longshoreman, the type of guy who manhandles fifty-five-gallon drums all day long for a living. No one had ever accused the investigation lieutenant of being frail.

He landed with a meaty thud. He escaped broken bones because the ground was soft and mushy from the recent rain and cushioned the fall.

Simmons was first out of the plane. "I ain't afraid to die," he boasted to the lieutenant.

"Well, I can sure help you along with that if you don't do what the fuck I tell you to do right now!" Donnie told him, while reaching for a short-barreled .357 Magnum revolver holstered on his hip.

"That seemed to take some of the starch out of his sails," Donnie recalled. "He wasn't the sharpest knife in the drawer and had a tendency to say things without thinking them all the way through. He needed to understand this wasn't a Clint Eastwood movie. Ken Nesbitt, on the other hand, was a gentleman and didn't give us a moment's trouble. He never did, except when he tried to ram us."

Pickles turned out to be a quick study and wisely waited until the helicopter's skids touched wet grass before disembarking. The two game warden supervisors and the two suspects held a parley. Back then, it wasn't unusual for the suspects to drive their own seized vehicle back to a convenient spot where the wardens could take possession of it. Donnie seized a Browning 12-gauge shotgun, ammunition, and a couple of knives from the plane. Nesbitt was given specific instructions to fly back to the Clewiston Airport. The wardens would follow in the Bell Ranger. Dusk was fast approaching, and they wanted to reach the airport before dark.

Everything went fine, up to a point, with Lance flying formation to the right rear, or about the five o'clock position in relation to the Piper. Being a former spray and combat pilot taught him to develop a keen eye for dangerous hazards that a lot of pilots might not pick up on. That would include the vague, needle-like silhouette of an unlit, two-hundred-foot radio antenna[1] looming out of the gloom ahead, the steel guide wires all but invisible.

"See what he's trying to do?" Lance asked.

"Yeah," Donnie replied. "Nesbitt's trying to run us into that antenna. I can barely see it in this dim light."

"He's a clever guy. He lined up with it a long way off so there wouldn't be any last-minute deviations in his flight path that we would notice."

Lance deftly avoided disaster by shifting the Bell Ranger to flying formation off the Piper's left rear as the fixed-wing buzzed past the antenna.

Donnie was beginning to have second thoughts about how nice Nesbitt really was.

There was no way to prove Nesbitt's specific intent to do bodily harm to the officers, although he was later charged with "operation of aircraft in a reckless manner."

After landing safely at the Clewiston Airport, Curtis Simmons asked Lieutenant Pickles if he was related to another game warden by the last name of Pickles who used to work in Hendry County.

"Yeah," Ken said, "he was my brother."

"I used to run from him all the time," Simmons bragged, his hands now cuffed securely behind his back. "He never caught me."

"Well," Pickles told him, with no small amount of satisfaction, "you didn't do a very good job of running today."

Case Disposition

Research into what Ken Nesbitt and Curtis Simmons were actually charged with and the final outcome of their cases proved challenging. The GFC records have long been destroyed, and none of the wardens kept copies of the actual charging documents.

---

1 The three lawmen inside the Bell Ranger all agree Ken Nesbitt tried running them into an obstruction. What they couldn't agree on was what exactly that obstruction was—Donnie, power lines; Lance, radio antenna; and Ken Pickles, a fire tower. Since Lance Ham was the pilot, his version is represented above.

Glades County Courthouse shows Nesbitt was found not guilty by a jury on the charge of "possession of turkey during the closed season." Interestingly, George Pottorf has no recollection of having ever been called as a witness for the state in a trial. Simmons was also charged with possession of illegal turkey. His case was nol-prossed—thrown out by the prosecution. The Piper Cub was returned to Nesbitt. Any possibility of the plane's forfeiture was eliminated when he was found not guilty of the turkey charge.

Hendry County Courthouse records show Nesbitt and Simmons pled guilty to the charge of "armed trespass." They were given two years' probation, which meant they could not possess a firearm during that period. The reckless airplane charge against Nesbitt was nol-prossed by the state.

Phase II

The human condition dictates that most everyone learns from their mistakes. Ken Nesbitt certainly did. Legal depositions between the wardens and his criminal defense attorney revealed precise details

A surveillance photograph of Ken Nesbitt's plane during Phase II of the Sky Poachers case, 1989. Nesbitt painted over the J-3 Piper Cub's original bright yellow with a distinctive, palmetto-fan camouflage pattern.

of how undercover game officers operated behind the scenes. Having gleaned these heretofore unknown tidbits of intelligence, Nesbitt set out to right his wrongs and never make the same mistakes again.

One thing Nesbitt learned was the Piper Cub's bright-yellow paint job made an easy target for a trailing GFC patrol plane to follow—even from a considerable distance. Another was how easily he'd been watched and monitored by plainclothes game and fish officers on stakeout at the public airports he flew from, particularly, how often he'd been seen loading a gun into the plane. Nesbitt figured both problems could be easily solved. In the future he'd hide his rifle near a private grass airstrip in a remote part of Hendry County and paint the plane to blend in with the countryside.

Apparently, it never occurred to him to give up the life of a wildlife crook.

Nesbitt was back in full swing two years later. The wardens, of course, got wind of what he was up to. The Piper's new paint job was distinctive—a palmetto-fan camouflage pattern made up of various shades of muted greens and browns. Nesbitt also used the switch in paint color to thumb his nose at the game commission with a familiar, if not so subtle message: "Catch me if you can."

As always, the wardens remained resolute in their determination to engage the now thirty-six-year-old pilot in a battle of wits and wills. They moved full steam ahead with what became known as "Phase II" of the investigation—once again, headed up by the indefatigable Lt. Donnie Hudson. Only this time, the inherent dangers of rural patrol would catch up with them, providing some sketchy moments for all involved.

A Weekday in September 1989, 4:00 p.m.

Warden George Pottorf crouched behind a lone wax myrtle bush. As far as bushes went, this one wasn't very big and just large enough around the middle to hide his upper torso and head. The brittle, woody-stemmed lowland plant stood at the tail end of a half-mile-long grass airstrip located in Hendry County. In the past it had been used by hefty DC-3 twin-engine cargo planes. A metal hangar built alongside the middle of the unimproved runway housed enough DC-3 parts to completely refurbish a whole plane. George wasn't sure why a DC-3 would be landing out here in the middle of nowhere, but he had his suspicions.

At the moment, the only plane on the desolate runway was the palmetto-camouflaged Piper Cub that had just touched down. Ken Nesbitt jumped out carrying a rifle, darted off the runway, and disappeared out of sight. A couple of minutes later he returned minus the gun.

Nesbitt cranked up the Piper and taxied down the runway. By pure happenstance, he aimed the nose straight at George along with his only means of concealment, the solitary wax myrtle. About one hundred yards of useable airstrip remained before it ended abruptly in a copse of trees. As the plane accelerated, it didn't leave the ground as quickly as George would have liked. He began to rethink the wisdom of having picked this particular plant to hide behind. Sweat beaded up on the warden's forehead, and it wasn't just from the stifling heat. The Piper barreled ahead, the propeller blades cutting through the air in a cacophony of thundering claps. George melted into the ground. The plane lifted off, flying five feet over his head in an ear-splitting roar. The prop wash knocked his camouflaged ball cap off while snippets of the wax myrtle bush rained down around him. "Christ!" George thought, panting like he'd just run a short sprint. "That was close."

Pausing in a moment of sober introspection, George concluded there would have been no glory having been found with his head cleaved in two by an airplane propeller. He made a personal commitment not to get caught in that sort of bind again.

The warden ran down to about where Nesbitt had disembarked from his plane. Where the pilot had stepped out was hard to judge. But an old, abandoned dump truck, heeled over on two sagging tires, caught his attention. Using both hands, he wrenched the passenger door open. The bottom of the bench seat was nothing more than bare metal springs and scraps of rotting cloth. Stale dirt and crushed beer cans covered the floorboards. On a hunch, he grabbed the back of the seat and muscled it forward. At first glance, nothing appeared out of place, but once his eyes adjusted to the shaded interior, a semiautomatic .22 Magnum rifle became visible wedged in between rusted seat springs. He pulled it out and saw an empty shell casing jammed in the ejector port. He jotted down the serial numbers in a pocket notebook and returned the gun to its original hiding place.

George hiked back to an unmarked patrol truck hidden in an orange grove more than a mile away. He was ready to call it a day.

The following afternoon he returned with Investigation Lt. Jerry Lord, who would operate a video camera during the stakeout. They wanted irrefutable proof that Nesbitt had put his hands on a firearm. Since Nesbitt was on probation, he could not legally possess a gun. Prison waited if he were caught and convicted.

The wardens need not have worried. Indeed, they were about to get their irrefutable proof and then some.

At four o'clock, the camouflaged Piper swooped down from a crystal-blue sky, touched down on the grass airstrip, and taxied up to the abandoned dump truck.

George and Jerry lay along one edge of the runway, looking at the rear of the truck from about fifty yards away. Dressed in full camouflage, including green and brown wax face paint, they had little worry of being detected.

Nesbitt headed straight to the truck, removed the gun, and walked around to the back bumper. Dressed in faded dungarees and a torn white T-shirt, the Piper pilot pulled out a screwdriver and dug into the rifle's ejector port. He rooted and poked and prodded until the stuck shell casing popped out. His gaze wandered back and forth in the tall weeds around him. Finally, he spotted an empty beer can. He picked it up in one hand and cocked his arm. He quizzically looked north, then south, and finally to the east, directly where George and Jerry lay hidden.

"Oh, no," whispered George in a contained panic. "He's going to throw the damn can toward us."

Sure enough, of all the points on the compass Nesbitt could have picked, he chose to toss the can in the wardens' direction. George was about to learn that no matter how well one planned, sometimes, "Shit happens!"

Lt. Donnie Hudson holds a handheld radio while on stakeout of the remote airstrip Ken Nesbitt used during Phase II of the Sky Poachers case, 1989.

The can landed about ten yards in front of Nesbitt. He shouldered the rifle, *crack*! The copper-jacketed bullet ricocheted off the ground and buzzed over the wardens' heads, like a bumblebee on steroids.

The video camera rocked unsteadily. "He's shooting at us," Jerry uttered excitedly, a statement that served more as a cathartic stress reliever than to convey a message that was patently obvious.

"Yes, yes, I can see that," George answered.

George needed some relief. In an act born out of sheer desperation, he shoved his metal citation book and binoculars out in front of him and crossed his arms over his head. A kind of impromptu but ineffective shield should an errant bullet fly his way.

Jerry glanced away from the view finder. "Like that's going to help," he remarked sarcastically.

"Well, it may not," George whispered harshly, "but it sure makes me feel better."

Nesbitt continued to wield the screwdriver. The gun was jammed again. A few seconds passed, and then he slid the bolt forward, chambering a fresh round. He threw the gun up and sighted, *crack*!

Thwack, the bullet lodged in the limb of a pine tree shading the wardens. As the rifle's action loosened up, the bullets started flying with more rapidity and with greater accuracy. The video shows the camera violently shaking as Jerry tries to maintain some semblance of professionalism. One bullet came winging a foot or two above George's head.

"Enough," George muttered, deciding to throw in the towel. He rolled down a shallow slope and out of the line of fire. Jerry followed right behind with the camera snuggled tightly against his chest. They'd captured enough of Nesbitt on film and planned to take it to an assistant state's attorney for review. It would provide the evidence for a future felony charge.

What the two lawmen had really wanted was to catch Nesbitt flat-footed with a dead deer or turkey in hand. It's in the DNA of every game warden.

Three Days Later, 2:00 p.m.

Lt. Donnie Hudson and Investigation Lt. Steve Blissett hid their unmarked patrol truck on the edge of a 1,200–acre orange grove, waded across a chest-deep canal, and took up a surveillance position on top of a tiny knoll at the west end of the remote runway. The hump of ground wasn't a whole lot more than eight feet in height, but a significant topographical feature in a land where only a foot or two in elevation can make the difference between swampland and high ground.

The mile-long hike had cooked both men. The heat was an incredible 98 degrees, the humidity so thick and choking that every breath felt like sucking oxygen through a soda straw. The sweat ran down their faces in tiny rivulets while they readied their gear. Donnie wiped the stinging salt from his eyes with the sleeve of his camo jacket. Then he pulled out a video camera, tripod, and camo tarp from a military backpack. Steve was a few feet away clearing out an area behind some scrub oaks for a hide. Neither man noticed the dark clouds gathering behind them, although a minute or two later they did feel a noticeable drop in temperature as a cool breeze drew air back into the gathering storm.

Phase II of the Sky Poachers case. Lt. Donnie Hudson shoulders a military back-pack while wading across a south Florida drainage canal, 1989.

Donnie nodded toward the west, where the weather was building. "We'd better get this stuff covered up."

Steve agreed.

Donnie began to rise from his knees. He grabbed an old boot stem at the base of a ten-foot-tall cabbage palm to steady himself.

At that instant a blinding white light and a deafening *POW!* blasted both men off the knoll. They landed, dumbstruck, at the edge of the canal. The odor of burnt gunpowder lingered in the air. Though Donnie never lost consciousness, he was left with a horrible ringing in his ears. The back of his neck hurt something fierce. His first thought: "Booby trap."

"What happened?" Steve patted his side. "Where's my gun?"

"Your gun's been blown off," Donnie said, noting the loose stitching hanging from Steve's gun belt. He still wasn't sure if it had been an improvised explosive device or a lightning bolt.

The men felt around in the murky water and recovered Steve's gun still snapped in its leather holster.

Camouflage was the uniform of the day for wardens conducting stakeouts in the Sky Poachers case, 1989. *Left to right:* Donnie Hudson, George Pottorf, Steve Blissett, and Jerry Lord.

Torrential rain, along with cloud-to-ground lightning strikes came in a fury. The bolts blew out treetops all around them, as every ten to fifteen seconds pinkish-white flashes of superpowered electricity coursed from the sky. It seemed as though the hounds of hell had been let loose. It was enough to convince Donnie a lightning bolt had struck near them.

"If we stay here, we die!" Donnie shouted, to be heard over the clamor of thunderclaps.

Their patrol truck was too far away. The men had to get to an area of low ground, clear of trees, fast.

They ran bent over into the middle of the grassy runway and dropped prone, keeping the antennas of their handheld radios flat against the ground. From horizon to horizon the heavens had turned a solid black while sheets of water fell in gusting waves. For the next hour the two lawmen just sucked it up and prayed. The canal banks overflowed, gradually filling the airstrip with water. Soon the tips of the grass were covered. The men raised their heads in order to breathe. In the course of one hour, five inches of rain fell. By the time the sky brightened, the landing strip had become a foot-deep pool of shimmering water.

The men packed their gear for the return trip. Only this time they would have to swim the canal using an awkward half sidestroke while the remaining arm held their equipment aloft.

The runway was so soggy no plane would be able to land or take off for several weeks. Donnie and the other investigators also had a stack of fresh wildlife crooks queued up to investigate. The investigation lieutenant decided to put the detail off until the dry season, give everyone some time to work through the backlog of cases, and then pick the detail back up in early spring of the following year.

But fate stepped in and permanently nixed those plans.

Thursday, January 25, 1990

The headline for the *Clewiston News* lead story read, "Joy Ride Turns into Tragedy":

"An airplane ride to view wildlife ended in tragedy this weekend when the plane crashed and burned in an orange grove east of La-Belle, authorities said.

"Veteran pilot James Kendrick 'Ken' Nesbitt, 36, of Clewiston, and Angela Atkinson [stepdaughter of Curtis Simmons], 16, of Moore Haven in Glades County, both died of 'multiple traumatic injuries' in the Saturday afternoon accident, according to a spokesman at the Lee County Medical Examiner's Office."

Final Thoughts

Closing the Sky Poacher case due to Nesbitt's death brought no satisfaction to the wardens who had spent uncounted hours planning, tracking, and on stakeouts. The high they normally experienced putting cuffs on an offender or hearing a guilty verdict was replaced by the tragic loss of two lives. What they gained from the case was a new appreciation for the ingenuity of lawbreakers. They had to always be alert and expect the unexpected whenever they dealt with wildlife criminals because even if they made one mistake, it could be their last.

THE CASKET CASE

If there's such a thing as a hunter hierarchy, the bottom-feeders in the food chain have to be groups of dog hunters gone rogue. They care little for the land, the animals they work with, or the creatures they hunt. They'll set half-starved hounds loose from metal cages wedged into the beds of four-wheel-drive pickup trucks, onto the scent of any deer. "If it's brown, it's down," is the popular catchphrase often drawled into citizens band radio mics upon first glimpse of a deer's tawny hide flashing through an open glade.

Legal antler length (one antler must be at least five inches long) is ignored, as any deer pursued are meant to die—by shooting or, less often, mauling. Secret code words for illegal shorthorn bucks and does killed are "camp meat," verbal shorthand for, "it will be eaten in camp," the easiest way to dispose of contraband meat.

Game wardens didn't cotton to outlaw dog hunters, thinking of them of as the "bad apples" of the hunting fraternity, a surly and troublesome bunch.

One thirty-nine-year-old lawman who didn't put up with a lot of guff from illegal dog hunters, or any poacher for that matter, was Warden Mike Thomas. Mike's patrol beat was in the east-central Florida county of Volusia, where he often worked solo. Over the years he'd learned to rely on wit and raw determination mixed in with a good dose of courage when going head to head with those who disrespected the game laws. Mike's career read like the script from a reality-based cable television show. He'd been beat on and shot at; one guy tried to stab him with a long-handled sheath knife, another tried to run him over with a car, and he'd twice had a gun shoved in his face. And a chilling threat was made on the lives of his children, when one morning, he found a handwritten note stuffed in his newspaper box, saying, "Your kids won't be coming home from school."

Mike stood less than six feet on a well-proportioned frame, had penetrating blue eyes, fine blond hair, and a neatly trimmed mustache. When talking with suspected game law violators he was always friendly and courteous, but his gaze never wavered. Make one furtive movement and he'd be on top of you like a snake striking a rat.

January 6, 1991, Volusia County

The last day of deer season was winding up in the sprawling 59,000-acre Farmton Wildlife Management Area, when Mike hit the brakes, bringing his patrol truck to a hasty stop on the Possum Camp Grade. The grade was one of many elevated dirt tracks crisscrossing the public hunting area and offered east-west access to the Pine Barrens and oak hammocks and cypress heads of this otherwise flat, featureless terrain. Ahead of him lay a long line of mud-splashed pickup trucks parked at odd angles in a haphazard attempt to straddle the steep, earthen embankment that formed the road's shoulder.

"Just another day in paradise," Mike muttered to himself. Then he put the gear shift lever in park and clambered out. A call from dispatch had brought him to this location, where forty or so scruffily dressed dog hunters milled about a dead doe that lay in a clearing just off the road. Mike zeroed in on Jack Cooper, a rotund, white-bearded, bib-overall-clad Santa Claus–like character. The sixty-year-old still lived with his mother, but by self-proclamation and bullying had become the de facto ringleader for this group of wayward hunters. Mike slid down the embankment and walked over to him.

Without any preamble, Cooper shook one finger at the carcass: "Well, are you going to let us keep the deer or not? We didn't mean for it to die. The dogs just happened to run it down is all." He turned, spitting a syrupy stream of dark-brown tobacco juice onto the ground, and then looked back expectantly at Mike.

The deer's body lay in a patch of bare earth surrounded by volunteer pine saplings eight to ten feet high. The sun was near its zenith and had warmed the deer's guts so a faint stench of decomposition hung in the still air. Blowflies circled erratically above the mauled carcass—in gradual descent until they landed on the choicest spots of torn flesh.

Seventeen years on the job told Mike the hunters' dogs had killed the deer several hours before, and now the men wanted to take it back to camp and eat it. The thought that these guys would consider eating an animal with souring flesh wounds coated in gritty sand and bits of leaves and broken twigs disgusted Mike, though their request didn't surprise him. The ragtag bunch who called themselves the Camp Nasty Hunt Club had palates less discerning than a coyote's.

Cooper's question stuck Mike like a sharp thorn. Mike knew many of them were crooked, with a history of having no respect for game laws or the men who enforced them. He figured they let their dogs run the deer to death and now were singing a different tune—since a lawful hunter had notified dispatch he had seen the dogs catch the deer. The witness was the only reason Cooper and his fan club had not already made off with the deer. The only problem was—Mike couldn't prove their intent to kill it.

Mike stood there for a moment while he mulled over what to do next. The body lay before him in full rigor mortis, stiff and cold, with all four legs locked out as straight as a coffee table. He decided to roll the dice. He put on a pair of surgical gloves and turned the deer from one side to the other, carefully inspecting it for wounds. He hoped that somehow the heavens would open up and a bullet hole would magically appear among the torn flesh and ripped hide. Disappointed, he pulled the gloves off.

"This deer is illegal," he announced, as he stood up to address the group. "This is an antlerless deer, and you can't possess it."

"Just what are you going to do with it then?" Cooper asked.

"Well, normally we would take it to a charity, but this deer is too ripe, and it's torn to shreds. Not really fit to eat." Mike shook his head in wonderment that anyone would consider trying to digest it.

"That just doesn't make good sense. You should let us keep the meat so it don't go to waste," Cooper offered, turning around to look at his minions, who eagerly nodded in silent agreement.

"No, I can't let you have it."

"What are you going do with it?" piped up another one from the back.

"I'm going to dump it in the woods," Mike answered.

"Yeah, right," Cooper snarled. "You're going to take it home and eat it. We know what happens to the deer game wardens seize, and we don't trust you."

"All right then, I'll show you what I'm going to do with it. I'll bury it right here. And I better not come back and find any of you dug it up."

"Fine, but we're going to stay here and watch."

Mike looked at the deer and then at an area of bare, sandy soil nearby where he planned to bury it, trying to gauge the size of hole he would need. He retrieved a shovel from his truck, notified dispatch he'd be unavailable for calls, and began to dig a square hole, about the size of a half sheet of plywood, or four feet by four feet. He hacked away at pine roots so the hole would be deep enough to fit the deer down in. The deer had to be buried sideways, an awkward arrangement since the legs wouldn't fold. The clock ticked ahead, and the digging went slowly. He sweated and he chopped and he sweated some more, mopping his brow occasionally to keep the stinging salt out of his eyes. "I was quickly beginning to realize," Mike explained later, "that this wasn't one of my better ideas."

The dog hunters, however, thoroughly enjoyed the spectacle of the warden's discomfort. They chewed and they spit, while cussing and discussing the merits of the warden's decision to bury the deer as opposed to letting them keep it.

Forty-five minutes later Mike finally stood up and stretched. His back ached and his right hip was killing him, the result of a thirteen-year-old hunting injury, when he'd fallen twenty-five feet from the top of a live oak and hit the ground, hard. The broken hip had never healed properly.

The deer was buried.

Deep.

"You know," Cooper said, eyeing the freshly packed sand with keen disappointment, "you could have saved yourself a lot of trouble if you'd just given the deer to us."

Mike stared at him, unblinking, while his trigger finger gently tapped the holster safety guard.

"Hey," Cooper said, with a cocky smirk on his face, both hands held up in a mock surrender, "just saying is all, just saying."

Thoroughly miffed now, Mike shuffled into the wood line, limping on his bad leg. He returned with a couple of dead sticks about two feet long. He went to his patrol truck and came back with some twine and went to work. Before long he had fashioned a reasonably well-made cross and stuck it in the grave.

"Now," Mike said, stepping back to admire his handiwork, "I want you all to leave this deer alone, let it rest in peace."

Grumblings of discontent stirred within the group as they began to disperse. Mike planned to hang around for a while to make sure they didn't rob the deer's grave. But the squawk of his patrol radio broke the tense moment—another complaint from dispatch. He had to go.

Late that afternoon, when the sun had become a giant orange orb on the western horizon, Mike was bumping down the Possum Camp Grade in his patrol truck. "I was wore out, exhausted," Mike remembered. "This was the last day of hunting season and I was ready to go home. So I'm looking out through my front windshield and see a fresh mound of dirt ahead. My first thought was, 'Those nasty sons-of-bitches dug that darn deer up.' I was fuming."

A quick check confirmed his suspicions. He hit the gas and steered straight for Camp Nasty. Ten minutes later the howls of penned hunting dogs greeted him as he rolled to a stop inside the compound. Surrounding him was an awkward array of homemade fenced-in dog enclosures, hand-hewn shacks, run-down single-wide trailers, and tow-behind campers. Rank patches of pokeweed and dog fennel sprouted up from between the dwellings. Power was supplied by gas generators and water from a hand-pump, shallow-draft well. The ground was sun-cooked and offered not a single spot of shade. The cloying odor of dog excrement permeated the late-afternoon air.

The warden marched straight for a red Chevy four-by-four pickup caked with strings of dried mud on the rocker panels, and with a metal dog box in the back. Also in the back was a thirty-gallon blue plastic trash can. It was Jack Cooper's truck, and the trash can had not been in it that morning. The door from a port-a-let banged open, and Cooper emerged buckling his pants. He strode up to confront Mike. "What the hell do you want?"

"I want to know what you did with that deer." Mike jabbed a finger in the direction he'd come from on the Possum Camp Grade.

"I don't know what you're talking about."

On a hunch Mike spun toward the bed of Cooper's pickup and pulled over the trash can. Inside was the doe, with the legs cut off and stuffed crossways on top of the body, covered in ice.

"This is what I'm talking about." Mike looked up from the barrel's mouth and pointed at Cooper. "I'm charging you with illegal possession of a doe deer."

"Well ain't that some cheery shit," Cooper said, and pulled out a wad of tobacco from a foil pack and shakily crammed it into his mouth. The veins in his alcohol-fed bulbous nose had begun to swell.

"I was by myself," Mike recalled, years later, "and now close to a hundred of these guys began to gather up around me. It was not a friendly crowd.

A couple of years earlier Mike had run into a similar situation, in the same management area, when an angry deer poacher suddenly stuck a 12-gauge shotgun in his face. Mike was briefly held at gunpoint, until he wrestled the gun away from the guy without anyone getting hurt. "That incident was different than this one in a big way," Mike explained. "I had three officers with me for backup."

He quickly issued Cooper a citation, seized the deer, and got the hell out of there.

"Cooper was a rough man and crude," Mike said. "One time I kiddingly told him he looked just like Santa Claus. He told me, 'Yeah, but

I *come* more than once a year.' That's the vulgar kind of person he was. He and I had quite a history, and I'd arrested him before. I guess it was just a matter of time before he went off the rails."

Almost One Year Later, January 2, 1992

Mike got a call at his house in New Smyrna Beach, a sleepy coastal community on Florida's east-central coast, an hour's drive north from the Kennedy Space Center. It was Walter Dittman, a friend of Mike's and the check station operator for Farmton Wildlife Management Area. A fragile personality, Dittman hesitantly relayed a disturbing conversation he'd had earlier in the day with Jack Cooper.

Dittman had been eating a ham-and-egg breakfast inside the check station cabin when he heard a commotion outside. He swung the door open and froze, surprised to see an old bronze hearse parked out front with a half-dozen hunters staring in the back window. Cooper sat in the driver's seat. Dittman had never seen the hearse before; in fact, he'd never seen any hearse driven around inside the public hunting area, which was mostly the domain of old pickups, jeeps, and SUVs—vehicles built on a sturdy truck frame with good ground clearance.

"Raymond rolled the rear window of the hearse down," Dittman told Mike, "and showed me a casket with the initials 'M.T.' and a crossbones spray-painted in fluorescent orange paint on top of the lid. Then Cooper said, 'This is for Mike Thomas.' I told him, 'Mike wouldn't fit in there.' He answered, 'He will fit in there—in pieces.'"

"I tried not to let this information upset me," Mike said, who had received death threats off and on throughout his career. "But I had a tough time shaking it off. This was really over the top."

At seven the following morning, Mike and a reserve warden drove through the gate to Farmton Wildlife Management Area on County Road 442 to begin what they thought would be a day of routine patrol. They passed the bronze hearse coming out.

"The hearse went by me," Mike said, "and I spun the truck around and stopped it. The driver turned out to be a relative of Cooper's. Sure enough, inside the back was a wooden casket with my initials spray-painted on top. I couldn't believe it. I called for a supervisor to come

The hearse and homemade casket spray-painted with Warden Mike Thomas's initials and crossbones, 1992. Disgruntled outlaws threatened to kill Thomas on many occasions, but this was a whole new way of expressing their discontent.

to the scene. About the time my boss arrived, Cooper showed up. Cooper changed his tune and told us 'M.T.' stands for 'My Toolbox.' Of course, we weren't buying that. But we weren't sure what criminal laws he may have violated either. It was a very unusual situation—for any lawman. So I seized the casket and let them keep the hearse. The plan was for me to review this incident with the state attorney's office and let them offer us guidance."

In those days, wardens with the then Game and Fresh Water Fish Commission routinely kept evidence at their homes, with a couple of exceptions: drugs were stored at the local sheriff's department. Large items, like trucks and boats, were kept inside a locked, chain-link compound at the Ocala regional office, more than an hour's drive away.

"So I took the casket home with me," Mike said, "and propped it up against a wall near the dryer. I forgot to tell my wife. That discussion didn't go well. She told me point-blank, 'I can handle finding snakes in a bag or a live alligator tied up in the laundry room, but not a coffin with my husband's name spray-painted on it. No way!'"

"In hindsight," Mike reflected, "I suppose it was a bit much to ask."

Mike already had a pending criminal felony case against Cooper for possession of a concealed firearm and a misdemeanor traffic violation for driving with a suspended license. A week after the casket episode and a thorough review conducted by the state attorney's office, Mike filed a warrant against Cooper for "tampering with a witness," a third-degree felony punishable by up to five years in prison and a five-thousand-dollar fine. Volusia County sheriff's deputies arrested Cooper on the warrant. Judges usually take the charge of tampering seriously, because the squeaky wheels of justice would grind to a halt if crooks were left unchecked to intimidate witnesses.

Cooper's effort to scare Mike had suddenly backfired. He settled on a desperate course of action to delay prosecution.

Ill thought out and hastily conceived, Cooper's scheme showed why he would never be confused for an attendee at a Mensa conference.

A few days before Cooper's first court hearing on the tampering charge, Mike got a telephone call from a friend who lived on Lake Ashby, a large freshwater lake twenty-five minutes southwest of his home. "You've got to see a photograph I just got my hands on," he exclaimed, chortling with unbridled enthusiasm.

"What's so important about this particular picture?" Mike asked, curious to know why he should make a thirty-minute drive just to see one photo.

"I don't want to spoil it. You've got to come on over and check this out."

Later that day, Mike held a Polaroid still shot in his hands. The stiff-backed picture measured three inches by three inches. He turned it around at different angles trying to figure out what in the heck he was looking at. The best he could make out was a pair of shriveled grapefruits, very large and, well, swollen. "Alright," Mike said, "I give up. What am I looking at?"

"Those belong to Jack Cooper," the friend explained. "He pulled out his private parts, stretched them across a stump, and hit them as hard as he could with a claw hammer. You're looking at the end result."

"Oh, my God!" Mike shouted, and winced.

He brought the photo closer to his face. A shiver went down his spine, imagining for a brief moment the blinding pain that must have come from such a horrible act of self-mutilation.

"Apparently, this was his plan to avoid going to court," said Mike's friend, an incorrigible gossip who delighted in the warden's reaction.

A couple of days after Cooper's first court appearance, Mike happened to be riding in the courthouse elevator with a couple of assistant state attorneys. "I couldn't help but overhear their conversation," Mike recalled, "when one of them asked the other if he'd heard about the Casket case. I chimed in and said, 'That's my case.' Then he tells me Cooper came into the courtroom for a scheduled appearance, wearing bib overalls and a white T-shirt, shuffling along with his legs spread wide. Apparently he wanted the judge to feel sorry for him and let him off on the charge."

In a manner of speaking, Cooper did get his wish. He managed to duck future court appearances and a potential conviction on the tampering charge when he died from complications created by his self-inflicted testicular injuries.

The story has become legendary lore among lawmen and hound hunters alike as a prime example of "poetic justice."

MANHOOD TESTED

My prior life as a Florida game warden was an interesting one. I've chased outlaw commercial fishermen, survived boat sinkings, been shot at by a turkey hunter, tracked down hardened deer poachers, dealt with old-school gator hunters, and suckered wannabe Davy Crocketts with a lifelike dummy deer. But I never had an experience like I did one fine spring morning when I met a most unusual young man. My thoughts at the time, and even now, looking back some twenty-five-odd years later, was that he possessed two key attributes for survival in the wild: self-sufficiency and mental fortitude—core traits that would have served him in good stead had he gone on to join the U.S. Army Special Forces or to choose the unorthodox lifestyle of an end-of-the-world doomsday prepper. Since that day our paths never crossed again, but I'll always wonder what became of him.

On Patrol in Northeast Florida, April 1993

So it was on one bright Sunday morning that I turned onto the Holloway Road, a graded dirt track that ran straight as a billiard cue. The road surface was composed mostly of fine-grained sand, which we in the South affectionately call "sugar sand." To my right and left grew mature hardwood hammocks interspersed with tall stands of old-growth pines, and on the drier tops of shallow hills grew sand pines and scrub oak. Just ahead lay a small, flat bridge where Etoniah Creek flowed underneath. A faded-blue GMC van was pulled off on the road shoulder next to the bridge. A pleasant-looking woman in her mid-fifties paced back and forth beside it. She had short, curly brown hair and wore a blue short-sleeve blouse, comfortable white shorts, and plain sneakers.

My concern as a lawman made me stop and ask if she needed any help. Unperturbed, she calmly replied, "I'm waiting for my son to come out of the woods. He's been camping."

"How long has he been camping?" I asked, instinct telling me there might be more to it than that.

"Two months." She gestured toward a rough footpath leading out of the woods and volunteered that her son "should be back any minute."

That last snippet of information got me to thinking. I quickly flipped through a mental Rolodex of crimes her son may have committed: deer poaching, marijuana growing, and trespass, to name three. What concerned me the most, though, as I scanned the tree line, was that I was standing fully exposed in bright sunlight with no cover and no way to conceal myself. My patrol truck, a shiny green Ford Bronco with an agency decal blazoned on the door and an emergency light bar mounted prominently on the rooftop, was highly visible as well. Not good. A person walking out of a dark, shaded forest toward a clearing or roadway always enjoys the advantage of being able to detect the person standing in the open first.

And it was right about then that her son came out of the woods walking toward us down the footpath. Twenty-something, close-cropped brown hair, intelligent brown eyes, lanky frame, wearing a short-sleeve T-shirt, hiking shorts, and running shoes. He carried himself with the springy grace of an athlete. He was no Daniel Boone, though, at least not in appearance. Instead, he looked more like a college sophomore on weekend break. He carried a bedroll and miscellaneous camping supplies in a rucksack slung over his shoulders.

Still, I sensed something wasn't right. When he got to the van he introduced himself as "David." I went straight for the jugular. "Where is the gun?" I asked.

His eyes briefly turned away. He paused, and with a slight catch in his voice said, "I wasn't carrying a gun."

He lied.

"I tell you what," I told him. "How about you stow this gear in the van and then show me where you've been camping."

I let David take the lead. As soon as we broke into the trees I looked right, scanning behind tree trunks and under palmetto fronds for the telltale burnished-wood stock of a gun. Nothing. I checked left, and there it was, a .30–30 lever-action rifle with sling, leaning against a tree.

"Is this yours?" I asked, pointing toward the gun.

"Yes, sir," he replied sheepishly. "I carry it for safety."

I decided to let it go for now. I was curious to see where he'd been living. I slung the gun over my shoulder, and we trundled on down the trail. The creek was below us and to our left, down a fairly steep but even slope of about seventy feet. Fallen timber tented the narrow, twisting watercourse. Random breaks in the dense forest canopy allowed a smattering of sunlight to dapple the ground ahead. The air smelled good and pure, lightly scented with a mixture of dank forest humus, tender green shoots emerging from native hardwoods, and wild azaleas blossoming.

After a half mile we stopped. David pointed downhill toward the creek. My sight plane followed his finger, but all I saw was leaf litter and weathered sticks and limbs scattered randomly. I looked again, this time letting my eyes slowly wander down from the crest of the embankment, along the declining tilt of the land until it met the creek, where two feet of clear water gurgled across a white, sandy bottom. Frustrated, I said, "Okay, it's time you tell me what's really going on."

David pointed again with renewed emphasis and said, "There's the door to my cave right there."

Then I saw it. Several dead limbs had been tied together with dark-brown twine into a roughly triangular shape. They camouflaged perfectly with the surrounding ground clutter.

He half-walked, half-skidded down the bank. I followed right behind. David stopped about midway and pulled up the homemade door. With a sweep of one hand he invited me to have a look inside the exposed opening. I knelt down and peered into an irregular two-by-three-foot entrance dug out by hand tools. The odor of stale dirt wafted out on a cool draft of air. The smell reminded me of crawling around under the wood-frame house I was raised in to do plumbing repairs. After a few seconds my eyes adjusted to the dimly lit interior.

"I can't believe this!" I exclaimed. "You must have excavated seven to eight yards of dirt." My back ached thinking of the immense physical effort required to remove a dump truck load of fill. He would have to have chopped and dug sideways—alternating between an ax and a blunt-tipped shovel—through hundreds of gnarly roots stretching their tendrils down toward the creek in search of moisture.

Then the logical portion of my brain took over. "Where," I wondered, "had David put the sand tailings and the pieces of cutup roots?" There was zero sign of them downhill from the cave mouth or in the creek. Nor was there any sign of typical camp litter, plastic bags, cans, buckets, and so forth. The area was pristine, except for shoe scuff marks in leaves around the entrance.

"So where did you put the dirt?" I asked.

"Well, I read this survival book that said to sprinkle the shoveled out material into the creek," he explained. "You know, to hide the sign to my cave entrance. So I walked up and down the middle of the creek and threw the material in one scoopfull at a time, so no one spot would appear built up or look unnatural." This was a classic move, reminiscent of *The Great Escape*, a 1963 World War II movie about Allied prisoners who tunnel out of a German POW camp. The problem they faced was how to dispose of the excavated soil without alerting the guards. Through trial and error they chanced upon an ingenious method. The POWs filled their pants pockets with fresh dirt, then nonchalantly walked around the encampment yard while shaking the soil loose through a hidden hole (controlled by a drawstring) in their pockets. Gravity did the rest, allowing the material to pour out through their trouser cuffs and onto the ground. A quick scuffling of the feet smeared the new soil into the old.

While rolling over in my mind what I had learned so far of David's efforts to avoid detection, I took a moment to survey the interior of his recently vacated earthen living quarters. I was impressed. The cave had been dug back a good eight feet into the bank, widened to about six, and reached up to five in height. The ceiling had been shored up with a questionable combination of two-by-fours and bare plywood to keep loose sand from raining down on top of him while he slept and, presumably, to prevent a catastrophic collapse. Along one wall were mounted two one-by-twelve-inch pine boards for shelving. On top of them were five one-gallon plastic jugs of water. He'd cleaned everything else out. One could easily imagine the near empty shelves provisioned with bags of dried beans and rice and flour and assorted canned goods.

David told me he actually left the cave about a week ago and that today was the last of several trips to haul his stuff out. Then he explained why he'd been living inside a hollowed-out creek bank. "Listen, I hope I'm not in any trouble, but I just wanted to challenge myself. I wanted to see if I could handle living out here alone and making my own way for a couple of months."

"Okay, I get it," I told him. "But we need to talk about what you ate. Did you kill any deer with the .30–30?"

"No sir, I'm not much of a hunter. But I did kill some squirrels with a twenty-two rifle."

"So what else did you eat?"

"I set bush hooks in some of the deeper holes in the creek to catch redbellies [small panfish] and catfish. All the other food I ate, I either hauled in or picked edible wild plants to eat. The survival book taught me how to identify them."

"Give me the names of two edible plants you can eat out here."

"You can eat the tender tips of new-growth green briar vines, cook them like asparagus or green beans, and they're quite good.[1] The inner young stalk of palmettos can be yanked out, and the stem that is white and tender can be eaten, too. It kind of tastes like a raw potato but without the crunch."

---

1 The author has eaten small quantities of raw green briar (*Smilax*) with no ill effects. Others who have eaten large quantities report instances of stomach indigestion. For those who would like to learn more go the website of Green Deane, *Eat The Weeds and Other Things, Too*.

"Very good," I said, nodding my head in satisfaction. I had to give David his kudos. Most fellas his age would be in a college dorm room smoking pot or out juking at bars, but not him. He had decided to have his own coming-of-age party, and with his mother's permission! I couldn't believe it.

I gave him the obligatory safety lecture—albeit a little too late—on the dangers of building caves or sideways holes into soft Florida sand. More than one kid has lost their life when dirt mounds collapsed at the beach or construction sites, resulting in entombment and death by suffocation.

We hiked back to my patrol truck. I swung the driver's door open and reached for my ticket book but let my hand drop to my side, realizing this kid deserved a medal, not a trespass ticket. Then my mind shifted to something I had thought about earlier. I had to wonder, two months eating roots and squirrels and fish. I looked up at David and smiled. "Listen, I've got to know. All this time you've been living like a caveman, what did you miss eating the most?

"Oh, man," said David, with a dreamy expression on his face, "I wanted a big T-bone steak with mashed potatoes and green beans so bad. You have no idea."

I had to laugh. "David, you're free to go. Go get some real food."

ROGUE GATOR

By all accounts, Adam Trevor Binford was your typically precocious three-year-old. Full of life, the tousle-headed, brown-haired ball of energy loved his momma and continually sought her affections, which would be normal for any boy his age. The natural urge to please his mother, though, much like the childlike cravings for ice cream and apple pie, would ultimately be his undoing. It would lead to a sensational tragedy reported by big-city newspapers and television networks around the world. And it would all begin with the pretty yellow flower of a water lily.

Around noontime on March 22, 1997, Lorri Binford brought her youngest son, Adam, his older brother, Evan, eight, and a cousin, Cassidy Bass, nine, to Lake Ashby Park for a picnic. With them were the family dogs, Charlie, a small mixed-breed beagle, and Willie, a mongrel hound.

Located in west Volusia County, the sixty-four-acre rural park is an hour's drive inland from the Kennedy spaceport and a hidden gem. This is *Real Florida*, where local residents and nature-bound tourists can explore, fish, swim, canoe, or even water-ski on the 1,030-acre freshwater lake.

The Binford crew left their car in a central parking area where a wooden-framed, glass-paneled kiosk displayed maps showing various hiking trails that crisscrossed the area. One trail led west toward the lake. This was the one Lorri picked as she led the children in tow, cradling a paper carryout bag from Taco Bell and one large cold drink for everyone to share. Handmade signs directed them along the quarter-mile route. Not that Lorri needed directions, since she'd first begun visiting the park as a young child. The well-trodden footpath of flattened earth took them beneath moss-draped trees and across a board-plank bridge that spanned a clear stream. The trail eventually broke out into an acre-sized picnic site, a clearing of coarse grass and patchy sand that formed a knob-shaped contour of land on the lake's eastern shore. The area offered an expansive three-sided vista across slate-gray waters darkened by an overcast sky. On the far side of the lake the uneven contour of an old-growth pine forest shadowed the horizon.

Lorri sat down at a wooden picnic table. She dug down in the bag and took out a handful of beef tacos for the kids to eat. They'd take a nibble and then run and play along the beach before circling back for more. The picturesque scene represented a tender moment in everyday America, like an iconic 1940s Norman Rockwell print for the *Saturday Evening Post*.

Adam wandered down to the lake's edge. He waded out alone into a patch of cow lilies, or spatterdock, barely deep enough to wet his knees. The pretty yellow flowers nestled among the shiny green lily pads had caught his attention. He held a small bouquet in one hand and bent down to pick another, thinking perhaps, of his mother's warm smile and appreciative coo when the heartfelt gift was presented.

Lorri glanced up and saw Adam kneeling down in the shallows. She called his name, warning him to come ashore and keep back a safe distance from the water's edge. He turned his head and looked up at his mother. Their eyes briefly met, and then a big splash erupted from the water, enveloping the boy in a curtain of spray that blocked Lorri's view of him for just a moment. "Only for a millisecond," she would later recall. By the time the cascade of water droplets had collapsed back into the lake Adam was gone. In the blink of an eye Lorri's world had turned upside down. The thirty-one-year-old mother of two was living her worst nightmare: her youngest son, Adam, had vanished. The only trace left of him was a boil of churning ripples. Deep down inside, the native Floridian knew the horror of what had happened to her son.

Terrified, heart pounding, Lorri ran screaming into the water, frantically searching the area where little Adam had stood just moments before. Evan and Cassidy took it upon themselves to run back up the trail for help. They remembered seeing a pay phone next to the bathrooms at the central parking area.

The 911 call came in as a possible alligator attack on Lake Ashby. Game and Fresh Water Fish Commission wardens, Volusia County sheriff's deputies, and Volusia County Beach patrol units were notified immediately of the boy's disappearance.

Warden Mike Thomas was at home on his regular day off. He was in the backyard preparing his saltwater flats boat for a fishing trip with his grandson when he got the call around one in the afternoon. As Volusia County's senior warden and acting supervisor (his lieutenant

Warden Mike Thomas sits astride a ten-foot alligator caught on a nuisance alligator complaint, Volusia County, 1975.

had been out on extended sick leave), he'd be responsible for taking the lead in coordinating the search with other law enforcement and search-and-rescue agencies.

Mike was sitting at "five till five" in his career. He had only had a few months left until retirement. He'd become a well-known and respected figure, even a legend, to many of the four hundred thousand–plus residents of Volusia County, having worked the same patrol beat for nearly twenty-five years.

To Mike, being a game warden was a calling, not a job. Any thoughts of the fishing outing he'd planned were quickly pushed aside. He hung his rods and reels back up in the garage and went inside the house. He hastily changed into the green and tan uniform and strapped on his 9mm service pistol. As he began to gather the rest of his gear, Mike considered the possibility of a real gator attack on Lake Ashby.

Earlier in his career, before the Nuisance Alligator Trapping Control Program was implemented in 1978,[1] Mike had caught and relocated hundreds of alligators alive, releasing them into remote watercourses ringed by dense swamps that would never be touched by a developer's backhoe. The hope was that these wilderness areas would offer less opportunity for them to come into contact with humans. He drew upon these experiences as he prepared to leave the house. "At first, I was very leery Adam had been taken by an alligator," he recalled. "Up to this point there had been nine documented fatal alligator attacks in Florida since 1948. We only knew that the boy's gone and none of the family members had seen what happened. They'd only heard a big splash. The logical course was for us to explore two

---

1 Prior to 1977, wildlife officers were tasked with catching and relocating nuisance alligators at an annual cost of $250,000 to the GFC. The time taken to capture these alligators diminished the ability of officers to effectively enforce game and fish laws. In 1976, the GFC petitioned the U.S. Fish and Wildlife Service to change the alligator's status from endangered to threatened, thereby allowing the legal harvest and killing of nuisance alligators for profit, which became the foundation for the Nuisance Alligator Control Program. The program was fully implemented in 1978 as a less costly method of controlling rogue gators that presented a threat to humans or livestock. Nuisance trappers were hired to work on a contract basis for 70 percent of the profit from alligator hides sold. The GFC took the remaining 30 percent to cover the cost of their administering the program.

possibilities for his disappearance: Adam either drowned or a gator had attacked him. We worked it from both angles."

When Mike rolled up to the scene, sheriff's deputies had already arrived. A half-dozen green-and-whites were parked haphazardly between the picnic tables and the beach. Electronic voices echoed clipped police codes from external speakers mounted inside patrol-car grills.

Sheriff's department and Wildlife K-9 cadaver dogs arrived within the hour. They rode in patrol boats, their noses eagerly pointed into the air, sniffing for any rising scent from the area Adam was last seen. Dive teams crawled along the bottom in deeper drop-offs. Another team of thirty to forty officers made a shoulder-to-shoulder line from the shore out into the lake and then walked parallel to it. They used sticks to slowly probe the hard sand bottom and in between clumps of lily pads. "We repeated this search pattern over and over and over," Mike said. "There were no happy faces among any of us. This was grim work. All of us were thinking of our own children and grandchildren who were close to the same age as Adam, and might very well have been the victim if circumstances had been different."

The *whup, whup, whup* of spotter helicopters filled the air as they circled above the lake's borders searching for any visual clue to the missing boy.

Patrol craft not assigned to carry cadaver dogs conducted extended visual sweeps, successively working farther out into the two-mile-wide lake.

"By three o'clock it was beginning to look more plausible that a gator attack had occurred," Mike said. "The depth of the lake is only about seven feet at its deepest point. Adam should have been found just offshore from the picnic area if he'd drowned. The most important thing we could do now was turn it over to the nuisance gator trappers. They had the gear and the expertise to hunt down a rogue gator."

Earlier in the day, nuisance alligator trapper Curtis Lucas had been down in Christmas, a tiny community fifteen miles east of Orlando that prided itself on having "Swampy," the world's largest faux alligator. Shaped out of concrete and reinforced steel, the enormous, algae-green-painted crocodilian stretched for two hundred feet and served as a legendary landmark and headquarters for the Jungle Adventure Nature Park. It seemed oddly coincidental that Curtis had gone to Christmas to help grade alligator hides at a private processing facility next door to the "World's Largest Alligator," albeit one constructed from common building materials.

The quarterly sale is an event where central Florida trappers brought salted alligator hides to be appraised and sold according to the quality of the leather. After the sale, the hides would be shipped out to tanneries around the world to be fashioned into belts, purses, wallets, boots, and other crocodilian knickknacks.

GFC dispatch called Curtis around one in the afternoon. He pointed the nose of his Ford F-150 north. He stared blankly ahead through the windshield, numb with fatigue. He looked and felt like he'd been on a weekend bender. Instead, he'd been up the night before hunting gators. He'd killed three, butchered them, and had the boned-out meat packaged and stored in a walk-in cooler at his personal processing facility by daylight. Then he'd rushed off with a load of hides to the sale.

Curtis adjusted the rearview mirror and saw red-rimmed eyes. He wondered what they would look like by the following morning. He knew he'd have good help, though, for what would likely be a grueling effort to find the right gator and then kill it.

Before leaving Christmas, he'd made a telephone call to his uncle, Sam Driggers. He asked Sam to get the boat ready and ran through a mental checklist of the necessary items: headlamps, hatchet, harpoons, snatch rods, rotted beef lung, shark hooks, 1,200-pound-test braided nylon line (to tie the hooks on for a hanging set-bait), and his favorite rifle, a .270 Remington bolt-action with a 3 × 9 Leupold scope. The plan was to meet his uncle at the public boat ramp on the east shore of Lake Ashby.

As a former warrant officer, thirty-eight-year veteran of the U.S. Marine Corps, and survivor of the Vietnam War, Sam Driggers was no stranger to the term *prepared*. He was built like a fireplug and as

Professional gator hunter and state nuisance trapper Curtis Lucas stands with two twelve-foot alligators harvested during a late-morning guided hunt, 2004. He and his two clients quit for lunch and came back in the afternoon to kill a third gator that also measured twelve feet. (At the time of this writing—in the spring of 2016—Lucas reckons he's killed close to five thousand alligators.)

solid as lighter stump. He once had a seven-hundred-pound bull gator whip its massive head around and clobber him in the lower right leg. The blow had landed dead center. It left the leg severely swollen, the skin tinged in an ugly black and blue that wrapped all the way around to the back of the calf. When a doctor examined the wound, he gawked in amazement. He told Sam if he hadn't been as thick and heavy-boned as he was, the blow would have snapped the tibia.

In contrast, Curtis, thirty-seven, was the polar opposite of his uncle in physical appearance. At five eleven, he stood a little taller and was lean, wiry, and agile. Being blessed with lightning-fast lateral reflexes and the ability to dart backward in an instant had served Curtis well throughout his gator-trapping career. He'd never lost a finger, or any other appendage for that matter, and he was darn proud of it.

Curtis arrived at Lake Ashby before Sam. He wore the same clothes he usually wore on gator hunts: knee-high rubber boots, faded blue jeans, and a bright blue T-shirt with a large oval logo on the back that read, "Florida Alligator Trapper." A frayed but serviceable gray denim ball cap shielded his face from the afternoon sun.

By now the picnic site had been turned into a mobile command post, where all search personnel staged from. Off in the distance, two helicopters hovered fifty yards above the water, blasting up huge curtains of spray.

Curtis walked along the shore with a pair of binoculars to see if he could spot anything. "I was looking for a gator to stick his head up," Curtis recalled, "maybe a piece of clothing, or an object floating, something that just didn't match. It could be the least little thing, like the way the ripples break as a gator submarines beneath the surface."

Then the helicopters headed toward Curtis. He asked for them to be sent away. "An alligator ain't going to poke his head up with all that racket," he said.

Sam arrived towing a twelve-foot Duracraft Jon boat, powered by an electric trolling motor clamped to the transom. Curtis believed in keeping a low profile when hunting gators. No million-candlepower Q-beam spotlights, huge outboard engines, or any fancy stuff. His daddy had started hunting gators with a carbide headlight. The beam wasn't a whole lot brighter than a match struck in the dark. "That's how I learned the business," Curtis explained. "Big lights may work just as well, but I was trained on a dim light, and that's what I've stuck with ever since."

Curtis and Sam, along with another nuisance trapper, met with GFC Captain Wayne King for a briefing.

King had a hard bearing. He wore a military flat-top haircut, crisply pressed uniform, shiny brass bars, and patent leather shoes buffed to a mirror finish. Direct and to the point, the captain had no problem in deciding what should be done. By now the media was apoplectic for blood. Gator blood!

The four men stood on the damp sand along the lake's shore. "Look," King said, using emphatic hand gestures to drive his point home, "you go kill me the first gator you can find. We've got to have a dead gator to show the press. Understand?"

"Up to that point," Curtis said, "my opinion of King was not good. I'd never had any personal dealings with him, but I knew he sent officers undercover to catch the commercial fishermen in the Astor [a tiny fishing hamlet, ten miles east of Lake Ashby on the St. Johns River] area I grew up in. But I understood where he was coming from on that day. The media were cordoned away from us, but you could tell they were in a feeding frenzy."

Wayne told the men a couple of the cadaver dogs had hit on the boy's scent near where he had last been seen. "He asked us what we thought," Curtis said. "I told him, 'That's where the gator lay on the bottom with the boy, but had probably eased off a little ways with all the noise from the helicopters and boats running around.' I really didn't expect us to see anything until dark."

Curtis and Sam put over and headed out into the lake, the shallow-draft aluminum boat cutting quietly across the surface. "We piddled around until dark," Curtis said, "and didn't see a thing. I knew there were a lot of gators in this lake from having come out on previous complaints. But they were pretty well spooked from the noise."

By now the sun lay low on the western horizon, casting a final golden glow across the lake's glassy surface. Soon it would vanish behind the scraggy silhouette of a distant tree line. Curtis and Sam made ready for the night's work. Each man put on a ball cap with a 50,000-candlepower coon-hunter's light mounted above the bill. Powered by a rechargeable battery belted to their waists, the incandescent lamp could last for several hours and was adjustable from flood to spot and from dim to bright.

Darkness settled in, and the two men began to hunt. Sam worked the trolling motor while Curtis moved his head slowly back and forth cutting a bright swath through the inky black. The beam followed wherever Curtis looked. That was the beauty of using a head-mounted lamp as opposed to a handheld, where one hand was always in use and the light not always pointed exactly where the holder's eyes were looking. Curtis also understood the basic rules for how best to detect and judge the age of crocodilian eyes at night with a light: The closer human eyes are aligned with the beam of a light source—in this case his headlamp—the better chance of seeing the retinal reflection in the animal's eye. In young alligators, the eyes glow a pinkish orange and are the size of twin pearls set close together. In an old gator, the eyes radiate a brilliant pure orange, have a wider spread between them, and resemble a jumbo marble in size.

"We caught one five-foot gator on a snatch hook," Curtis said. "I let it hang alongside the boat while it flopped around. I told Sam, 'We can't pass this off as the gator that caught the boy.' I kept looking at it, debating about what to do. I would have been embarrassed to bring it in. About this time it wiggled loose and swam away. That solved the problem for us."

★

Later that night, 11:30 p.m. Three hours had elapsed and the men still hadn't come across an alligator other than the one five-footer. They'd made their way to the north shore where it roughly paralleled a two-lane blacktop that was State Road 415. They were about a hundred yards offshore from Lake Ashby Mobile Home Park, when Curtis caught an orange glint reflecting back at him. "There's something out there next to that eye, a bit of shadow," Curtis told Sam, as he stared down the beam of his headlamp. "It could be a deer, or a big garfish, maybe even the boy."

Curtis knew gators often carry a kill in their jaws to protect it from other alligators and to let it decompose and soften up so they could shake pieces loose to eat (an alligator's jaws are not designed to chew).

"I'll ease you up to him," Sam said, barely loud enough for Curtis to hear.

Curtis kept his light trained on the eye. It blinked out at about fifty yards away.

Sam cut the trolling motor. The boat continued a silent drift forward. The gator had turned so the back of his knobby head was facing the light. It was difficult to see. In appearance it looked like a lump of black coal—about the size of a hotdog bun looking at it from that angle—floating on the lake's surface. "I can't see the eye anymore," Curtis said, straining to make out what the strange object was next to the head, "but the shadow's still there." Based on how the object appeared now, he reconsidered, telling Sam, "It could be a piece of trash, or maybe even a wad of lily pads that broke loose. I can't tell much at this distance. Let's ease ahead."

Sam turned the throttle handle, and a low hum from the 2 HP electric motor clicked on. Water gurgled softly. The flat-bottomed hull slipped quietly through the night.

The shadow disappeared, leaving a small area of disturbed ripples behind. "Okay, he's definitely got something in his mouth," Curtis said, with an intensity Sam had not heard his nephew use before. "We're going to hunt this gator down and kill him. He's certainly big enough, probably around eleven feet."

Curtis reached up to the bill of his cap and toggled the light off. They sat in silence, except for the steady *whoosh* of passing automobiles along busy 415 and the intermittent barking of dogs from shoreline homes.

Twenty minutes passed. Curtis switched the light on, swept it for a few seconds, and then shut it back down. A slight sea breeze crept up out of the east and pushed the boat away from where the gator had sunk. By habit, Sam steered them back into position and shut down. Then the air began to swirl, and a slight puff, barely a kiss of a breeze, pushed them slowly in the other direction.

Every time the wind nudged the lightweight aluminum boat out of position, Sam brought them back around to where they'd started. Light on. Light off. The lights-out strategy was a trick to try to get the gator to relax and pop his head up.

Two thirty in the morning. Still no gator. Not a single flash of an eye. The battery for Curtis's light started to go dead. "Sam, I've to get some sleep," Curtis said, yawning, "and we need fresh batteries too. All I need is an hour and I'll be good to go."

"Not a problem," Sam said. "I'll get us geared up while you take a nap in the truck."

"When we come back, we'll wait right here. That gator isn't going anywhere."

The captain saw the green and red navigation lights approaching the command post and met them at the shore. "Why did you come back in?" King asked curtly.

"Captain, I have to get some sleep," Curtis said. "I hunted all last night and was grading hides down in Christmas when I got the call."

"Alright, but make it short. We need to kill that gator." With that, the captain spun around and returned to the command post.

An hour later Sam knocked on the windshield of Curtis's truck. "Time to get going," he said.

The two men headed back to the spot where they'd last seen the gator. This time Curtis ran the boat up into the sandy shallows near shore, jumped into the water, and dragged it up on the bank. They could at least move around and stretch their legs while they waited and watched for the gator to reappear. The cramped interior of a twelve-foot metal boat has never been known to have many creature comforts.

★

The life of a hunter is one that requires infinite patience. The ability to wait for hours until the quarry eventually appears has been an invaluable trait since men first carried clubs and spears. In the spring of 1997, Curtis had been a nuisance gator trapper for eight years and had killed close to two thousand alligators in that time. The education earned in taking that many animals gave him a strong sense of confidence and a heightened understanding of their habits few could claim, or would ever understand.

★

The predawn came with a lightening of dull gray in the eastern horizon.

Still no gator.

As the building natural light gradually erased the gloom of night, the two hunters could vaguely make out distant objects with the naked eye. Interestingly, with an incandescent light turned on, a gator's eye would still reflect. This time of day only lasts about fifteen minutes and happens once at dawn and once at dusk.

During this odd time of natural light transition, Curtis swept his headlamp beam and saw the orange glow. The gator was still in the same area. Only now it was on the move, with the back up and tail sweeping unhurriedly back and forth, cutting a V-wake through the water.

Curtis saw the other trapper making his way around the far side of the lake in a powerboat. He was on a full plane while sweeping the powerful beam of a Q-beam spotlight. Curtis cut his light off to watch. From a half mile away, the other trapper flashed his light once over where the gator was, and it went down. He continued to follow the shoreline's contour. Ten minutes later he motored around to the north side of the lake and inadvertently ran over where the gator had sunk, passed by Sam and Curtis, and headed back to the command post.

Curtis knew the other trapper had not seen the gator from a distance of a half mile, nor had he seen them as they sat quietly on the bank with his headlamp extinguished. Curtis wasn't the least bit perturbed. This was all part of gator hunting.

"Sam, set your watch," Curtis said, who had never worn a watch in his life. "Let's see if we can get a pattern on this gator."

The two men grabbed the bow and shoved off. Sam jumped in first, followed by Curtis, who sat in the bow.

Twenty minutes later the gator rose to the surface, swimming slowly away from them and parallel to the shoreline.

The men pulled their headlamps off and stowed them in a plastic five-gallon bucket. It was light enough to see without the aid of an artificial lamp.

Sam steered the boat closer to the gator, when it sounded.

"Set your watch again," Curtis said. "And ease me up to where he sank. I'll try to snatch him off the bottom."

Often when a gator sinks, it will lie still on the bottom or crawl along it. If they crawl, a string of fine bubble trails will float to the surface, giving its location away.

Curtis picked up a stout fiberglass bass rod affixed with a level wind reel and spooled with thirty-pound-test monofilament fishing line. He cast a weighted treble hook over where the gator had sunk and dragged it slowly across the bottom. He cast again and again and again. An early-morning breeze kicked up and pushed them away from the site. Sam brought them back around. The gator surfaced at twenty-two minutes. The men gave slow chase, and it sank again. Curtis continued to sling that treble hook, but still no gator.

The dance of the hunter and the hunted repeated itself four more times; each time the men gradually inched closer. A pattern was beginning to develop. The gator was surfacing for air every eighteen to twenty-two minutes.

Finally, Curtis was about thirty-five yards from the gator when it ducked under. He cast once, twice, and on the third toss hooked him.

The rod bent double while the drag screeched, line tearing furiously from the reel's spool. Curtis leaned back, arm and shoulder muscles straining, and cranked the handle. He pumped the rod up and down like a deep-sea angler hooked to a massive grouper. He studied the line and saw how it sliced from side to side through the water, causing a pronounced swaying in the rod tip. "We got a problem," he announced. "It's a tail hook."

A tail hook is the worst possible way to snag a gator. It means one of the three hooks is partially embedded in the toughest part of the tail, the bony armor-plated scute ridge. The violent thrashing of the tail can often shake the hook loose.

The fight lasted thirty minutes until he wrenched the tail up to the surface, the head and body slanted down and out of sight beneath the dark tannin-stained waters of Lake Ashby. Given the shallow depth, the gator's head was likely bumping along the bottom.

"Do you think you could jab the harpoon through the tail?" Curtis asked. He'd forgotten all about the guns (one of the wardens had also given them a riot shotgun to use in addition to Curtis's rifle) because they were not part of the gear he normally carried. Nuisance trappers are not allowed to use a firearm unless it's an emergency.

This was an emergency!

"Sure," Sam said. "But why don't we use the shotgun instead? Less risk of losing him if something goes wrong."

"Okay, I'm going to give him a little slack and let him lie on the bottom. When he comes up to take a breath of air, shoot him. Look at your watch and tell me what time it is."

"Eight-oh-three."

"We've got about twenty minutes to wait."

Eight twenty-three. Both men stood up. Sam stood on a flat metal seat behind and above Curtis's shoulder. Curtis stood on the deck in front of him just behind the bow seat.

"I can feel him crawling, Sam. He's coming up."

Sam stood silently, watching for the water to break. Curtis cranked away. He wanted to make sure when the gator did surface, it would happen alongside the boat and not off a ways. The shotgun Sam held had an open bore. With no constrictions in the barrel, the buckshot would begin to pattern wide immediately upon leaving the muzzle. The shot needed to be taken at close range.

The tail came up, and now the head and body began to surface. And then the outline of the boy emerged, clamped tightly in the gator's jaws.

"I can see the kid," Curtis said through clenched teeth. "Blow that gator's damn head off when he lifts it up!"

Curtis was not a war veteran like Sam. This was the first time he'd ever been exposed to such a disturbing scene and the anguish he felt when he looked at Adam, framed a ghostly pale white against the dark waters of the lake.

Seconds ticked by. No shot. "Why doesn't he pull the trigger?" Curtis wondered, anxious to get it over with.

Sam didn't have the same visual as Curtis did. If he'd shot the gator's head when it first broke the water's surface, he would have hit the boy. Sam didn't want to do that.

With the gun shouldered and the brass bead held right between the eyes, Sam patiently tracked the gator's movements, hoping for a better shot.

A few seconds later the gator cocked his head.

The boy was clear.

Booomm!

A geyser of water shot up as the load of 12-gauge double-ought buckshot punched through the skull right between the eyes. "He's dead," Curtis announced.

Then the gator started pitching and rolling and slapping its tail in the final death throes. Curtis continued to apply pressure with the rod.

"Sink a harpoon in the bottom," Curtis said. "The divers can use it as a marker to find the boy, and we may need it to retrieve the gator if he throws the hook."

Sam rammed a twelve-foot harpoon into the solid sand bottom. Made of one-and-a-quarter-inch wooden dowel, it would make an easy reference point.

The gator sounded again, and Curtis allowed line to unspool from the reel while keeping it taut as it slid between his fingers. The extra slack allowed him go to the bottom. Adam floated quietly to the surface.

The men motored over to him and gently placed him in the boat. Curtis saw the resemblance to his two-year-old son.

"Sam, he looks a lot like Josiah," Curtis said.

"Hey," Sam shouted. "Quit looking. It can come back to haunt you later. Don't look at him anymore!"

Curtis did stop looking, but not before he closed his eyes and bowed his head. In a silent prayer, he thanked the Lord for letting them find the boy and prayed for Adam's family and for his soul. He opened his eyes. "Sam, our job is done here. How come none of the boats from the command post have come to us?

"When I shot down into the water, it muffled the sound. I know how to get their attention." Sam lifted the shotgun high into the air and pulled the trigger three times.

Moments later they heard the welcome drone of four patrol craft headed their way.

Curtis and Sam ran the Jon boat's bow onto the beach at the command post. Adam's body had been loaded into one sheriff's department patrol boat for transport. Captain King met the two gator trappers on the shore. "Curtis, you and Sam did real good," Wayne said, in a caring tone Curtis had never heard before. "It takes a lot of grit to see something like this through to the end. You can go now. If either of you have any problems, call me."

Curtis and Sam drove away from the command post in separate trucks. "As soon as I left the parking lot," Curtis recalled, "I started praying. 'Lord I've been through something I've never been through before. I don't know everything about it, but if there is anything from this experience that would be bad for me, I pray that you take it away from me.'"

Then Curtis wept. He cried like a baby for a couple of miles until he reached the intersection of Highway 44 and State Road 415, where he had to fuel his truck up. "My shirt was soaked to my hips with tears," Curtis remembered. "I kept praising the Lord, saying, 'Whatever is inside of me please take it out.' By the time I got out to pump gas, I'd stopped crying. Everything had been cleansed out of me. It hasn't bothered me since. Prayers do work."

Curtis's dad owned Halls Restaurant in Astor. Wayne stopped by a few days later. "He talked to my dad," Curtis said. "He told him, 'I want you to keep an eye on your boy. He's been through some bad stuff. I don't want anything to happen to him. If you see something going wrong, get with me and we'll get him some help.'"

"I had the greatest respect for Captain King after that. He cared enough to stop and check on me."

Final Notes

Lake Ashby Beach, March 23, 1997. The headline above the color photograph published in the *Daytona Beach News-Journal* read, "Tragedy at Lake Ashby." It shows Warden Mike Thomas, head bent, leading a solemn procession of law enforcement and public safety personnel in a protective cordon around the body of Adam Binford. "I called for a prayer," Mike recalled. "I asked everyone to line up like they were guarding Adam to show respect for him and his parents.

"It was the most horrific experience in my law enforcement career. I still get chills looking at the newspaper picture."

A second color photograph in the *News-Journal* shows the dead alligator curled up in the bed of a green GFC pickup truck, the bloody gunshot entrance wound clearly visible between the eyes. Four TV cameramen hefting heavy shoulder-mounted cameras lean in as they film the beast.

Wildlife biologists measured its length at eleven feet and its weight at four hundred pounds.

The majority of gator attacks result from someone feeding them. Working from that premise, wildlife investigators canvassed every home on Lake Ashby in an attempt to determine who might have been feeding the alligators.

Mike believes he found the culprit—an old man living on the west side of the lake who raised chickens and ducks and geese. According to a neighbor, whenever a fowl died, he would toss the carcass into the lake behind his home instead of incinerating it.

"Another investigator and I went to talk to him," Mike said. "We checked in the backyard, and there was this huge gator lying just off his beach. Now we'd been all over this lake and hadn't seen a gator, but there was this gator floating in the water unafraid. Then it all made sense to me. When I asked the old man if he tossed his dead ducks in the lake, he said, 'Oh, no, I wouldn't do anything like that.'"

Mike never found a witness willing to testify in court. Other than a strong hunch, he had no proof of the old man's alleged shenanigans. No charges were ever filed.

Mike wrapped up his take on the tragedy with these thoughts: "Most of the nuisance alligator complaints I've ever responded to, the gators have been fed. A tragic death like Adam's most likely could have been prevented. People think feeding alligators is cute. What really happens is they're conditioning them to associate humans with food. Not good. Often they start with little ones. Little ones become big ones. Big ones eat people.

"If folks would just stop feeding the alligators, we'd all be better off."

Other Possible Causes of the Attack

During my research for this story I also interviewed GFC Investigator Curtis Brown, who'd canvassed several residents living in the vicinity of the county park. He received credible information about an individual who'd been feeding gators at the beach where Adam had been attacked. Again, there was not enough evidence to corroborate a criminal charge for prosecution.

Another possible cause of the gator attack is that the Binford dogs might have enticed the gator to come close to shore. It is a well-known fact that barking dogs are like candy to an alligator. I did not feel comfortable in speculating on this possibility as my telephone interview with Lorri Binford ended before that topic was broached. (She had only granted one other official press interview, and that was to a journalist from *National Geographic*.)

Postscript

Lorri Binford visits Lake Ashby Park once or twice a year. She goes to a quiet place hidden deep in the woods. Hanging on a red maple tree is a private memorial to Adam decorated with angels and plaques. She prays for him in heaven.

SOME PEOPLE
JUST DON'T LEARN

"A policeman's lot is not a happy one," or so goes the ditty created by nineteenth-century playwrights Gilbert and Sullivan. Nor, I might add, is a game warden's, unless fully engaged in the pursuit of bringing wildlife crooks to justice. At the moment, I considered my lot to be a sorry one too, as I sat inside my home buried elbow deep in a stack of monthly reports and arrest summaries.

Outside it was a glorious October day. The scent of fall was in the air, the temperature a perfect 65 degrees. The urge to be outside was hard to resist. It wouldn't take much to tempt me.

I pulled another form off the top of the pile, scanned it for mistakes, then scribbled my signature with a ballpoint pen above the line for patrol supervisor. An unexpected telephone call from dispatch broke my concentration.

"Betty-Sue just called again," the dispatcher informed me.

"Oh, no," I said, in exasperation. "And what did she complain about this time?"

"Well, she actually sounds lucid today. She says she's found where a deer has been killed near her home in Hoot Owl Ridge subdivision. Isn't that over near where you live?

"Yes, she lives just a couple of miles from me. I'll give her a call."

To be fair, Betty-Sue wasn't a bad person. She could even be quite affable at times. It's just that she had a way of looking at things that was a lot different than normal folks. She had visions, and so far her visions had not turned out to be anything I was interested in. I wouldn't put her up in that rarefied category known as "batshit crazy," but she certainly had her moments. I picked up the telephone receiver, took a deep, calming breath, and punched in her number. This would make the tenth time I'd spoken with her in the last two months.

"Betty-Sue," I said, "what's going on today?"

In a hushed, conspiratorial whisper, she replied, "Well, earlier this morning I heard a gunshot behind my house near the state park. And later, when I took my dog for a walk in the woods I found a pool of blood along a trail. Looks to me like someone killed a deer."

"What color was the blood?"

"It was kind of a bright, candy-apple red."

She had my attention now. After you talk to enough people you can get a feel if there's anything of substance to what they've told you. And this was the first time that it sounded like Betty-Sue had hit pay dirt. It was a lot better than the night she had seen Martians driving pickup trucks hovering above the ground while shining bright spotlights all around her home. (Clichéd, yes, but this is how she reported it to me.) Being an eternal optimist, I took this to mean deer poachers were afoot in the woods near her single-wide trailer. But when I drove out at one in the morning to check, I found zip. No fresh truck tire tracks or signs of extraterrestrial beings, either.

My men and I had done some business in vacant wooded parcels behind her home from time to time, privately owned thirty- and forty-acre tracts of land that abutted the Dunns Creek State Park. So we were familiar with the area and also aware of one young man who lived not far away. He had a problem in the same way that some people are alcoholics. His problem, though, had nothing to do with overindulgence in high octane-spirits. No, his problem was that he liked to kill deer.

Daniel Connors began his life of crime at the tender age of sixteen when he killed a four-hundred-pound heifer, tied it off to the tow bar of his all-terrain vehicle, and dragged it up behind his parents' house.

When the owner of the heifer discovered one of his prized livestock had gone missing, he did what most ranchers would do. He went looking for it. The first thing he checked was the boundary fence lines. Within an hour he'd found where a four-strand barbed-wire fence had been cut, drag marks, and patches of loose black hair—suspiciously like that of the other two hundred head of prize Angus beef cattle he kept on his property.

In short order, game wardens and sheriff's deputies descended on the area. They followed deep, wide grooves in the earth that led them to the back of Connors's parents' mobile home, where he was doing a not-so-good job of butchering the deceased beast. This earned Connors a stretch in a juvenile detention facility, which was an unusual punishment for someone under the age of eighteen. But Putnam is a rural county, and you don't shoot another man's cow. Period.

By the time I had spoken with Betty-Sue, Connors had turned twenty-two years of age. We'd received occasional tips about deer he'd poached since the cow killing, but until now we hadn't received a solid lead. In my experience, most folks who endure the shock of getting caught "flat-footed," or in the act, try to improve on their technique when they commit subsequent wildlife crimes. It would be interesting to see whether Connors had devised a more sophisticated plan to avoid detection or would stick to his earlier method of operation, which was wholly in need of tweaking.

Encouraged by the telephone conversation with Betty-Sue, I called up Warden Eric Meade, an officer who worked under my command. His patrol beat was in the adjoining county of Flagler. I was the only one on duty in Putnam County, so I thought I'd invite Eric over to help out.

Most of my wardens knew Connors and have always maintained a good working relationship with him. After all, he was a client. He's an introvert, so he never yells or screams or uses expletives when questioned. My bet was that Connors would be less likely to talk to us because of his previous arrest and the attendant lawyerly advice.

There was, of course, the possibility no wildlife crime had been committed. It was muzzleloader season, a time of year when a deer with at least one antler more than five inches in length can legally be harvested. The firearm used must be loaded from the barrel's end, or muzzle, by dropping in a powder charge, followed by a bullet, and sometimes a lubricated patch that is then tamped down firmly with a ramrod. Whether Connors had killed a legal or illegal deer or someone else had shot the deer would have to be sorted out. Eric and I hoped to have that done by the end of the day.

At 8:00 p.m., Eric picked me up from my house to check out the pool of blood. We'd decided not to go during daylight, just in case one of Connors's friends or relatives saw us driving into the sparsely populated subdivision where few secrets are kept. Things tend to work out better when the element of surprise is on your side.

Eric is the kind of officer any supervisor would be proud to have work for them. He was twenty-seven years old, blond hair, blue eyes, easygoing, and even-tempered, with the physique of a college wrestler and an effervescent smile. He lived the dream as a game warden and loved every minute of it.

Stiff branches scraped the sides of our Ford Bronco patrol truck as Eric maneuvered us down a narrow dirt track barely wide enough to accommodate a full-size vehicle. Headlight beams briefly illuminated a patch of moldy aluminum siding through an opening in the tangled brush ahead. It was Betty-Sue's trailer. We drove past, following the off-road trail that wound through a copse of spindly sand pines and scrub oak. We parked our patrol truck out of sight from Betty-Sue's residence, disembarked, and quietly pressed our doors shut until we heard the locks click. We didn't want to wake her up.

We flicked on our flashlights and swept the beams back and forth as we walked down a woods road that led us across a sand ridge covered with a stand of live oaks and long-needle pines. Underneath the dense canopies grew a sparse understory of crooked-wood, high-bush blueberries, and a scattering of huckleberries. The road came to a "T" at an overgrown logging trail many years out of use. We turned right.

This was the path that Betty-Sue had taken on her walk earlier that morning. We'd traveled two hundred yards when Eric broke the night silence with the magic words, "Got blood."

Immediately in front of us lay a large pool of coagulating blood that had begun to darken from oxidation. Still damp, it reflected brightly in the pure white light cast by our flashlights. There were small clods of dirt, acorns, and other forest debris mixed into the jelly-like pool that bore an uncanny resemblance to the whole cranberry sauce my wife is so fond of serving with our Thanksgiving meals. Though not in taste, I was sure.

It looked like a neck shot. The animal likely collapsed on the ground and bled out within a minute or two from a fatal wound to the carotid artery.

We explored around the area of blood and discovered one fresh foot track of about a size 12 running shoe. There were no other prints, because whoever had killed the deer dragged it behind him, inadvertently brushing his own tracks away as cleanly if it had been swept with a broom. What remained was a beautiful drag of scraped sugar sand and rolled-up clumps of pine needles that had turned over underneath the deer carcass as it was pulled along.

We followed the drag marks for a quarter mile before I stopped and faced Eric. "Listen, we can save some time if we go straight to Connors's house and chat him up. I bet we find these drag marks coming up behind either his house or his dad's."

"Sounds good to me," Eric replied. "And if that doesn't work out we can always come back and finish walking it out."

Connors lived on a quarter-acre lot in a dilapidated, single-wide mobile home beneath a massive live oak. A disassembled motorcycle sat out front along with spare parts and an oil drain pan nearby. The front door hung precariously from sagging hinges. It was apparent no one had bothered to replace it or tried to fix anything else on the property. It had been like that for a long time.

His dad lived in a double-wide next door. Over time, it had morphed into a community of smaller-sized dwellings that spread out in different directions from the main residence. Yellow and orange electrical extension cords crisscrossed his yard to axle-less camper shells and an old ice-cream truck that sat atop stacks of cinder blocks run four courses high. I suspected none of the ad hoc living quarters had been approved by the county building inspector.

When Eric and I drove into Connors's front yard there were no lights on, in or outside the trailer. Connors, however, was standing outside alone in the dark. I hadn't a clue why. Our high beams lit him up as we rolled into the front yard and parked. With a disheveled mop of hair and a wiry frame, he eyed us with caution as we approached. He had a heightened sensitivity to green and tan uniforms.

"Hey, Dan," I said. "What's happening?"

"Not much," he answered, with a desultory shrug.

"Listen, I know it's starting to get late, but Officer Meade and I just need to talk to you about something. Do you have a few minutes?"

"Sure."

"There was a deer killed earlier today about a mile from here. Do you know who killed it?"

He looked down and pushed some dirt around with one toe before he offered a reply, "No, ah, I don't, well, you know, don't really know anything about it."

Eric gave me a side glance. Connors had lied. Either he killed the deer or knew who did.

I explained to Connors a little more about what we saw. He stuck to his story, claiming he knew nothing about a dead deer.

"Listen, I said, "it's hunting season. You're allowed to kill a deer. It's okay if you killed a legal buck. We just have to check it out. It's part of our job."

"Sorry, I don't know anything about it."

"Okay, would you mind humoring us just a little bit longer? Can we take a shortcut through your yard to the power line behind your house? I believe I can show you what we're talking about"

"Okay."

He walked us through the backyard. We dodged old washing machines, generators, a busted backhoe, and other flotsam from his life. We came to a sandy service road that ran beneath the high-tension power lines. Eric and I probed the ground ahead with our flashlight beams but saw nothing of interest.

I turned to Connors. "Let's try on down a little farther behind your dad's home."

He walked right beside me. I dropped my flashlight down by my side and shined the beam behind where Connors had just stepped. Bingo. His track looked like an exact match to the one at the kill site. When we got behind his dad's home, we found the drag trail where the deer had been pulled up to an old wooden gate at the back border fence of his dad's property.

"Looks like somebody killed a deer," I said, "and dragged it onto your dad's property."

"I don't want to get in trouble," Connors said, clearly nervous. "I've already gone to jail, and I don't have a hunting license."

"Listen, Dan, a hunting license is no big deal; it's just a civil infraction. We need to see the deer to make sure it's legal."

Connors face contorted while the mental gears inside his head worked furiously to fabricate an explanation for the drag marks leading into his dad's backyard. After a few seconds his expression abruptly changed. He looked relieved. He'd finally come up with a plan. "I killed the deer," he blurted out. "I shot it with my dad's muzzleloader."

"Excellent," I said, nodding my head in a show of appreciation for his cooperation. "How about letting us go into your father's yard so we can see where you skinned the deer?"

We walked through the gate and followed a well-worn foot path that led us to a low wooden deck that fronted the double-wide. Connors pointed up to the bare rafters of an eave that overhung the deck and was also directly above the front door. "I hung the deer there," he told us.

Eric and I looked down at our feet; fresh blood and pieces of viscera were smeared across the entryway. Bloody shoe prints went every which way. It looked like Hannibal Lector had paid them a visit. Not the oddest place I'd ever seen for a gutting though. That prize went to a guy who hung a deer above his dining room table and disemboweled it there. Scenes like these always felt primal and real. It helped to narrow our focus and energize the soul. We weren't cold-trailing Connors anymore.

"What kind of gun did you shoot it with?" Eric asked.

"My dad's .50-caliber Hawkins," Connors said. He then paused for a moment and quickly added, "But I've cleaned it. I used black powder."

"I understand completely," I told him. (Most folks who shoot real black powder clean the weapon soon after firing to prevent the highly corrosive, salt-based residue from eating into the lands and grooves of the barrel.)

Eric walked inside with Connors and came out a minute later holding a percussion-cap Hawkins rifle with a blue-steel octagonal barrel. The nine-pound gun was a replica of larger calibers used by the Great Plains buffalo hunters two hundred years ago.

Eric hefted the weapon in his hands while admiring the beautifully waxed and polished hardwood stock and brass hardware. Then he casually looked up at Dan. "What kind of bullet did you shoot it with?"

"A .50-caliber patched round ball," Connors answered.

"Good job, Eric," I thought. Earlier, as we were walking through the gate, Connors told us he shot the deer in the neck from a distance of fifty yards. That's some pretty fair shooting with a gun that averages a two-inch group (greatest measured spread of bullet holes in a target) when shot from a bench rest at the same distance using iron sights. What that really meant was to shoot this gun offhand, or with no rest, he would realistically be shooting a four- to six-inch group. The neck of a Florida deer isn't much wider. That makes an offhand neck shot a tricky and unlikely hit using iron sights on a .50-caliber Hawkins.

"You made one heck of a shot using a gun like this," I said, hoping to play to his ego.

Connors shrugged.

Eric and I knew without even speaking to each other that Connors thought he was on a roll. That we had sucked down the bait, hook, line, and sinker. And that's exactly what we wanted him to think.

"One more thing, can we see the antlers from the deer?" I asked.

"Sure," he said, "they're back at my house hanging in a tree."

Eric and I followed Connors back to his trailer and looked at the rack. It was a three point, and one of the antlers was six inches long. The deer was legal.

"Well, Dan," I said, "it looks like we're about to wrap this up. I want to thank you for being so cooperative. But before we go, maybe there's one more thing you can help us with."

"Well," he said tentatively, "if . . . I . . . can."

"Great, we need to see where you dumped the deer carcass."

"No way, you'll write me up for littering."

"I promise you, Dan, no litter tickets tonight. We just need to check the remains out real quick. Hey, it's part of our procedure," I said, with an apologetic shrug. "We're just doing what our bosses tell us to do."

He sighed. "Oh, alright."

We put Connors in our truck and drove out into the woods a quarter mile from his house. He told us where to stop. We all piled out, and he pointed to a metal culvert that emptied into a weed-choked ditch. Eric and I shined our lights down into the drainage channel where the hide, neck, and boned-out carcass of the deer lay scattered in pieces. Eric picked up the crumpled hide and shook it out to unravel the creases. Then he spread it on the ground, fur side down, so we could examine it for holes. I bent over for a closer look. Eric placed one finger next to a neat round hole in the neck region. It looked like it came from a .30-caliber (just under $\frac{5}{16}$-inch) projectile, certainly not one of a .50-caliber ($\frac{1}{2}$-inch) diameter. There were two short slashing cuts in the body of the hide. My past deer-cleaning experiences told me these were likely caused by Connors when his knife accidentally slipped. I gestured to the hole in the neck and looked up at Connors. "Looks like this is where you shot it."

"Oh, no, I didn't shoot it there," said Connors, emphatically pointing to one of the knife cuts in the body. "No, I shot it here."

"Not a chance," I thought. But I didn't push it. We were almost to the point where we would need to read him his Miranda rights.

"One last thing. How about showing us where you were standing when you shot the deer?"

"Alright."

We clambered back in the truck and drove over to the kill site. Connors pointed to a spot about fifty yards away from the pool of blood where he said he'd been standing. Eric shined his light on the ground and found a freshly fired .30–30-caliber cartridge casing.

Eric held up the shiny brass casing between two fingertips for Connors to examine. It was a subtle play at theatrics. Hit them with the facts and hope they break.

It was finally time to read Connors his Miranda rights. He acknowledged understanding them.

"Will you talk to us?" Eric asked.

"Not without my lawyer."

We put him back in the truck and took him home. Eric issued him a couple of citations for license violations. We told him—without any hesitation—that we would see him in court for the unlawful use of a modern firearm during muzzleloader season.

All we had to do now was prove it.

We returned to the dump site and seized the hide and the neck. The next day Eric made an hour-and-a-half drive down to central Florida, where he'd previously made an appointment with the medical examiner's office in Leesburg.

Eric arrived promptly at two in the afternoon. Under one arm he cradled a heavy-duty plastic garbage bag with the chilled deer hide and neck inside. He was greeted in the front lobby by the medical examiner, an enthusiastic forty-something woman wearing a white lab coat. She was petite, tanned, with jet-black hair and beautiful brown eyes that twinkled with an intense curiosity. This was a first for both of them: She'd never forensically examined evidence in a game case. Eric had never been inside an autopsy room.

"I was kind of awestruck," Eric told me later. "There were dead naked bodies everywhere. I'll never forget this one guy. He was lying flat on his back with his arms and legs stiffened straight out, pointing toward the ceiling. His chest was split open so his ribs were showing. I'm not sure what all that was about, but it impressed me in a creepy sort of way."

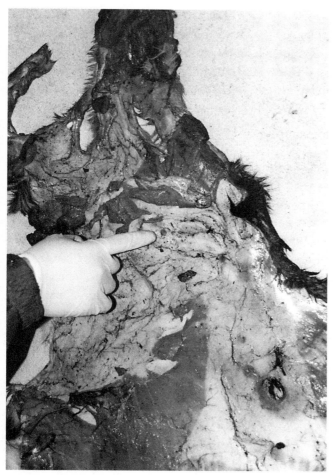

Warden Eric Meade points to a .30-caliber bullet hole in the neck of a deer hide seized during an investigation of David Connors, 1998. The suspect tried to convince Meade and the author that the knife cut (*lower right*) was the actual bullet hole. Cuts like these often happen when the skinner's knife slips during the butchering process.

Eric pulled the hide out and laid it on a stainless-steel examination table. "The medical examiner was really into it," Eric recalled, "fascinated by what I'd brought. That was until she found something she hadn't planned on finding. Suddenly she jumps back and shrieks, 'Oh, my God! There's a tick!' Like it was the most horrible thing she'd ever seen. I laughed, and then she started laughing. I had a little fun with that, and then she got down to business."

The medical examiner held the items for a month before issuing her report: The circular hole in the hide's neck area was slightly elliptical in shape and measured .29 caliber. The bullet wound in the neck came from a high-velocity copper-jacketed bullet. She also gave Eric a small plastic evidence bag containing fragments of the disintegrated copper jacket removed from the bullet wound track in the deer's neck. If needed, we would submit them to the Florida Department of Law Enforcement for further testing.

The construction of a copper-jacketed .30-caliber conical bullet stands in stark contrast to a .50-caliber round ball made of solid lead and spherical in shape. A bullet made with a copper jacket has a lead core. Upon striking an object, the jacket often disintegrates or is partially or fully peeled back away from the core. Thus, when wound channels of these two bullets are compared side by side, forensic examiners note substantial differences. The differences in velocity also play a key factor. Round ball slow. Conical fast—when fired from a .30–30 high-powered rifle.

Eric filed the paperwork with the Putnam County State Attorney's Office. Connors later pled guilty to the wildlife crime of illegally taking deer with a modern firearm.

That got me to thinking about Betty-Sue. So I called her up. It was a couple of weeks before Christmas. "Betty-Sue, the fella who killed that deer received a conviction. But guess what?"

"What?" She asked, suspicious of my exuberance.

"You're eligible for a Wildlife Alert Reward!"

Her demeanor abruptly changed. "God bless you," she said, and then choked a little. "I'll be able to pay my electric bill this month."

A couple of days later Eric and I drove up to Betty-Sue's trailer and handed her a plain white envelope. Inside was $250 in cash.

Postscript

Connors's enthusiasm for committing game violations was in no way diminished by his encounter with Eric and me. The following hunting season he killed another illegal deer. He dragged it to the back of his single-wide and butchered it. Thinking that we just might show up, he took the added precaution of burning the remains in a fire pit behind his home. My guys were too good for that. They were able to pull out enough charred bones to make a case against him.

The next hunting season he poached yet another deer, using the same method of operation, but this time he kept the entire gut pile and bloody skeletal remains inside of his home in a thirty-gallon garbage trash can.

His plan was to wait until garbage pickup day to put the trash cans out by the roadside. Then he'd be safe once the cans were emptied into the lumbering trucks and the back-bin compactor had squished the deer remains into unrecognizable parts.

Wrong again.

My men ferreted out some neighborhood witnesses, including a family member of Connors who told them they had seen him skinning a doe (illegal deer) in his backyard. When Connors felt the weight of his neighbors' accusations, he simply gave up and allowed the wardens into his home, where they recovered the fruits of his crime.

Some people just don't learn.

10

CLOSE-QUARTER COMBAT

Nestled between the sand dunes of Anastasia Island and the St. Augustine Lighthouse is Salt Run, a tidal lagoon that serves as a dedicated anchorage and free home for sailboaters. Many of the boats lying at anchor are known as "live-a-boards"; with hulls encrusted by barnacles and poles bare, they rock gently with the clacking of worn rigging. Most of the owners are merely eccentrics, harmless characters who fancy themselves as living out a bit part in a Hemingway novel.

Others, however, have a darker side.

Sunday, October 6, 2002

The Atlantic seas were running three to four feet in front of a waning nor'easter when the twenty-five-foot Mako rode out to meet them. The solid-gray hull with diagonal green stripes down the sides heaved onto the first ocean swells as it left St. Augustine Inlet. Warden Randy Bowlin nudged the throttle forward, comforted by the steady rumble of twin 225 Mercury outboards running in perfect sync. He stood erect at the helm, his eyes scanning a limitless horizon, where a solid-blue sky met the pewter-gray expanse of the Atlantic.

Diesel trawlers dragged heavy shrimp nets off the beach, while expensive motor yachts and offshore sportsfishing vessels headed inshore, prows tipped high, hurling back thick trails of white frothy foam, on a homeward course to safe harbor. By five in the afternoon, most recreational boaters had become weary of rattling around in the ocean and were ready to call it a day.

With the seas backing down, the air temperature comfortable in the mid-60s, and the tangy smell of crisp sea salt in the air, the start of his patrol shift, it seemed to Randy, was shaping up to be a pleasant one.

★

Randy Bowlin had arrived in northeast Florida a few months earlier, having requested a transfer up from the Keys. The twenty-eight-year-old warden was a six-year veteran assigned full-time water patrol duties on the Intracoastal Waterway, or ICW, and the Atlantic Ocean, based out of the nation's oldest city, St. Augustine.

The young warden stood an even six feet, and his trim, lean frame fit FWC's green and tan uniform as if it had been precision stamped from a mold. He was a minimalist—shaved head, no facial hair. The only jewelry-like adornment he allowed himself to wear was a waterproof diver's wristwatch, and that was more for job functionality than image. He had a certain vibe—calm, reassuring, unflappable, even stoic at times. But it wasn't until he was engaged in lighthearted banter around close friends that an understated streak of dry, comedic humor surfaced.

The former land surveyor had a mind and eye for detail that reflected in every facet of his work. A keen shot and an admitted "gun buff," he kept his 9mm Glock 17 well oiled and clean. The lines in his patrol boat were coiled neatly, the deck scrubbed spotless upon returning to port. He'd made up reference notebooks with charts and pictures of marine fish, ducks, and other hard-to-identify wildlife, each section carefully catalogued within clear plastic sleeves in a three-ring binder.

Indeed, the conservation lawman was, to borrow a nautical cliché, "squared away."

★

Warden Randy Bowlin (now a lieutenant) stands atop the St. Augustine Light-house with Salt Run, Anastasia Island, and the Atlantic Ocean in the background, 2007. Salt Run (*far right*) is the general vicinity where the suspect's blue Tartan sailboat was anchored.

Randy's first order of business was to take care of a delicate cargo that required a special home. On the stern deck lay a small crate with fifteen baby sea turtles—endangered species—that had been reha-bilitated from earlier injuries. Hatchling hawksbill, green, and logger-head turtles spend the first year of their lives or more living in dense mats of floating sargassum grass that ride with the ocean currents. The self-sustaining biomass of brown-colored seaweed provided food and cover from hungry predators.

Fifteen miles offshore, Randy spotted a large patch of drifting sar-gassum grass as it gently undulated with the crests and troughs of the ocean swells. He nosed the patrol craft's bow up into the grass, threw the shifter into neutral, grabbed the crate, and upended it over the side so the turtles splashed down safely on top of the tangled carpet of seaweed.

With his first mission of the day accomplished, Randy turned his attention to other matters.

In the past week, he'd received several complaints of commercial shrimp boats trawling less than a mile from the beach, an illegal activity normally conducted under the cloak of darkness. Because he was already far offshore and sunset only an hour away, he decided to wait there—drifting in the currents until nightfall.

When dark fell, Randy brought the boat up on a plane. He ran black (without navigation lights) through a sloppy following sea as he worked his way back shoreward. Once he was just off of the beach, he turned south, running a parallel course to it. As he scanned ahead with his radar, the display screen showed six bright blips ten miles away. All outlaw shrimp boats fishing inside the mile limit.

Randy mashed the throttle and set a course to intercept them. As he closed with the shrimpers, they picked him up on their radar and scuttled back to the safety of legal waters before he could catch them. He came alongside two of the trawlers, careful not to get hung up on taut lines hanging down from the swaying outriggers. Frustrated, he felt like shaking his fists at the boat captains, but he took a deep breath instead and gave them a stern warning not to fish less than a mile from the beach.

Even if Randy had caught one of the boats fishing in illegal waters, it was usually an uphill battle to win the case in court. Fines could be stiff, the gear and saltwater product seized worth tens of thousands of dollars. Outlaw shrimpers familiar with this penalty often planned ahead. They'd claim a steering arm broke or their GPS navigation system malfunctioned, causing them to veer off course.

During a court trial, this strategy sometimes won cases for the defense because it negated being inside the prohibited area as an intentional act, which the prosecution had to prove.

Since he was already so far south, Randy decided to complete the "loop," one of his favorite patrol patterns that began from the Mako's wet slip at Camachee Cove Marina, in St. Augustine. From there it ran out through St. Augustine Inlet, hooked south, ran fifteen miles down the beach, entered Matanzas Inlet, and then north on the ICW, and back to the marina. The course clockwise circumnavigated Anastasia Island, a narrow barrier island fifteen miles long by up to three wide.

★

With a steady hand on the wheel, Randy squinted into the dim glow of a Garmin GPS, careful to keep the vessel's course on track with a set of predetermined waypoints. The squiggly yellow line was all that would keep him from running aground on the treacherous shoals at the unmarked entrance to Matanzas Inlet.

The snakelike track brought the warden uncomfortably close to the beach before it abruptly veered southwest, cutting diagonally across the inlet and into a narrow channel that ran beneath the A1A Bridge. Randy throttled back, letting the hull settle fully into the water. He idled between the concrete bridge pylons and into protected inshore waters. He finally loosened his grip, relieved at having safely navigated the dangerous route, where less-experienced boaters often ran afoul of shifting sandbars. As he approached Fort Matanzas Park, he spotted one of the rangers standing under the glow of a dock light and pulled alongside to talk with him.

As they chatted, the subject of officer-involved shootings came up. The park ranger told Bowlin about two of their guys who'd just been shot at by drug smugglers in Arizona. The ranger offered Randy a friendly caution before they parted, "You be careful out there." At that moment, neither man could have predicted the true meaning of an offhand comment between friends.

Randy gave his buddy a parting wave, pulled away from the dock, and headed north on the ICW. His shift was about to end.

All he had to do was make the trip back to St. Augustine safely, secure his patrol boat at the marina, and head for the house.

The fiberglass V-hull rode smoothly through the night. Randy kept the Mako centered between the blinking red and green navigation markers, careful not to stray out of the twisting channel and onto shallow banks encrusted with oysters.

Off to his right, Crescent Beach formed one of five communities on Anastasia Island. The strip of ancient sand dunes now sparkled with the bright lights of multistory condominiums, oceanfront hotels, and million-dollar beach homes. To the port (left) side lay darkened glades of spartina grass that ran uninterrupted for nearly a mile, until it melded into a barely distinct, inky-black tree line along the western horizon. Two different worlds, right modern, left primal, defined in separation by a narrow tidal waterway.

At about 11:00 p.m., he passed under the Bridge of Lions in St. Augustine. He glanced to his left, taking in the sculpted lawns and brightly lit ramparts of Castillo de San Marcos. Built in 1672–95, it is the oldest masonry fort in the continental United States and a U.S. National Monument. The iconic landmark annually draws up to 6 million tourists to the Ancient City. The massive structure faded away behind the patrol boat's stern as the channel curved east into Matanzas Bay.

Salt Run lay ahead on the right.

"It was very dark," Randy recalled, "and I was looking for an unlit green channel marker that was hard to see. My boat was just on a plane, when out of my peripheral vision I saw a small boat go by—whoosh—off the port side of my boat blacked-out. I turned around and looked and for a moment thought I had run him over."

Randy spun the wheel hard, bringing his patrol boat around in a wrenching one-eighty, to check on the safety of the vessel and its operator. As he pulled alongside, he shined his spotlight onto a seven-foot blue dinghy powered by a 2 HP Johnson. A tall, thin-framed man with a patchy beard, augmented by a salt-and-pepper mustache, sat on a flat-board wooden seat near the stern. He was shirtless, wearing white shorts, with greasy brown, collar-length hair stringing from beneath a black bandana. Beside his feet sat a red plastic party cup partially filled with an amber-colored liquid. He had one hand on the motor's tiller, puttering along at a leisurely pace toward the entrance of Salt Run.

Randy ordered him to "Stop!" several times. The dinghy operator stared ahead with glazed eyes, ignoring the commands. Finally, Randy eased his vessel in front of the dinghy and forced it to stop.

As Randy bent over the Mako's gunwale to speak with the man, the odor of hard liquor wafted up to him. The dinghy operator's slurred voice and loud talk was enough to alert him. He was one of the friend-liest drunks Randy had ever encountered. "Just great," he thought. "I would have to run into this knucklehead when I'm about to go off shift."

Randy then asked *the question*, one that every traffic cop has asked since the first drunk-driving law was legislated. "How much have you had to drink?"

"Two-and-a-half cups of rum since sunset," replied the dinghy op-erator, mouthing the words carefully.

As they talked, Randy detected a German accent in the man's speech. The operator said he was a cabinet maker from Germany and had recently come over to the States on his sailboat. He said his name was "J. Michael Giairod" and that his passport was on his sailboat, anchored just ahead of them in Salt Run. He claimed he didn't have a driver's license, which was believable to Randy. In his experience, a lot of sailboaters didn't own a car or a truck so would never be in need of one. The dinghy was not registered, and the operator had no paperwork on him.

Randy had Giairod do a couple of sobriety tasks to determine if he was indeed drunk. Giairod flunked the eye-movement test first. Then he tried the finger count next. Dazed, he stared at the tips of his fingers; seconds ticked by, and nothing happened. Finally, by way of a cotton-mouthed explanation, he muttered, "Man, I really am drunk."

Randy tied the dinghy off to his vessel so it was rafted alongside and put the engines in gear, moving toward the sailboat at two to three knots. He ran Giairod's name through dispatch, trying to verify his identity. Dispatch kept responding with, "No record found."

When Randy reached the sailboat—a powder-blue, thirty-foot Tartan single-mast sloop—he ran its registration numbers, and it came back, "No record found."

"I admit," Randy said, "that by now I was completely puzzled and a little frustrated, because the sailboat's registration numbers should have come back to someone. My intention was to get his identifica-tion, then take him over to the Lighthouse Boat Ramp, which was a quarter mile away, and finish giving him the field sobriety tasks on firm ground that was flat and well lighted."

Giairod continued to joke around. He showed no signs of nervousness to Randy, who considered himself a good reader of people.

But Giairod's nice-guy routine was all a smoke-and-mirrors act. Inside his head roiled a jumbled bunch of thoughts. He was in tremendous psychological turmoil. He knew he was one step away from a life behind cold steel bars and solid cement walls if the warden discovered his true identity. He considered his options and thought, "Lord, it's going to be a night to die." Through the hazy fog of rum spirits, he'd finally come to realize the enormity of his predicament. And he began to hatch a plan.

"Can I go on my boat to get my paperwork?" Giairod calmly asked.

"Do you have any guns on board?" countered Randy, who didn't think Giairod's request unusual under the circumstances.

"No guns, I hate guns. Only some knives and a bow and arrow."

"We'll board the vessel together," Randy instructed. "I'll remain a few feet behind you. When we're close to where you keep the paperwork, you will point it out to me so I can retrieve it."

Both men entered the cabin through a narrow companionway (entrance) on the stern deck, which led down three wooden steps into a galley. Randy ducked his head as he entered the cramped doorway that allowed only two inches of room on either side of his shoulders as he squeezed through. The already claustrophobic space had been made even smaller, cluttered with assorted gear from deck to ceiling: five-gallon containers for potable water, a wooden toolbox, engine parts, marine-band radios, five-gallon plastic buckets, a portable CD player, sacks containing life vests, an electric fan, a fire extinguisher, power tools, a Coleman two-burner cookstove, and folded clothing were stuffed or stacked in every available space along the cabin's walls and countertops. The two men threaded their way forward and into a tight hallway that led past a tiny kitchen to a dead end. Ahead was a triangle-shaped berthing area whose inner walls fit snug against the V-shaped bow.

"Where is the paperwork?" Randy asked.

"Underneath my mattress," Giairod said.

By now Giairod had stopped in front of the mattress, which butted up flush to a narrow doorway with bulkheads made of cheap wood

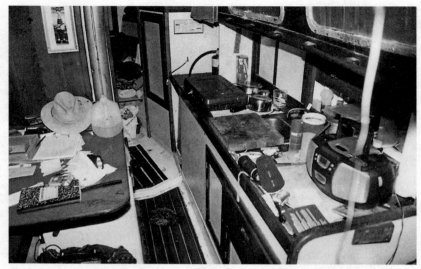

Warden Randy Bowlin squeezed through the narrow hallway (*upper right*) to access the berthing area where James Forney, a.k.a. J. Michael Giairod, engaged him in a brief shootout, 2002. Bowlin then retreated while continuing to fire through the wood-paneled walls at where he believed Forney was. Note the two bullet holes in the vertical pipe and two more bullet holes in the gallon plastic water jug.

paneling on each side. The bed was a mess; a dark-blue comforter lay crumpled on top mixed with bunched-up garments in need of laundry. The cloying odor of unwashed clothing hung in the still air. Giairod turned and sat down on the mattress facing Randy. Then he lit a cigarette with his left hand.

Randy eyed Giairod with increased intensity. His pulse began to tick up. Something did not feel right. He bladed his body, right foot forward, left foot back, to create a smaller target and a more stable fighting stance. He placed the palm of his left hand on the grip of his duty weapon.

Giairod's demeanor did a sudden one-eighty, and now Randy picked up subliminal cues that something was very wrong. Giairod looked down at his feet and would not make eye contact. He refused to answer any more questions. And he was leaning back on his right hand, which was now just behind the bulkhead hidden from the warden's line of sight.

"I kept the best reactionary gap that I could," Randy recalled, "which was eight to nine feet, about the best you can do in a sailboat. I unsnapped my gun and rocked it out of the retention—keeping it level with the holster along my side. My first thought was, 'He's going to charge me with a knife.'"

"What's in your right hand?" Randy asked.

No response.

He repeated the question, "What's in your right hand?"

Again, no response.

In a firm tone, with each word perfectly enunciated, Randy said, "Let me see your right hand real slow."

"He quickly leaned to his left," Randy remembered, "pulled his right hand in tight to his chest to get around the bulkhead and punched his arm straight out holding a pistol. So now I was looking right down the muzzle of his gun. I pulled my gun up from the hip and punched out three—*Bang! Bang! Bang!* One from the hip, one at midstroke, and one pointed."

Simultaneously, *Bang!* Giairod shot at Randy. Once. He missed, though Randy didn't realize that at the time.

"I knew I'd hit him," Randy said, "because he had fallen back on the mattress with his upper torso lying behind the bulkhead. All I could see was from his legs down. And I could see blood."

The warden quickly shuffled backward, continuing to fire rounds downrange, even after he'd lost sight of Giairod and entered the galley backing up. He shot through the bulkhead walls, adjusting his line of fire according to where he imagined Giairod to be on the other side.

As Randy bumped into the companionway steps, he pulled the trigger again; time seemed to stand still. He watched the slide come back and the shiny brass shell casing slowly spin away from the ejection port. Up to this point, no more than two to three seconds had elapsed since he fired his first shot.

Giairod screamed, "You've killed me, you motherfucker! You've killed me!"

"What was really weird," Randy recalled, "was when I spun around and began to run up the stairs. It felt like my feet were stuck, like they were superglued to the wooden steps. I could not make them move fast enough. If you had asked me right then, I would have bet a paycheck that I was going to take a round, because the suspect was wounded, angry as hell, and in possession of a loaded pistol that could punch holes through those thin wood-paneled cabin walls like it was going through tissue paper.

"I had made up my mind that I was getting out of that boat—unless I was hit in the head or neck—because I had body armor on. I was mentally prepared to take a bullet in the butt or the back of my legs. I thought it would feel like a baseball bat hitting me. But no matter what, I had to get out of that boat!"

Randy raced out of the galley and onto the top deck. He dove between two guy-wire supports for the mast, slicing one arm open before slamming onto the forward deck of his patrol boat. He hastily undid the bowline, cranked the twin 225s, and slammed the throttle forward. Seconds later he came off plane and idled up to the dock at the Lighthouse Boat Ramp, where he could safely call for backup.

In less than a minute, St. Augustine Police Department officers, St. Johns County sheriff's deputies, and Randy's supervisor, Lt. Bill Head, were dispatched and en route.

Randy didn't have to wait long before cop cars, state four-wheel-drive pickups, county green-and-whites, and emergency rescue vehicles began streaming into the parking lot at the Lighthouse Boat Ramp. Blinking blue and red strobes flickered across manicured lawns and into the ornate shrubbery of nearby homes, while the blue Tartan sailboat lay quietly at anchor less than a quarter mile away, with an armed man who had already attempted to kill a state law enforcement officer and was known to be wounded, which could make him even more dangerous.

Under the pinkish glow of sodium vapor lights, the burly lieutenant—a twenty-five-year veteran who had spent his entire conservation law enforcement career patrolling St. Augustine's waterways—met with all of the lawmen to come up with a game plan. Their two main concerns were that Giairod was in the sailboat bleeding to death and, of course, that he still needed to be apprehended.

Their plan was a simple one: Lieutenant Head would captain the

Mako, while two St. Johns County sheriff's deputies and two St. Augustine Police Department officers formed an assault team.

Before they shoved off, the lieutenant explained to Randy he would have to stand down on this detail. The assault team needed to be composed of officers who had not been in a violent confrontation with the suspect. The appearance of impartiality needed to be maintained should they engage Giairod in a gunfight. It was standard police procedure.

"I backed away from the dock," Bill recalled, "spun around, and killed the lights on the patrol boat. It was the dark of the moon, but we had enough ambient light from shoreline dock lamps and homes to partially illuminate the vessels that lay at anchor in Salt Run.

"I placed a shotgun on the deck by my feet. The other officers were crouched down behind the bow, with their guns drawn, trying to stay as low as they could. I eased around behind the sailboat. There were no lights on. It was eerily quiet."

Powerful flashlight beams shined into the lower cabin. Giairod could be seen lying on his back. He held a pistol in his left hand across his chest.

Officers shouted, "Drop the gun! Drop the gun! Drop the gun!"

Giairod let the pistol fall onto the cabin deck.

"I nudged the Mako's bow against the sailboat's stern," Bill said. "On the touch, Sgt. Chris Strickland [St. Johns County Sheriff's Office] and Corporal Richard Warner [St. Augustine Police Department] were up and into the sailboat like pirates. You would have thought they'd rehearsed it a hundred times. While they were in the cabin, I was crouched down in the Mako, with one hand on the shotgun, the other hand on the wheel. The engines were still in forward gear, pressing the bow against the stern. I didn't want to tie off in case we had to make a hasty retreat.

"The other two officers stayed behind with me for backup. There wasn't enough room inside the cabin of that sailboat for more than two people to maneuver."

A bloody Giairod was cuffed in less than a minute. He began ranting as they dragged him out of the boat: "I lied to the officer. I lied

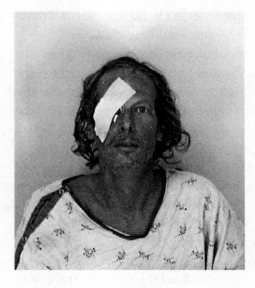

St. Johns County Sheriff's Office booking photo of James Michael Forney, 2002.

about my name. I knew I was in trouble. Just go ahead and shoot me in the head. Just let me die."

Then Giairod's mind whipsawed in a whole new direction. In a moment of apparent regret, or maybe it was just the fickle mind of a "rummy," he inquired about Randy's welfare, "Is he all right? Did I hurt him? I didn't want to do it."

The registration numbers were run again on the sailboat. This time it came back to James M. Forney, forty-three, wanted for questioning in a homicide by the Miami-Dade Police Department. The name Giairod was one of several aliases that Forney was known to use.

Forney was life-flighted to Shands Hospital in Jacksonville with gunshot wounds to his left knee and right hand and metal bullet fragments embedded in his right eye. He would later lose the eye.

Investigators from the Florida Department of Law Enforcement examined Randy's duty weapon, which showed he'd fired seven rounds. Forney had used a 9mm FIE-TZ75 semi-auto pistol; a spent shell casing was found stuck in the ejection port, indicating he had fired at least one round.

Upon Forney's release from the hospital, he was charged with: "attempted murder of a law enforcement officer," "giving a false name," "boating under the influence," and "operating a vessel without navigation lights."

Postscript

In early January 2001, nine months before Randy's encounter with Forney, fishermen found the remains of a thirty-five-year-old prostitute, Gina Marie Roberto, in a south Miami-Dade canal. She had been beaten, stabbed, and mutilated with slice marks on her neck, wrists, and genitals.

During the third week of June 2008, James Michael Forney was tried for her murder in the Broward County Courthouse. He represented himself, while wearing a black patch over the eye lost during his shootout with Randy. Apparently his arguments to the jury were less then compelling. According to an article published in the south Florida *Sun-Sentinel*, "Forney told Broward County jurors he stabbed the prostitute eight times because she gurgled and it sounded like demons. He had to kill the demons, Forney said, explaining the multiple stabbings."

The jury deliberated for ninety minutes before convicting him of Gina's murder. He was sentenced to life in prison.

11

SCARED STRAIGHT

Game wardens often think about the meaning of luck. Sitting alone, in the dark, for hours and hours waiting for some wayward poacher to show up engenders these kinds of thoughts. Believe me.

Back in 1978, I met with my sergeant one day to tell him about a big commercial fish-poaching case I'd made. At some point in the conversation I mentioned the word "luck," as in random chance. He stopped me cold, saying, "The definition of luck is when preparation meets opportunity."

In the story below, luck in one form or another does come into play. Some might think it a roll of the dice or merely coincidence, while others might say it was someone who recognized an opportunity and seized it. I tend to think it was the latter.

North-Central Florida, November 20, 2005, 7:05 p.m.

A pale three-quarter moon rose above the pine forest, casting deep shadows across Forest Road 8 in southeast Marion County. FWC Lt. Gregg Eason steered his state ride, a silver Ford F-150 pickup, southbound on the two-lane blacktop doing 55. The nine-year veteran wasn't thinking about luck so much as he was wondering why a deer decoy stakeout he'd worked earlier in the day had turned up a big fat goose egg. Determined to make something productive come of this shift, he decided to change locations to an area closed to deer hunting year-round.

The Sunnyhill Restoration Area is 4,405 acres of public wilderness managed by the St. Johns River Water Management District. The upper Ocklawaha River basin drains through the property, leaving a vast marsh that spreads out to sandy ridges interspersed with oak hammocks, pine forests, and head-high patches of dense scrub oak thicket. A four-strand barbed-wire fence delineates the property boundary running along the west side of Forest Road 8.

Peering down the patrol truck's high beams, the lieutenant saw the reflection of taillights ahead. An unlit vehicle was parked on the west shoulder of the road next to the water management property. The taillight design told him it was a Chevy Z-71 pickup. As he whipped by the truck, two faint lights registered simultaneously in his side vision—a dim orange glow inside the truck's cab and a white flash, no more than a flicker, from deep in the woods.

The flash might have been a firefly, maybe the sliver from a flashlight beam, or Gregg's mind playing tricks. He wasn't sure. But, he had no doubt about what the orange glow meant.

Twenty Minutes Earlier

Inside the dark cab of the Chevy pickup, Ricky Stratton, twenty-three, sat alone behind the steering wheel. He shot a nervous glance into the rearview mirror before dropping his gaze to look through the front windshield and beyond. His vision alternated between the two sight planes so he could keep tabs on traffic approaching from either direction. He felt like the wheelman for a gang of bank robbers as he waited for two friends to slip out of Sunnyhill with a poached deer.

Ricky glanced at his watch—6:45 p.m. It was the fifth time he'd checked it in the last ten minutes. His fingers drummed impatiently against the steering wheel while he wondered how in the hell he'd let himself get talked into doing this.

Inside the truck's cab with the windows rolled down, biting mosquitoes smothered Ricky in a cloud. Fed up with the pesky critters, he switched on his ThermaCELL—a handheld-sized mosquito control device a little bigger than a television remote control. He laid it on the truck's dash. Within seconds, burning gas ignited, emitting a dull orange glow the size of a thumbtack. An invisible cloud of odorless repellent enveloped Ricky, while he settled back and tried to relax.

Lt. Gregg Eason recognized the orange glow as coming from a Therma-CELL, just like the ones issued to every warden in the state. To Gregg, the activated mosquito-repellant device meant only one thing—the guy sitting inside the parked truck had been waiting there awhile.

The lieutenant didn't let off the gas. He never tapped the breaks. Instead, he kept his speed constant, staying in the natural flow of traffic until he was about a mile down the road. Then he pulled over. He was far enough away so the man sitting in the Chevy wouldn't hear the telltale *wha . . . wha . . . wha* of heavy lugged off-road tires decelerating. He waited until the first northbound truck passed, then spun around and got in behind it. When they were one curve from the Chevy, he cut the lights and passed by the unlit truck, a dark shadow hanging in the slipstream of the vehicle ahead.

On this drive-by, he gave the suspicious truck a good hard look. He didn't see any lights back in the woods, but something didn't feel right. Instinct told Gregg he needed to check it out.

Back in 2004, Gregg, thirty-six, supervised six officers in Marion County. He is an avid deer hunter who targets trophy whitetails. He is also an ordained Baptist minister and a U.S. Marine Corps veteran.

In those days, his hair was cut in a rigid military flattop. He stood five ten, weighed in at a solid 185, and was a fastidious dresser, both on and off the job. Always composed, he spoke with a calm, subtle confidence, choosing his words carefully. When presented with a particularly vexing problem, he would consider all of the angles and then render a decision in a timely manner. Neither his peers nor his subordinates would ever describe him as "indecisive." Thus, he embodied "command presence," a desirable trait for those in the law enforcement profession.

Inside Sunnyhill Restoration Area

Earlier that afternoon, well before the Chevy truck would end up parked on the road shoulder of Forest Road 8, Bubba Spencer, twenty-four, slipped into the water management property and illegally killed a "good-sized eight-point buck." He dragged the deer to within two hundred yards of Forest Road 8 and stashed it behind a tree. He planned to come back for it after dark.

Bubba waited for a lull in traffic before climbing over the fence and crossing to the opposite side of the highway, where his truck was parked on the road shoulder next to the Ocala National Forest boundary. Bubba had a tree stand back in the Forest where it was open season and legal to hunt deer. He figured if the "game warden" checked him, he'd take him right to his hunting stand. Proof he was on the up-and-up.

Bubba rationalized daytime hunting in a closed area as a more "legitimate" form of poaching, one rung below the "real poachers" who hunted deer at night with a gun and light.

★

Gregg flicked his headlights on and rolled to a stop behind the Chevy truck. He walked up to the driver's door, flashlight in hand, identified himself, and asked, "Hey, what's going on this evening?"

"Oh, ah . . . I just had to stop for a minute to use the bathroom," Ricky replied.

"Is that right? How about showing me where?"

"Well . . . right over there," he gestured to a spot in the short Bahia grass, about twenty yards away next to the fence.

"How about you walk over and show me exactly where."

Ricky led Gregg to a spot near the fence, but Gregg's light didn't show any wet places on the grass. Instead, he saw where two sets of foot tracks entered the fence, made their way across a freshly plowed fire break and into the state property.

Suspicious now, Gregg tried a bluff.

"Listen," he said, "the gig's up. So far everything you have told me is a lie. You are the lookout for someone hunting in Sunnyhill. You have two choices: Keep digging a deeper hole by lying, or tell me the truth. Tell the truth and I won't put you in jail."

After a bit more coaxing, Ricky admitted to being the lookout/pickup man for Bubba Spencer and his cousin, Davy Metter. He told Gregg he'd dropped both men off thirty minutes earlier to pick up a deer Bubba had shot that afternoon.

"What do these guys look like?" Gregg asked.

"They both kind of look the same," Ricky answered, "around five six, short brown hair, and both wear goatees. Bubba tops out at around 275, and his cousin is little lighter. I'd say somewhere around 225."

"I guess I don't have to worry about a foot chase then," Gregg chuckled.

"Not a chance."

"Okay, so what's the all-clear sign?"

"One long honk of the horn."

"Have you signaled them yet?" Gregg asked.

"No," Ricky said.

"Do you expect them to come out soon?"

"They should be here any minute."

Gregg took Ricky's driver's license and shoved it into his back pocket. If Ricky disappeared he'd have the particulars to complete a warrant for his arrest. He told him not to leave. Before ducking through the barbed-wire fence and into Sunnyhill, Gregg gave the horn one good blast. Then he followed the foot tracks under the surreal glow of a waxing moon. The near daylight conditions made it tricky. Experience had taught him that if the men in the woods saw him standing in the open or profiled against the skyline, they'd spook and run.

Earlier, while Ricky was waiting in the Chevy and the lieutenant was driving past, Bubba and Davy were stomping through a tangle of brush and young oaks in the dark, trying to find the hidden deer.

Bubba was worried about turning on a flashlight. But he figured they were far enough back in the woods that no one passing by on the highway could possibly see it. So he took a chance and blinked the light on for only a "second or two," before they found the deer.

It was at precisely that moment Gregg happened to drive by the parked Chevy and peripherally saw a flash of white light. Bad luck for the poachers, good luck for Gregg. Seldom does coincidence present such a unique set of circumstances to a conservation lawman.

Dragging 130 pounds of dead weight across uneven ground is tiring. It took the two men a good fifteen minutes to manhandle the deer over blowdowns and around ragged branches that kept snagging on their clothing and the deer's antlers. Before long, they could see the Chevy through a gap in the foliage. The cab and hood shined brightly in the moonlight. Parked behind it was another truck, an F-150 pickup, with the darkened image of a decal on the door. While Bubba couldn't make out the lettering or colors in the moonlight, the oval shape told him it belonged to a game warden truck (unlike most FWC patrol trucks, this F-150 did not have an emergency light bar mounted atop the cab). Faint voices, barely audible, drifted back to the men watching from the brush.

Bubba and Davy backtracked down the trail, masking their retreat by padding softly through the dark. They came up with a hasty plan: leave the deer, circle around through the woods, come out onto the highway a quarter mile from the truck, and then walk back, casual like, just to see what was going on.

Bubba stopped for a moment. He pulled out a pair of wire snippers from his back pocket and stuck them in the cargo pocket of his camouflaged pants, where it would be more secure if he had to pick up the pace. He'd planned to use them to cut the bottom fence strand so the deer could be dragged underneath and out the other side without snagging on the barbed wire. No self-respecting poacher wanted to be caught in the bright headlights of a passing motorist while struggling to free his deer. It smacked of amateurism.

Halfway along the new route, Bubba thought he heard the roar of off-road tires fading away. He took this as a fortuitous sign; one that meant the game warden had left. Then a single horn blast reverberated through the night. Coupled with the sounds of truck tires dissipating only moments before, the men believed they were now safe and decided to abort their plan. They retraced their steps to where they had left the deer and crept up the sandy path toward the Chevy for a quick peek, just to make sure the coast was clear.

★

Bent over, the lieutenant quietly slipped between the barbed-wire strands. He used the ambient lunar light to follow the foot tracks into a path that was narrow and dark and twisting. It weaved through a tunnel of scrub oak that blocked out all but a dappling of starlight and the weak slivers of illumination cast by a low-hanging moon. Forty yards down the trail he paused to listen.

Silence.

Then Gregg stepped to one side, pulled apart some young saplings, and squatted to hide his silhouette in the thick vegetation. "What I was concentrating on really hard," he recalled, "was being able to see them coming toward me. We had some moon and a path of white sand leading away from me. I knew when they got to within thirty feet of me I'd be able to see them no matter what, because once they stepped on the bright white sand, their bodies would become black silhouettes against the lighter background."

Five minutes had passed when irregular shadows came around a turn in the trail. Peering into the gloom, Gregg strained to make out what they were doing. There was something weird about their gait. "It didn't dawn on me," Gregg said, "that they were dragging a deer, sat it down, and were taking a break."

A minute or two passed before two vague shadows began moving up the path. The lieutenant planned to take an unorthodox approach when confronting them. He wanted to catch them off guard. He didn't want them to think it was the "man" right of, and maybe fire a round downrange if they had a gun. By creating some confusion, a little hesitation, he hoped to gain an extra second or two to take control.

Having the advantage in what amounts to an ambush of sorts can make the difference between living and dying. Officers have been killed in similar circumstances.[1]

The two men filled the trail, husky young lads of large girth who resembled twin bears as they lumbered ahead. With a gun in one hand and an unlit flashlight in the other, Gregg whispered into the dark, "Bubba."

"Yeah," Bubba answered.

"Is this Bubba Spencer?"

"Yeah," Bubba mouthed the word hesitantly, heart pounding, unsure who stood ahead in the darkened scrub. He prayed it was Ricky.

"Game warden!" The lieutenant's flashlight flicked on. Ten feet away two ashen faces stared back at him, mouths agape, frozen in the bright white light.

Scared speechless, Bubba had only one thought, "Oh shit!"

A short time later, Warden Joe Simpson arrived to assist Gregg with processing the scene and the three suspects. Bubba decided to cooperate and tell the truth about what had happened. What the young poacher didn't realize was that once you start talking to someone like Lieutenant Eason, the man will pick your bones clean in short order.

Before long, Bubba admitted to illegally killing another buck—a trophy 10-point he'd shot in the same area a few months before. That time it was during archery season, and he had killed the deer with a high-powered rifle.

Wanting recognition that would give him sure-enough bragging rights for his prize deer, he posed for a picture with it, holding a bow and arrow, and then submitted the photo to a popular Florida

---

1 On Sunday, November 5, 1972, Sgt. Harry Charles Chapin was shot and killed while attempting to arrest three men for hunting at night, while on foot. As Sergeant Chapin and three other officers attempted to arrest the suspects— in a wooded area off State Road 159 in Gadsden County—they were met with 12-gauge shotgun blasts. Two suspects were apprehended at the scene. The third suspect was apprehended at his home a few hours later. Sergeant Chapin is survived by his wife and two children.

Lt. Gregg Eason with evidence seized in the Scared Straight case, 2005.

outdoor magazine. The publisher, unaware of the deer's history, later printed the photo as its feature cover shot.

After learning of the illegal 10-point, Gregg and Joe recovered the evidence at Bubba's dad's house located less than a mile down the road from the water management property. "We retrieved the cape out of a freezer," Gregg said, "thawed it out, and turned the hide fur side down to examine it for bullet holes. We found an entrance and exit hole of a bullet. About a quarter inch to one side was a star-shaped pattern where Bubba had poked a broadhead through the hide to make it appear it had legally been killed with a bow and arrow. But it just didn't stand up to close scrutiny, because he hadn't pushed it through the exact path made by the bullet."

While they were wrapping things up, the dad sidled up to Gregg and said, "Listen, you can't blame my boy. He learned from the best."

Follow-Up

The lieutenant met with Bubba and his pregnant wife, Linda, a couple of days after the arrest. Gregg needed to conduct a follow-up interview, but he also wanted to take that opportunity to speak with them as a couple.

"As you know, I'm an ordained minister," Gregg told me later during a ride-a-long. "I do try to keep it separate from my occupation. But there are times in my career when I see a crack in the door open, where I may be able to utilize my beliefs, because they're similar to the bad guy's beliefs. I could tell by talking to Linda that Bubba was completely deflated. She could have asked him to do anything at that moment and he would have done it. I saw that as an opportunity to maybe make a difference.

"This was Bubba's wake-up call, an intersection in his life where he could choose between the illegal hunting and carousing and going out at night, or settle down and become a family man.

"If after meeting with me they recognize that, *yes, I did wrong, but one mistake doesn't define me, and that I can still be a productive person for the rest of my life*, then that's how I want to leave them."

Six Years Later, September 21, 2010

It was a hot and muggy Tuesday afternoon when Gregg and I dropped by Bubba's home in the community of Summerfield, about fifteen miles south of Ocala. The modest mobile home had clean white siding wrapped all the way around, with a raised wooden deck built at the entranceway. Bubba was at work, but Linda was home and stepped out the front door to greet us barefoot. She was a pleasant-looking woman with an easy smile and wearing shorts and a T-shirt that said, "Born to Be Wild."

I thought her choice of clothing was more a reflection of what she found comfortable to wear rather than a window into her character. She struck me as being sincere and honest, and like many young mothers who have two children, wanted the best for her family.

When I asked what she thought about me interviewing her husband for this story, she seemed genuinely excited and thought he would be too.

"You see," she told me, "Bubba's made the turn. He doesn't poach anymore. We had a friend over for a cookout the other day, and he asked Bubba to go with him to hunt out of season on the water district property. Said he had it all figured out. Bubba told him, 'No way!'

"Bubba thought he had it all figured out too, but he lost his hunting license for two years and had to pay some pretty stiff fines. To be honest with you, I don't know if his heart could take being scared that bad again—once was enough."

12

GILL-NETTERS
IN THE DARK

As the sun set on a pleasant September evening in 2006, two rookie game wardens hid behind a shrubbery hedge at the Burnt Store Marina in Punta Gorda. One warden stood on the ground while he hefted up a bulging cordura bag. The other reached down, grasped the heavy-duty handles, and, with a grunt, hoisted it over the gunwale of a twenty-two-foot Angler, Grande Bay patrol boat. The boat rested on a sturdy, twin-axle aluminum trailer, which would remain there until they loaded and double-checked all of their gear. While the wardens were busy stowing their equipment, one thought stayed foremost on their minds, "Don't get caught."

Within the psyche of most game wardens lies an obsession to ensure one's work plans aren't compromised in any way. On that night, they would be targeting a loose-knit ring of outlaw commercial fishermen who made a habit of driving by the asphalt parking lots of local boat ramps, checking for silver pickup trucks emblazoned with green, black, and white decals that read, "Florida Fish and Wildlife Conservation Commission."

The wayward fishermen had every reason to be as wary and cautious as the lawmen who stalked them. They were professional wildlife crooks who stole stealthily into the night to poach valuable saltwater finfish using illegal gill nets. Getting busted meant an arrest for a third-degree felony, a trip to jail, and seizure of the fish, nets, and vessel. The penalties could run up a tab in the tens of thousands of dollars and shut them down for good.

The wardens spoke quietly, and a nervous anticipation seeped into their conversations. Finally, the patrol craft was ready. One man stood behind the helm, while the other backed the trailer down the ramp. Guide-on rollers creaked as the boat sloshed into the water. The truck was quickly driven out of sight and parked in a private compound away from the public parking area.

A few minutes later the Angler idled away from the ramp, leaving behind a faint V-wake of ripples as it passed luxury motor yachts, catamarans, and teak-trimmed sailboats moored to floating concrete docks. Clear of the marina, they turned south, into the protected waters of Charlotte Harbor. Behind them, the polished plate-glass windows of multistory condominiums receded into the skyline, reflecting the final rays of a setting sun as twilight faded into night.

If they had followed the open harbor on a southwesterly course for ten miles, it would have led them into the Gulf of Mexico's pristine waters. Instead, they continued due south for nine miles until they reached their destination, a state-designated aquatic preserve around Big Pine Island and Matlacha Pass.

The wardens switched off the navigation lights and for the remainder of their trip motored at a slow speed to reduce engine noise and remain undetected. A cell-phone call meant one of them would have to cover up with a rain jacket to blot out the telltale glow from the watchful eyes of a shoreline lookout.

The wardens' prey were clever and would stop at nothing to catch pompano, a common-looking, fork-tailed fish that rarely grew to more than six pounds. They are often served baked, and high-end chefs considered pompano a delicacy for their buttery, creamy taste and firm texture. With a thin supply and high demand, patrons of fine restaurants gladly paid exorbitant prices to dip their forks into a perfectly cooked pompano. Thus, greed became the motivating force behind an outlaw commercial fisherman's gamble to risk losing it all.

★

The full moon shone down upon the light-gray patrol boat, bathing the interior in a soft, pearly glow. The Angler lay nearly still, tethered by a slack line to a wooden channel marker in Matlacha Pass.

High tide had peaked.

The hull shifted slightly as Warden Rich Wilcox stood to stretch his legs. He scanned the horizon, peering into the eerie green glow of night-vision goggles strapped to his head. The instrument's image intensifier multiplied tiny amounts of light many thousands of times, framing the watery landscape of mangrove islands and backwater lagoons in near daylight conditions.

His partner, Scott Peterson, sat quietly beside him on a bench seat behind the center console. Scott pushed a button on his digital watch. The crystal face lit up—4:30. He leaned back, crossed his arms, and thought about how the night had gone so far. They'd done everything right, he hoped. At least as much as could be expected for two rookie game wardens, graduated from the State Fish and Wildlife Academy only five months before.

Scott's gaze climbed above the dark silhouettes of mangrove islands to a clear sky, where the stars were nearly washed out from an incredibly bright moon. They could not have picked a better night for a stakeout. One of the biggest tides of late summer had swept in from the Gulf. Even the shallowest backwater shoals and sandbars were covered with enough water to allow their patrol craft to navigate without fear of running aground. The extra depth put them on an equal footing with the shallow-draft, outlaw net skiff boats that could seemingly run in spit and turn on a dime (an advantage illegal gill-net fishermen from the nearby community of Big Pine Island—that bordered the southern shoreline of Matlacha Pass—never failed to exploit during a boat chase).

Scott marveled at Rich's tenacity. His systematic, full-circle sweeps of the horizon had to be mentally fatiguing. "How does the guy do it?" wondered Scott, who tended to tire from the monotony of waiting hours on end and preferred the busier work of an active daytime patrol.

Attention to detail was part of Rich's nature. His excessive diligence could be traced to an unquenchable curiosity and an unusual knack to visually detect sanity within chaos. If anyone could find the proverbial needle in a haystack, it would be Rich. He'd honed his skills on hidden-picture puzzle games as a kid, and now he was playing for real. With uncorrected 20/10 vision in both eyes, his powers of observation were keen as a hawk's.

The two men had become close friends during their six months in the fish and wildlife academy. Their assignment to the same duty station in southwest Florida was providential. When the news came down, they promptly high-fived each other and within two weeks had rented an apartment in Cape Coral to split the cost of living.

At thirty-six, both wardens were older and brought more real-world experience to the job than most new hires. Rich was a former Marine, and Scott, a soldier in the Army's 101st Airborne Division. Both men were veterans of the Desert Shield and Desert Storm wars in Iraq.

Although Rich and Scott had been patrolling solo for barely two months, they'd become familiar with the geography of these waters during frequent off-duty fishing trips together. The knee-deep, clear-water sand flats behind Captain Herman's Island—on the north side of Matlacha Pass—was one of their favorite spots to explore and fish with light tackle. These environs seemed like the perfect setting for a picture postcard: coconut palms broke the sun-drenched skyline above the island's mangrove-rimmed shore, and roseate spoonbills probed tidal pools for small crustaceans while pelicans and seagulls hovered above, waiting for the ripple of fingerling fishes.

Paradise.

But what they'd only begun to learn were the strategies of the "players," the men who made a living from poaching some of the richest inshore fishing grounds in the southeastern United States.

The rookie wardens needed help.

Enter Larry Jernstedt, a seven-year veteran FWC investigator who had an encyclopedic knowledge of every commercial fisherman (legal and illegal) who plied the coast for thirty miles in either direction. To Larry, catching commercial fish poachers was a cat-and-mouse game

Investigator Larry Jernstedt (plainclothes) and Warden Rich Wilcox collecting evidence in the pompano poaching case, 2006.

in the extreme, a mental chess match where stealth and cunning often determined the winner.

And Larry—like a professional sleight-of-hand magician—had a bag full of tricks. Creating the illusion of being somewhere you weren't was the first one he taught to Rich and Scott.

One night, he had them dunk their empty boat trailer into the water at a public boat ramp three times and then hide it in a vacant wooded lot before returning to water patrol. "The fake water trail," he explained to them, "would mimic a loaded boat trailer with bilge water pouring from a vessel's drain plug hole as it was hauled away." Anyone who had spotted the warden's patrol truck and empty boat trailer parked at the boat ramp earlier—while it was still daylight— would hopefully fall for the ruse and believe the lawmen had vacated the area for good.

The ploy worked. Rich and Scott made their first pompano gill-net case that night.

Craftiness counts. So does having a good coach and mentor.

★

In the lexicon of Big Pine Island commercial fishermen, pompano are known as "golden nuggets," due to the metallic-yellow sheen around the throat, belly, and anal fin. Wholesale commercial fish houses often paid a hefty price of $3.50 to $4.00 a pound for them whole. (In 2006, commercial pompano sales in Florida totaled $1,606,801.)

Easy money if you don't get caught.

During a previous summer, Larry arrested a sixteen-year-old boy left alone in an outlaw skiff at night, after his dad dove overboard and swam away—a typical method of operation in this area because juveniles are treated more leniently by the courts. Thinking this was a teachable moment, Larry told the kid, "You know you shouldn't be out here doing this."

The kid matter-of-factly replied, "Yeah, I know it, but I made fifteen thousand dollars last week as a crewman. Where else can I go and make that kind of money?"

Indeed.

★

Since biblical times and before, hand-sewn nets have been used to harvest fish. The Bible frequently mentions the use of cast and seine nets on the Sea of Galilee. Records show that as far back as three thousand years ago, the Japanese used gill nets made from natural fibers as an entangling device to catch fish.

Modern-day gill nets are made cheaply from high-test, plastic monofilament, sewn by factory machine into long lines of webbing. They have a lead line along the bottom and a cork line at the top to keep the meshes spread open throughout the water column. Any fish swimming into a mesh will be encircled around the gills by the monofilament and trapped.

The vessel commonly used to work a gill net is a flat-bottom boat made from marine-grade plywood, known as a "birddog boat." It has an outboard engine mounted in the center of the vessel, forward of amidships. A tunnel runs the length of the keel back from the engine to the stern. The configuration ensures an adequate volume of water for the propeller to run in to avoid cavitation—the collection of air pockets around the propeller blades. The advantage of this unique hull design means nets can be dropped and retrieved from the stern deck without risk of snagging on a propeller as they would on a conventional, transom-mounted engine. And since the weight is distributed more evenly across the hull, no one part of the boat is lower than the other, allowing it to run in waters far shallower than a typical vessel of its size.

Gill nets have long been the bane of saltwater sport fishermen. Unlike live-catch fish traps, where protected species can be sorted and released, gill nets can't distinguish between species of fish caught. Any fish swimming into a net will be entangled and die. In some instances, fishermen would set a net and never come back to pick it up. It would lie in the water and continue to trap fish—24/7—until a bloated mass of rotting carcasses floated the webbing.

Concerned sportsmen and conservation groups in Florida lobbied tirelessly to bring the issue before the people in the form of a referendum. In November 1994, an overwhelming 72 percent of Florida voters said "yes" to a constitutional amendment limiting marine net fishing. The amendment includes both a prohibition on the use of gill and entangling nets in all state waters (out to nine miles in the Gulf) and a size limit on other nets for the protection of saltwater finfish, shellfish, and other marine animals from unnecessary killing, over-fishing, and waste.

★

Rich pulled the night-vision goggles up over his head and massaged his eyes for a moment. "Well, what do you think?"

"Something needs to happen pretty quick or we'll draw a zip for this shift," Scott said. "We've been sitting here blacked-out all night and haven't seen a thing. Why don't we try doing the opposite of what we're supposed to do?"

"What did you have in mind?"

"Let's turn our lights on and run around Captain Herman's Island real fast to see if we can catch a boat hid up in the mangroves picking fish or with a net strung out. If someone sees us from a distance, they'll probably think we're a lost sport fishing boat trying to find their way back to the ramp."

"Let's do it."

Scott jerked the bowline once, and a slip knot broke free from the channel marker. Rich eased the throttle forward, and the 250 Mercury Optimax growled as it kicked the boat up on an easy plane. Scott directed the bright beam from a million-candlepower Q-beam spotlight into dark-green patches of mangroves and across shallow lagoons and narrow sloughs, looking for the distinctive shape of a blacked-out boat.

They began their circuit around the mile-long island from the north, cut in behind it, and rounded the south end coming into a small bay tucked between the mangroves only fifty yards wide. They had entered a manatee zone (mandatory slow speed) and were easing along at an idle when Rich suddenly shut the engine down. "Cut the lights. Cut them off now!"

While the Angler quietly coasted to a stop, Rich handed the night-vision goggles to Scott. "Look to the north. It looks like a working light."

Scott put the goggles up to his face. "You're right. I see the beam sweeping across the tops of the mangroves. It looks like a boat coming right to us."

By now, the whine of a big V-6 outboard reverberated through the still night air, along with the *whoosh, whoosh* of the flat-bottom hull as it slid from side to side, weaving between the little islands of sturdy vegetation.

Rich cranked the engine. The wardens waited in the dark, bow pointed toward a narrow gap, no more than ten yards wide, where the approaching vessel would emerge.

The boat blew out of the gap and swung their spotlight onto the wardens. Instinctively, the operator wrenched the steering wheel. In a blur, the boat swapped ends, turning within its own circumference like a zero-turn mower and fled back in the direction it had just come. A washing machine–like wake spread out in all directions.

"Hold on," Rich shouted, as he mashed the throttle and simultaneously hit the wave crest rolling toward them. The hull flew up and then slammed down into the trough with a teeth-rattling jar.

Scott regained his seat after having nearly been catapulted into the bow. He flipped on the emergency lights and siren and turned on the handheld spotlight, illuminating the other boat in a cone of brilliant white light. As the warden's boat shot out of the hole, the other vessel, a twenty-four-foot homemade wooden net skiff boat, powered by a center-mounted 150 Yamaha, shut its lights off and disappeared into the mangroves.

The last thing the wardens saw before the fleeing boat ducked out of sight was a big man hanging halfway out of the boat. He wore a white T-shirt and orange bib rain-slicker pants and was clinging to the starboard gunwale for his life. He'd been flung out of an unsecured lawn chair when the driver of the net boat performed the radical one-eighty.

Rich flared the hull, rolling the Angler into a tight righthand turn, and flew into the narrow passage. He rode the bubble trail and wake wash of the fleeing vessel. A quarter mile brought them to within sight of the net boat's transom as it zigzagged through the twisting course. The bitter odor of burnt outboard fuel washed over the wardens as they followed in the vessel's slipstream.

The two boats approached the north end of Captain Herman's Island in tandem. They dodged and weaved through a mangrove jungle filled with a puzzling maze of hidden paths and narrow, twisting water corridors. On either side of the boats, heavily leafed mangrove branches whipped by in a blur. The saltwater shrubs' leaves shined with alternating hues of brilliant green in the artificial light.

The driver of the net boat used one hand to cover his face with a black rain jacket and the other to steer. He hooked hard right, hugging the island's outer edge, and crossed over a shallow sandbar, a scant eighteen inches deep. Mangroves slapped the boat's sides, leaving behind a shower of leaf litter and broken branches in the propeller wash.

The foot of the Angler's outboard began to rub the hard sand bottom. Rich trimmed the engine up and gunned it.

Ahead, the big man crawled and lurched his way to the stern of the net boat.

In order to deploy a gill net, a "let go" buoy and weight are tossed over the stern while the vessel is under way. The device anchors one end of the net in place while the vessel circles a school of fish, 2006.

"He's setting out the 'let go' buoy," Rich shouted, to be heard over the roar of both engines. "It just caught—the net's coming out. Hang on."

"Be careful, be careful," Scott shouted back, as the net furrowed over the transom and into the water.

At that moment, both wardens realized how prescient the advice from one of their academy instructors had been when he cautioned the class to be vigilant for this particular hazard when chasing a gill-net boat.

Rich swung hard to port. "I got it, I got it," he said, as he barely escaped being wrapped up in the mass of monofilament webbing streaming out of the fleeing vessel. Clear, he swung the bow to starboard, inching closer until just an arm's width separated them from the net boat's port side. So close, that every nick and scratch in the skiff's gray paint showed under the warden's light.

The Angler rode the trailing wake like a surfboard, tipping precariously from side to side as Rich feathered the steering wheel to keep the keel centered over the wave's crest.

"We were danger close." Rich would later say, a term he picked up as a Marine in Iraq. "The moment seemed so surreal. It was definitely slow-mo, but crazy. It reminded me of when my Humvee got blown up by an IED during the war—everything became a time distortion. But I loved chasing that boat. It was a beautiful thing. Everything was in our favor that night, faster boat, big tide, full moon. They couldn't get away from us as long as we didn't make a mistake."

"I was focused on my life at that moment," Scott recalled later, in a more sober assessment of what it felt like to be the passenger. "I was worried we would ramp up onto the stern of the other vessel or possibly run over the passenger if he tumbled overboard. I kept an iron grip on the guardrail with one hand and guided the beam from the spotlight into the face of the boat operator with the other. I was trying to blind him with it and at the same time let Rich see the boat. I also wanted to be at the helm of our boat that night. I like to be in control and think my reaction only normal under those circumstances. It was a horrifying experience."

Thirty seconds later, the entire load of gill net had been jettisoned. Six hundred yards of corks and plastic monofilament lay bobbing in the turbulent backwash of the vessels. The net boat continued to fly through the night.

The big guy went back to work.

"He's dumping fish! He's dumping fish!" Rich yelled. "He's trying to lighten the load."

Desperate to increase the outlaw vessel's top-end speed, the big man emptied one orange plastic laundry basket after another filled with jack crevalle overboard.[1]

Surprisingly, the net skiff began to throttle down. Then the driver pulled up smartly to a tiny mangrove island and stopped, while a thin plume of blue-black smoke gathered around the engine's exhaust

---

1 Jack crevalle were considered near worthless as a food product. The wholesale commercial fish houses on Big Pine Island wouldn't accept a load unless the fishermen brought in a minimum of 300 pounds. They were often confused for pompano by the commercial fisherman at night when they picked their nets in dim or no light.

ports. It was running at idle, the gear in neutral. By all appearances, it seemed like the wardens' night had come to a satisfactory close.

As the Angler came off plane, Rich and Scott shouted instructions: "You're under arrest. Raise your hands."

At first the driver of the net boat appeared to yield to the wardens. As Rich slowed down to almost a dead stop, the outlaw boat suddenly jumped up on a plane. The Angler glided over the watery depression left in its wake, and Rich punched the throttle. The Angler chewed up the bottom, spitting out huge gouts of sand and spray before making it back up on top, barely. The driver of the net boat had set a trap. He knew about a deep trough in the sandbar. Had the wardens' patrol craft been a few feet to either side, they would have grounded out. And as one might imagine, Rich and Scott were on a mission now.

The race continued out into an open area of sand flats. The outlaw boat continued to twist and turn, trying to shake the wardens. To Rich, the figure eights and sudden course changes were like a well-choreographed dance, like two fighter pilots engaged in intricate maneuvers, always seeking the advantage.

Unable to shake his pursuers, the driver of the outlaw boat nosed up into a little mangrove island known as Bear Key and shut down. The wardens pulled up behind them, guns drawn.

"Hands on your head! Hands on your head now!" they shouted in unison.

The big man complied. But the driver—a tall, muscular guy, with a shaven head sporting a purple Mohawk—became a blur as he dove headfirst over the side. The wardens heard a splash, then sounds like someone was trying to pick their way through gnarly mangrove roots. The tide was still high and had pushed twenty to thirty feet up into the dense plants.

The wardens had a problem: the guy who went overboard wasn't just anyone. He was William "Bad Bill" Jackson, a thirty-something Golden Gloves boxer and Mixed Martial Arts fighter who'd won a couple of light-heavyweight Tough Man Contests in the Fort Myers area.

Even though Bad Bill had never been a problem in the past, neither of the lawmen wanted to take a chance on having to go one-on-one with a man whose favorite hobby was beating someone to within an inch of their life. This included Rich, who stood six foot three and weighed in at a solid 240.

Rich and Scott gave spirited verbal encouragement for Bad Bill to come out of the dark and surrender.

But Bad Bill had a reputation to uphold. He fancied himself a renegade of sorts and at various times in the past had referred to himself as the Grey Ghost, Billy the Kid, and other assorted folk heroes from the 1900s. He was the ringleader for several illegal net boat operations, made close to a six-figure income, and drove a brand-new Chevy Z-71 pickup.

The big man stood silently on the stern deck of the net boat. He was in his early fifties and had an exceptionally broad back. He'd also had surgery on both shoulders as a result of having hauled fishing nets for more than four decades. He physically could not put his hands behind his back. The wardens put a supersized life vest on him and used three pairs of handcuffs to comfortably secure him. He told them he'd been asleep in the lawn chair and didn't have a clue what had happened until he was almost thrown out of the boat. He denied having thrown any fish overboard or deploying the gill net. He didn't know why Bad Bill had fled. As to forty-one pompano left in two laundry baskets, no comment. Apparently the pompano were too valuable to throw overboard.

Rich called dispatch and requested Investigator Jernstedt be called out to the scene, as well as their supervisor and an FWC helicopter. They had a net boat to seize, a gill net to recover, and a search for Bad Bill to conduct.

Rich turned to Scott. "Are you good with me going to look for the net? I'm worried someone in another boat will pick it up before we can get back to it."

"I'm good," Scott replied. "I've got my handheld radio if something happens."

Rich climbed into the Angler and sped off into the night.

After Rich left, Scott's status suddenly became more serious. He was alone and realized that Bad Bill might be armed. Bad Bill could have circled back and tried to ambush him or climb up over the side and tackle him. But the other concern was that he was underneath the tunnel in the net boat Scott was now standing in, or hidden up in the motor splash well waiting to ambush him.

Scott mentally braced himself for a fight as he panned the waters all around him with his flashlight beam. He began to issue loud verbal commands: "Bad Bill, if you're anywhere near here and have a plan to come at me with a knife or a stick or a gun, I'm going to kill you. If you're swimming, you better keep on swimming." He really expected Bad Bill to come out of the water with a spear that night.

Meanwhile, Rich had motored up to the gill net, taken the GPS coordinates, and hauled it in, along with a pile of wiggling fish already entangled in the meshes. The job took forty-five minutes, and then he started the hunt for Bad Bill.

He began a slow circle around Captain Herman's Island, manually sweeping the water and probing the mangroves with the beam of his spotlight. He entered a cut, and the only thing he saw were crab-trap buoys. Then off in the distance, maybe a hundred yards across an open bay, on the dimly lit fringe of the illuminated area, was a red buoy. "That's odd," he thought, "because all of the others are white." Curious, he had to check it out. As he got closer, the circular red ball swiveled around. It was Bad Bill, crawling through three feet of water on his hands and knees with a red T-shirt wrapped around his head. He looked up at Rich through tiny slits in the cloth. Rich stared back at him, momentarily stunned by the uncanny likeness to Spider Man from the neck up.

Rich pulled up to him. "Bad Bill, it's over with. Get in the boat."

"Don't put that felony fleeing on me," Bad Bill begged, as he unwound the T-shirt from his head.

"Everything's set in motion. We got backup coming, and a helo will be here shortly. There's nothing I can do for you."

Bad Bill stood in thigh-deep saltwater wearing cutoff jeans. His dampened purple Mohawk glistened brilliantly under the intense spotlight. Then he abruptly changed gears and engaged Rich in a lively philosophical discussion. His keen green eyes radiated enthusiasm. "You know they'll be writing folk songs about me long after you're gone. They'll never remember your name."

"I didn't take this job to have folk songs written about me," said Rich, who decided to humor Bad Bill. Perhaps this little talk would open up a window into his psyche.

"You know what, Rich? This is our destiny."

"What do you mean?"

"You're my Wyatt."

"Your Wyatt?"

"Haven't you heard of Wyatt Earp before?"

"Sure."

"Yeah, you're my Wyatt Earp. I always said that one day Wyatt would catch me."

"I guess that brings us back full circle then, because you're under arrest."

The dim gray of first dawn gathered quietly over the tiny fishing village of Matlacha, an island community of cozy waterfront cottages and small motels, boutique shops, colorful art galleries, and roadside seafood restaurants. On this fine morning, though, the action was at the double-lane public boat ramp, where several FWC officers gathered around Rich and Scott to help them tie off the seized vessel and their patrol boat. The prisoners had been marched off to one side of an asphalt parking lot. Larry Jernstedt strode up to Rich and Scott; a big grin split his face as he shook hands with them. "Good job, guys. You managed to catch two of the most elusive outlaws on Pine Island. This is the first time Bad Bill's ever been caught in a boat chase. Have they made any statements yet?"

"None that counted," Rich said. "Bad Bill spent most of the time telling me how famous he is—or maybe I should say infamous."

"That sounds about right," Larry said. "He's definitely a folk hero in his own mind. Now listen, you all have done a great job, but we still need to put a bow on this package.

"What do you mean?" Scott asked.

"We need them to confess or at least make an admission. Few suspects ever challenge a case in court if they confess or make an admission that shows their intent to commit a crime. So here's the plan,"

Warden Rich Wilcox (*left*) with the seized birddog boat at the Matlacha Boat Ramp, 2006.

Larry said, pointing to a Lee County Sheriff's Office Suburban sitting in the parking lot. "I'll hide a digital recorder in the SO truck, and we'll put Bad Bill and his buddy in the backseat and let them stew for awhile. I think the conversation will tell us everything we need to know."

The two handcuffed prisoners settled into the back of the Suburban, the door shut, and the recorder with a hidden mike switched on.

BIG GUY: (after a few grunts and a slew of expletives, intermixed with some odd and out-of-place references to the Bible) Tell you one thing, they were out to catch us. . . . I could have jumped out with you driving. . . . I was trying for anything. I was hoping he [Rich] get caught in the net . . . [or] . . . you'd go up Pine Island Creek [a trick to get the wardens' patrol boat stuck on shallow bottom].

BAD BILL: The tide was too high.

BIG GUY: I know it.

BAD BILL: It wouldn't have mattered where I went. They've seen this high tide at night. High water, big moon, that's why those fuckers were out. I don't understand why I did that [flee]. Can I plead temporary insanity?

BIG GUY: Stress, post–ban net syndrome, yeah. They get people out of jail all the time for stupid shit like this. [The Big Guy looks up and sees several high-ranking FWC supervisors standing around their net skiff boat.] They brought all the big wheels out here. You know why? Because we're Butch Cassidy and the Sundance Kid.

Postscript

Before this case could be disposed of by the courts, Bad Bill decided to double down and try his luck again. In December 2006, he was arrested a second time within a three-month period for fleeing and attempting to elude and unlawfully fishing a gill net in state waters.

A review of his rap sheet was an experience in itself. I needed a calculator to track the citations, arrests, and court dispositions he'd racked up (and this was only for Lee County). Since October 22, 1974, he'd been either cited or arrested ninety-six times. A good many of them were for low-level wildlife/boating and traffic infractions. The rest were for a mixed bag of drug violations, grand theft, burglary, battery, resisting a law enforcement officer without violence, criminal traffic, and major saltwater fisheries and criminal boating violations. Of these, twenty-four cases had been tossed out by the court.

The Big Guy had a brief criminal history. The misdemeanor charges Rich and Scott had filed against him were dropped. Not unusual in the bustling courthouse of Lee County, where cases were often bundled to push them on out the door. Since Bad Bill was charged with two third-degree felonies—the fleeing and attempting to elude and fishing the gill net within state waters—he took the financial wallop.

By 2007, Rich and Scott had transferred to different counties in north Florida. That left Larry to keep an eye on Bad Bill. During a telephone conversation I had with him, he summed up Bad Bill's present situation: "He came by the office a few months ago hanging his head. A lot of his equipment had been forfeited by the courts, and he's had to pay thousands of dollars in fines. He's a broken man now."

Then he paused for a moment to reconsider. "But when I think about it, maybe he hasn't made the turn completely. On one illegal gill-net case, he had to sign a form when his salt water products license was suspended for ninety days, and he was civilly fined five thousand dollars. So he signed the document and handed it back to me. I couldn't believe it. Above the signature line he'd written, 'Billy the Kid.'"

13

TERROR IN A NORTH FLORIDA SINKHOLE

Warden Dwain Mobley stood with his arms crossed, shivering in the March cold, as he peered through a tangle of brush into a remote clearing. The dim, predawn gray slowly faded, replaced by the morning sun casting pale light across the grassy opening. As each minute passed, what had been the barely discernible outlines of a camouflaged tent blind, turkey decoys, and a hanging barrel feeder set up by his "target" gradually became more distinct.

The target was a turkey poacher from the rural town of Live Oak, population 7,117, in north Florida, twenty-two miles from the Georgia line. Dwain had been keeping close tabs on the man because sources told him the guy would be turkey hunting that morning—six days before the legal gobbler season opened.

Eight o'clock came. The timer-controlled feeder cycled on with a gravelly whir, spraying cracked corn onto the ground. Eleven turkeys—two gobblers and nine hens—ran up to the feeding station, pecking and scratching at the bite-size yellow kernels. But there was no poacher.

"This guy's a no-show," Dwain thought. "It's time to go." The young warden knew his prey. His suspect had to be at work at a small retail business in Live Oak by nine o'clock. Dwain had other places he needed to check.

The warden had done his homework, embarking on daily scouting trips during the weeks before. He'd flown, driven, or walked selected portions of the 692 square miles of rural Suwannee County—his patrol zone—searching for suspicious tire sign and foot tracks. The type of grain left on the ground at the end of these tracks could be a telltale clue as to whether someone was out to illegally entice turkeys or simply maintaining a legal deer stand for the next hunting season.

Cracked corn, milo, millet, or wild bird seed mix sprinkled on the ground meant turkey bait. Whole corn or enriched pellets were more likely intended for deer. Turkeys cannot be hunted over or within one hundred yards of a bait site. Wild turkeys only feed in the daytime, roosting in tall trees for predator protection at night. These strict diurnal habits make them as easy to shoot as the proverbial "duck in a bathtub" when baited. Thus, like many game laws, prohibiting the taking of turkeys over bait is based on the principle of fair chase.

Dwain had located other potential turkey poaching sites that looked as promising as this one. He needed to move out now while the morning was still young.

The warden shouldered his backpack and hurriedly pushed through chest-high palmettos toward his all-terrain vehicle, hidden a hundred yards away in the tall grass of a dried-up pond. Dwain climbed onto the Yamaha Kodiak 450, cranked it up, and headed off. This was his third morning working the stakeout. Every time he came and went he'd break a new trail so as not to beat down permanent ruts in the palmettos—a precaution to keep the suspect from noticing the bike's tire sign.

Earlier that morning, temperatures before daylight had hovered in the upper 20s. Dwain had dressed accordingly in multiple garments—an Under Armour shirt, long-sleeve rough-duty uniform shirt, lightweight uniform slicker jacket, and a fleece jacket topped off with a camouflaged Bug Tamer jacket. Dressing in layered clothing would normally be a good choice for the fast-warming Florida weather. But for the next twenty minutes or so of the warden's life, it would become an unforeseen obstacle to his survival.

Dwain stood up on his bike, feathering the gas as he scanned the terrain ahead, between longleaf pines and across the ragged tops of saw palmettos for a horizontal slash of white: the elevated lime-rock road that would take him back to his patrol truck. He hadn't eaten breakfast and eagerly anticipated a large omelet before heading back out on patrol. That thought, however, became a distant memory when the ground suddenly opened up beneath him.

★

On that March day in 2007, Dwain was a thirteen-year veteran with FWC. Each year, he'd logged hundreds of hours on his ATV while patrolling the pine forests and river swamps of Suwannee County. But beneath the sandy soil ran a treacherous layer of limestone bedrock. Over time, slightly acidic groundwater had hollowed out voids and cavities in the substrata, and when the ceiling could no longer hold the sediments above, the unsupported ground collapsed into sinkholes. Dwain understood the dangers of patrolling solo in this rugged and uncertain terrain on a four-wheeler. He'd become adept at dodging the craters and climbing the crooked, often treacherous rocky embankments of the nearby Alapaha River.

In addition to his everyday work as a conservation lawman, he was a defensive tactics instructor at the FWC Academy. In his classes he also incorporated skills learned as a recreational jujitsu player. At five feet seven and 196 pounds, his compact, muscular frame was well suited for the job. He liked the ground-fighting style taught in jujitsu because it addressed the age-old problem of what to do when one combatant was larger than the other. The techniques had proven their worth when Dwain grappled with bigger guys on the mat.

Dwain, thirty-seven, had jet-black hair trimmed into a neat military flattop, and dark-brown eyes that expressed feelings of warmth and fairness. He was soft-spoken, at times animated, and always courteous, with an easy grin that won friends and calmed adversaries. He lived with his wife, Leslie, and four-year-old son, Morgan, in Live Oak. The same town where he grew up, went to high school, and played varsity baseball and football. He also lifted weights—his best bench press, an impressive 385 pounds. His physical prowess would play a pivotal role in whether he survived the misadventure that was about to befall him.

★

Dwain recalled the moment the earth dropped away beneath his four-wheeler. "From my field of view, I couldn't see anything. I busted through those palmettos and boom, there was nothing there. The bike didn't drop straight down like going off a cliff. Instead, it skidded out of control down a steep slope before slamming into the bottom of this sinkhole, chunking me over the handlebars and into the dirt."

He got up, brushed himself off, and found he was standing in a calf-deep soup composed of sodden forest debris and black muddy water in the bottom of a cone-shaped hole, similar in shape to a paper water-cooler cup. The hole was eight feet deep, about twelve wide, and three across at the bottom.

Dwain paused for a moment to take stock of his surroundings and consider his next course of action. As far as holes went, this one seemed pretty benign. The sides had eroded over time, smoothing most of the rougher edges from the inside slopes. Pine-needle straw and dead sticks littered the soil-lined interior. Rooted into one wall were twin pine tops growing out of a common bole. Looking above, Dwain could see the needled green canopies framed against a bright-blue sky. The pine-scented air smelled crisp and clean. There was no hint of peril.

"I climbed back on the bike and engaged the four-wheel drive," recalled Dwain, who was confident he could drive it out. "I tried one wall, but just as I would get to the top, the front wheels would begin to stutter and bounce. It wasn't getting enough traction, so I'd back down and give it another go. It was kind of like a marble rolling back and forth in the bottom of a bowl. Finally, I looked to my left and saw the angle wasn't as steep. 'I can do this,' I told myself."

What the warden couldn't see was a gnarly palmetto root sticking out from below the rim of the hole, hidden by a palmetto fan. "If only I could have looked into a crystal ball then," Dwain sighed. "I would have walked back to my truck and retrieved the four-wheeler later."

Instead, he gunned the ATV, shooting straight up the incline.

When the front tire grabbed the palmetto root, the bike and Mobley rocketed straight up into the air.

"I remember the bike revving real loud as it fell over backward, landing upside down on top of me," he said. "Then everything went black for a second or two. I woke up hearing this loud buzz. It was just like in football when someone whacked me in the head. As I gathered my senses, I realized I was living my worst nightmare. I was trapped underwater and I couldn't breathe."

Dwain's fear of drowning bordered on paranoia. As a young child, he'd developed an unshakeable phobia of drowning in a car, helped along by Hollywood movie scenes of graphic sunken car crashes. And not learning how to swim until the age of twelve only heightened his anxiety.

"I was lying at an angle," Dwain continued, "with my head jammed into the mud at the bottom of the hole. The handlebars, along with the nose of the machine and all of its weight (591 pounds), pinned my head and shoulders beneath the muck. In that one brief moment, I knew I was going to die."

Mobley furiously struggled to work his head and shoulders from underneath the handlebars. But he couldn't. His backpack was snagged on something, preventing him from wiggling out. The pack bulged with gear. His kit included many odd-shaped items—binoculars, metal-covered citation and warning books, night-vision goggles, GPS, camera, first-aid kit, a water bottle, and a Nextel phone, all pressed against the pack's outer shell and into the unrelenting grip of clinging mud.

Events swirled through Dwain's mind so fast he had a hard time grasping reality. One moment he'd been fantasizing about an omelet, and now he was upside down, trapped under ice-cold, muddy water fighting for his life. He needed to breathe soon or he'd drown.

Dwain grabbed the handlebars and shoved, straining with a Herculean effort, pushing straight up, grunting and heaving, until every joint and muscle and sinew bulged to near bursting. During that one brief, but grave moment in his young adult life, he called up every primal fiber of his caveman DNA.

The machine budged.

He held it up long enough to slide a few inches to the left, before the machine fell back down on top of him. His effort worked, at least in part. By pressing down with his left hand and elbow into the muck, he could elevate his face high enough so that his eyes, mouth, and nose were just out of the water, barely.

"I took a second then to praise my Savior," Dwain said. "I couldn't believe I was still alive."

Garbled voices floated to his ears. Their origin seemed to come from some obscure place above and outside the hole. But the words were unclear, kind of like a deaf-mute trying to speak.

"I wanted to ask for help, until I realized the sounds came from my own throat," Mobley said. "It was me hollering and gagging, while I coughed up muck and peat and leaves that I'd inhaled while shoving so hard against the bike. And all of that crud was falling back into my eyes, blurring my vision."

By then the ATV engine had died, but gas and oil drained into the hole, creating a foul concoction that made circumstances even more dangerous because of the noxious petroleum fumes collecting into an invisible layer at the bottom.

Nobody knew Mobley's location, except for FWC dispatch, which had recorded him signing off the radio before daylight in the general vicinity of a three-thousand-acre block of woods, a chunk of remote wilderness within a sparsely populated county. His agency handheld radio was in his backpack, too, buried in the muck and dirty water beneath him. Dense palmetto bushes overgrew the sinkhole's rim, making it unlikely—if a search were begun—for ground rescue teams or spotter planes to detect the bike or Mobley hidden in the dark recess of the hole.

Self-rescue was his only option.

He wormed a hand down to the Leatherman tool on his gun belt, and carefully worked it back up along his side to the strap around his left shoulder.

"By this time," Mobley said, "I'd gotten a huge adrenaline dump. I was shaking so bad I could hardly keep a grip on the Leatherman tool. I couldn't get at the strap because it was cutting deep into my clothing. The Leatherman tool kept catching my outer jacket. The harder

I tried to get at the strap, the more it got hung up. Finally, it slipped out of my hand and dropped into the water. My range of motion was such that I could put my hands together like a raccoon, but I couldn't reach down to retrieve the Leatherman tool.

"I pulled out my folding knife then. The blade is four-and-a-half inches long and razor sharp. I sliced at the strap a couple of times, but all I did was cut through several layers of jackets. I worried I'd make a mistake and cut myself. Then I'd end up bleeding to death in that stinking pit. So I put the knife back in my pocket."

Survival experts say that the first thing someone does when faced with a life-threatening situation is to draw upon their previous life experiences for a solution. Mobley had already used the bench press to get his face out of the water. Next, he would rely on his ground-fighting skills.

Without thinking, he did what came naturally to him and gradually executed a series of small, almost imperceptible maneuvers with his hips and legs to worm out from underneath the bike, just like he would if an opponent had him pinned against the mat.

After twenty minutes of constant struggle, he managed to slip his hips out to the left of the machine. But he still needed to get free from the backpack that remained hellishly stuck to the sinkhole's bottom. Having his hips out to one side of the bike allowed him more room to maneuver. Now he could posture up with his shoulders, which increased his ability to leverage more pressure. With a gut-wrenching effort, he broke the right strap and freed himself.

He scrambled out of the hole and into the bright sunshine, dragging his backpack with him. He could finally take in big gulping breaths of fresh, clean, sun-washed air. It felt heaven-sent.

Dwain's waterlogged handheld couldn't transmit, so he tried his Nextel cell phone and called fellow warden Matt Tyre, who arrived first at the scene.

"Dwain thought he only needed my help in winching his ATV out of the hole," Matt recalled. "But he was in shock and suffering from borderline hypothermia when I first saw him. He had a big knot on his forehead and a puncture wound in his left eyebrow that was oozing blood. He needed to go to the hospital to get checked out. A few

Warden Dwain Mobley immediately after he flipped his all-terrain vehicle in an overgrown sinkhole, 2007. Look closely and you can see the upside-down bike partially covered by palmetto fans.

minutes later our lieutenant arrived along with another officer. Together we convinced him to go to the hospital."

Mobley recovered fine from the scrapes and bruises. But the toxic goop that had flooded his lungs had a lingering effect. He came down with a severe upper respiratory infection that lasted for weeks.

In reminiscing about his experience, Mobley summed it up on a lighter note: "Perhaps if I'd been thinking less about a triple-egg omelet and more about what I was supposed to be doing, I might have avoided the entire situation. From now on I'm going to eat my eggs before I go out on patrol."

After all, the experts do say breakfast is the most important meal of the day.

14

UNDERWATER ALLIGATOR WRESTLING

Normal human beings don't jump in to the water to wrestle alligators. But if you ever met Roger Gunter, you may not think him a normal human being. The notorious poacher, former Eighty-Second Airborne paratrooper, scuba diver, deadhead logger, outlaw commercial fisherman, and expert woodsman, had had his share of hair-raising adventures. I should know, because I spent a good portion of my thirty-year career as a Florida game warden chasing him without, I am loath to admit, a whole lot of success. Since my retirement in 2007, we had come to an informal truce.

I met with Gunter, seventy-six, to interview him, curious to learn more about this gator-wrestling business. I had to know what in the heck motivated someone to willingly jump on top of a living relic from the dinosaur era.

Gunter talked to me in that loud raspy voice of the near deaf as he explained the proper technique for crocodilian hand-to-hand combat while free diving with a snorkel and mask. His wrestling mat, in a manner of speaking, was the gin-clear waters of the Ocklawaha River

Roger Gunter on his favorite playground, the Ocklawaha River, 2014.

in northeast Florida. An incongruous mix of verdant beauty and primal danger, the twisting watercourse flowed through a dense riverine swamp that could have been a scene straight out of *Jurassic Park*.

Gunter talked with his hands as he explained the basics: "I perfected this technique where I'd spot one lying on the bottom, dive down and catch 'em by a front leg, and grab him around the jaw with the other hand. Now when he goes to rollin' and wallerin,' sometimes your hand will slip off his jaw and his teeth will go to gnashing and get caught up in your T-shirt." Chuckling, he tugged at the chest of his shirt to mimic how their teeth could get caught in the cloth. "It's hard to hold one for very long that's much bigger than five or six foot," he explained in earnest.

But that never stopped Gunter from trying his luck with the real monsters that thickly populate this junglelike waterway.

Gunter told me of one day when he was snorkeling in the Ocklawaha, catching crabs below Rodman Dam with his then eleven-year-old son, Lance, and a friend, and he spotted a twelve-footer lying still on the bottom. Gunter waved them over. "Hey, boys, I just want to show you all something," he said, jabbing one finger down below.

"Usually," he said, "they'll swim away whenever you try to slip up on them. But this one happened to have his nose jammed right up against a log. So I swam down and caught that big-assed alligator by the tail. He tried to go, but his nose got hung up under the log. Now this son-of-a-gun was that big around," Gunter made a circle with his hands and arms, big enough to fit around a fifty-five-gallon barrel, "and was trying to crawl into a hole beneath the log instead of backing out."

The big gator tore the sandy bottom up as sticks and limbs and leaves swirled in a miasma of tumbling river litter and alternating currents caused by the violent and abrupt course changes. Gunter gamely held on, tossed about like a dishrag in a washing machine. Finally, in one massive whip of its tail, the gator slung him loose.

Gunter casually shrugged his shoulders. "He was just too big to hold onto," he explained matter-of-factly. "But it was one hell of a ride while it lasted." His mouth twisted into a crooked grin, satisfied he'd covered all the highlights worth telling of this particular adventure. This eye-opening revelation convinced me he was as much an adrenaline junkie as he was a poacher, and a little bit crazy too.

As Gunter warmed to the storytelling, the level of risk gradually increased. I didn't know if he had planned it that way, or if he was a natural raconteur, saving the best material for last.

"So one night," Gunter continued, "a friend and I were camping on the Ocklawaha down at Davenport Landing. The plan was for us to take the boat out monkey-fishing (illegal electrocution of catfish). Naturally we were drinkin' beer, and then we had some whiskey. So I told my buddy, 'I know where this one gator should be layin' up. Let's go catch him, just for the hell of it.'"

About two in the morning, they pushed off from shore and motored down the creek. Summer rains had flooded the swamp, creating a critter smorgasbord for gators that lay in wait to ambush a hapless raccoon or opossum as it swam by. Gunter shined his 6-volt headlamp beam between the trees and around the brush growing out of this shallow-water no-man's land. Two orange orbs glowed deep in the dark. Gunter silently motioned ahead with his hand. His buddy cut the engine. The boat drifted noiselessly to a stop in knee-deep water. Gunter climbed out and waded straight toward those twin burning embers. Then he leapt.

"Let me tell ya," he said, "when I jumped on him, he come alive! He wasn't no catchin'-size alligator. He was about ten to twelve feet long!

"I grabbed him up, and we went to rollin' in the mud and water, round and round, smashin' into cypress knees and roots and such. He was just a'flailin' and a'thrashin' away with that tail making a big fuss. I looked up, and all of a sudden his head was right here." Gunter mimicked a set of gator jaws by touching two calloused palms together at the wrists, spread them open, and then laid them beside his face.

I could easily imagine the frightening picture of him pinned to the bottom by a quarter ton of angry gator. Somehow Gunter got his head up out of the water that night, just enough to catch a gulp of air. He kept blinking his eyes to clear the mud and leaves. Gradually his vision cleared enough to see the gator crack its mouth open. In the stark beam of the headlamp gleamed two jagged rows of white pointed teeth. "As you might imagine," Gunter said, "I was starting to sober up mighty quick and thought to myself, 'Good Gawd Almighty, Lord help me now!' So I turned the alligator loose, and he went on about his business, and we went on about ours. That alligator could have caught me by the head, you know what I mean?"

"So why do it?" I asked, curious to know what made him tick.

Gunter looked puzzled, dumbfounded I could even ask such a question. "Because it was fun!" he told me, stating what he thought must surely be obvious.

Clearly, my powers of deductive reasoning were lacking.

I had to shake my head as I took a moment to mull over his reply. Alligators are a protected species. Technically what Gunter did is considered molesting wildlife. But if I had been on patrol and come across someone wrestling alligators, I would have to wonder who was molesting whom.

Author's Note

For those who would like to learn more about Roger Gunter, check out my first book, *Backcountry Lawman: True Stories from a Florida Game Warden.*

15

WHEN KEEN EYES COUNT

Ten thousand years ago the ability to spot a coiled poisonous snake in tall grass was often the final arbiter between life and death. Nowadays, sitting behind a computer monitor in the confines of a thin-walled cubicle does not require this type of keen vision. The skills needed to patiently stalk prey while keeping a lookout for prehistoric danger has basically been bred out of us.

Even though we live in the twenty-first century, certain traits inherent to the hunter can still be of great benefit when applied to outdoor professions, like conservation law enforcement. Regrettably, the human genetically designed to spot a four-leafed clover in a sea of green is a rare breed.

Warden Richard Wilcox, however, happens to be one of them.

★

Ever since he was a little boy, Richard has had a knack for finding lost items. Just ask his mother, Kathy Wilcox, who vividly remembers Richard as a child with eyes that saw things no one else seemed to see.

"If anything was ever lost around our house, we would put Richard on it," Kathy recalled. "And eventually he would find it. His successes got to be so regular that we nicknamed him Finder."

Young Richard, heady from his triumphs as the Finder, sought new challenges beyond the confines of home. Surely, there must be more to discover.

Indeed, once he started attending Lakeside Elementary School in Orange Park, Florida, the mile walk home from school each day opened up a whole new universe to explore. "He'd catch a patch of color lying in the tall grass along the road shoulder," Kathy said, "like an old baseball cap or a shoe, and stop to check it out. He was curious that way, very meticulous in picking out the odd items most people wouldn't pay attention to. Of course, he always brought these relics home to us as gifts, telling us, 'This is worth something.' And we were delighted to receive them."

Interestingly, Richard didn't keep the curiosities he found. For him, the enjoyment was always in the hunt.

Richard, thirty-nine, grew into a mountain of a man with an appetite to match. At six foot three and weighing in at a solid 265, he rarely feels full. Only after eating two meals of what any normal person would eat is he finally sated. And then, after two or three hours have gone by, the cycle of replenishment begins anew.

His temperament, fortunately, does not mirror his size or his appetite. Those who have had the pleasure of his company would agree he is a person of perpetual good humor, talkative and friendly, with an uncanny knack for making people open up. Even the bad guys he so fervently pursues eventually fall sway to his powers of persuasion and often cough up the truth, albeit reluctantly.

The former Marine and Desert Storm veteran joined FWC in 2005. His first duty assignment was a two-year stint in southwest Florida. It didn't take long before his talent for seeing the not so obvious quickly garnered the respect of seasoned peers and supervisors. His powers of observation were also aided by unusually acute eyesight— Richard was blessed with 20/10 vision in both eyes.

One day he was on water patrol with his field training officer in southwest Florida when they received a tip about a motor fishing yacht coming into Matlacha Pass with an unlawful catch of marine product on board. Both wardens searched the vessel from stem to stern and came up empty. Then Rich volunteered to go below for one more try. He carefully studied all of the fixtures and appliances in the galley. A wall-mounted refrigerator caught his attention. The metal brackets holding the unit to a wood panel had holes for six small screws. Four of the holes had screws missing while the other two had Phillips screws inserted with stripped threads. The refrigerator was warm to the touch. Richard removed the appliance. In the back was a hidden cold-storage compartment holding more than a hundred undersize stone crab claws and dozens of illegal snook filets sealed in plastic Ziploc bags.

A few months later Richard and another warden were involved in a nighttime boat pursuit with the infamous Big Pine Island gill-net poacher William "Bad Bill" Jackson. Bad Bill dove overboard in an attempt to give the wardens the slip. Richard spotted him hiding neck deep among an array of crab-trap floats with a red T-shirt wrapped around his head. Crabbers paint their floats every color in the rainbow. But in this particular set they were all white except for what looked like a red one barely discernible in the outer fringe of his spotlight beam. Richard checked out the oddity and caught the culprit (see chapter 12).

In 2007, Richard transferred to St. Johns County—located on the Atlantic coast in northeast Florida and also adjacent to Putnam and Clay Counties to the west—as a land patrol warden. Within a few months of working in his new patrol beat, his childhood talent for finding what no one else seemed to see would be put to the test two more times. The first incident would be a warm-up, the second a matter of life and death.

Suicidal Man

On the sun-baked afternoon of August 1, 2009, Richard and his lieutenant, Ben Allen, helped in the search for a Clay County man who had threatened to commit suicide inside Bayard Conservation Area, 10,371 acres of turkey-oak sand ridges, tall pine forests, and dense bottomland hardwoods that wind for seven miles along the western shore of the St. Johns River.

Apparently the search was to be by invitation only. When the lieutenant first heard about it, he spoke to an on-scene law enforcement supervisor from another agency and volunteered to help. The supervisor told him they had it covered, had a K-9 Unit hot on the man's trail heading west, he said. It just didn't seem right to the lieutenant that they wouldn't be utilized in some fashion. "I didn't feel good about leaving as long as the search was going on," Ben recalled. "After all, this is a public wildlife management area our officers patrol, day in and day out, and are intimately familiar with."

Since most of the searchers were piled up near the western boundary of the search area, the lieutenant and Richard decided to head east.

The suicidal man's wife had called the sheriff's department saying her husband had used his cell phone to call her from inside the wildlife area, telling her he was going to shoot himself. She heard one gunshot and nothing more.

Local sheriff's deputies arriving first on the scene found the man's cell phone, a spent shotgun shell, and an empty shotgun case on a public walk-in area to the management area. But the man was gone, along with his gun.

Tensions ran high among the fifty or so law enforcement officers who combed the thickly wooded tract in an intensive ground and air search for the man. They knew that people who threatened suicide sometimes shot those attempting to rescue them.

Richard and Ben found it odd that no one was watching Highway 16, where it crossed the Shands Bridge at the northeast boundary to the search area. The area was shaped like the right angle of a carpenter's square, a corner pinch point formed by the intersection of the mile-wide river and a major two-lane highway. It seemed like a natural trap, a kind of funnel, to draw someone heading that way on foot.

Richard drove to the bridge and parked his F-150 state pickup where he had an unobstructed view of the river's shoreline and back down Highway 16 until it curved out of sight. He waited four hours, then cranked the truck up and steered along the sloped road shoulder at the glacial pace of 2 miles per hour to meet with his lieutenant. Lieutenant Allen had taken up a watch post on the highway's curve six hundred yards west of Richard's station. Each man had a clear visual of the other and anyone who might try to dart across the road between them. Ben needed to meet with Richard for a few minutes to talk about an alternative game plan if what they were doing didn't pan out.

Richard, however, needed to find the suicidal man. At that moment his concentration had a singular focus. Nothing else mattered.

Ben fully understood the machinations of Richard's mind. He also thought Richard wore a golden halo of sorts. "More often than not," Ben said, "whatever the task, Richard had a way of making things work out. He had the Midas touch." The lieutenant leaned back in his seat, content to let Richard do his thing.

Richard's patrol truck jerked up and down as the tires bumped unevenly across clumps and bunches of uncut Bahia grass. One hand lightly gripped the steering wheel while he peered out the driver's window to scrutinize the roadside brush. He'd traveled about a quarter mile when he suddenly hit the brakes.

A couple of hundred yards to the west, Ben grabbed the steering wheel of his patrol vehicle and jerked himself upright. He'd seen the front bumper of his warden's truck abruptly dip before it ground to a halt. The lieutenant cranked the engine, checked his side mirror, and pulled out onto the highway. It was right about then that Richard called him on the radio.

Back under the deep shadows cast by a clutch of cabbage palms Richard had spotted a bulky man wearing a blue polo shirt and cutoff blue jeans sitting on a log, wet and covered in mud. Richard glanced back at his laptop computer screen. The face of the 300-pound man staring at him matched the driver's license photo of the suicidal suspect. He reached down to the radio console and picked up the mic. "I got him, Lieutenant."

The big man was only twenty yards away. Well within shotgun range. Richard put his patrol truck in park, shoved the door open, and shouted, "Put your hands in the air!"

The man lifted his hands up.

"Where is your gun?"

"I left it back in the woods hanging in the crook of a tree," he replied, looking utterly exhausted.

Richard walked the man out to the road shoulder as Ben ran up. They handcuffed him and then turned him over to sheriff's deputies. "In my opinion," Ben said, "the gentleman knew he had caused more trouble than he had intended to and was sitting back in the woods, half-hidden, while he tried to figure a way out."

A K-9 unit from a nearby prison followed up on the man's trail and located his shotgun forty yards back in the woods, stuck in the Y limb of a sweet gum tree.

Now some would say that Richard's good fortune in finding the missing man was nothing but pure happenstance. Or, to borrow a saying from the Florida backcountry, "Even a blind hog can find an acorn once in a while."

Perhaps.

Missing Woman

Kymberly Meredith, twenty-one, had attractive long brown hair and a bashful smile. She was a shy, socially reclusive young woman who lived with her parents in a modest white stucco home a few miles east of Melrose, in west Putnam County. Fearful of being alone in the outdoors, she was not the kind of person who would lace up a pair of hiking boots and go for a nature walk by herself. In fact, she never traveled anywhere unless accompanied by her mother.

Sometime around 2:00 a.m. on Thursday, September 17, 2009, Barbara Meredith and her husband checked their daughter's bedroom and discovered she was gone. A brief search of their property found her sitting in the family car parked in the front yard. Barbara sat outside with her daughter for a couple of hours, talking to her about some problems her daughter was facing.

Kymberly suddenly bolted from the car, ran out of the fenced yard and down a single-lane dirt road in the direction of Highway 26. The Putnam County Sheriff's Office would later report she had darted off into the night barefoot, wearing a blue denim skirt, and a garnet-colored Florida State University hooded sweatshirt.

Minutes later, Kymberly's cell-phone records showed she called her brother, but he could only hear background noise. A few minutes after the call to her brother, she called 911, but the operator could not hear anyone on the line.

By Tuesday of the following week, Kymberly had been missing for six days. Multiple law enforcement agencies, including FWC, had conducted intensive ground and air searches. Helicopters with special heat-sensing equipment had flown at night, and K-9 units along with officers on four-wheeler patrol had scoured the area during the day. So far, searchers had found no sign of the young woman except for her disassembled cell phone located a thousand feet from her house.

Investigators believed she was in grave danger. Generally, a human can survive three days without water and up to three weeks without food. If she was lost in the woods, could she have survived that long under a harsh Florida sun, on her own, with no knowledge of how to build shelter, start a fire, trap forest animals, signal for help, find water, or navigate by the sun or stars? Search-and-rescue personnel had their doubts.

Richard arrived at the command post, located a half mile from Kymberly's home, around noon on Tuesday to meet with Lt. Ben Allen. The two conferred under the shady canopy of a live oak tree to get some relief from the scorching 95-plus-degree heat and choking humidity. A prodigious sweater, Richard continually mopped his brow with a hand towel while Ben explained the search area would be shifted south of Highway 26 into the Ordway-Swisher Biological Station, a 9,100-acre wilderness tract owned by the University of Florida. The property is a research center for university students participating in outdoor research classes.

At 1:30 p.m., Richard entered the area on his all-terrain vehicle with instructions to search the east side. As he drove along, the warden started calculating the probabilities of where the young woman might be if she was inside the UF property. His mind churned through

Warden Rich Wilcox (*foreground*) and Lt. Ben Allen check out the GPS route Wilcox followed on the day he found Kymberly Meredith, 2009.

various outcomes with an intensity most people would find exhausting. He was "hyperfocused," as he likes to call it.

Richard, who has an affinity for all manner of electronic gadgets, brought his laptop computer, keeping it secured in molded fiberglass box mounted across the front of his four-wheeler. He would stop occasionally to check his position using a Google Earth mapping system that would also track where he had been.

"I tried to put myself in her place," Richard recalled. "Where would I go if I was depressed? That's when I rode up on an old cemetery about two hundred yards directly across from the road leading to her home. For some reason it gave me hope. I thought it might be a place of solitude for someone who was upset. A place Kymberly might gravitate to if she knew it was there."

Richard slowly picked his way through the cemetery, probing the open spaces inside thickets and clumps of brush by nosing the four-wheel bike up into them and then backing out. Then he'd continue on to next likely-looking spot where the young woman may have sought shelter. Finding nothing, he headed across an area of dried ponds, kicking up a trail of dust as he made a mile-long loop, then continued east, bushwhacking through palmettos and low-bush scrub oak. Dried sticks and brittle, woody-stemmed shrubs cracked and popped beneath the bike's V-ribbed tires. It hadn't rained in weeks. Then he glimpsed two white flashes—about 150 yards away—through a thinly wooded area with tall pines and fallen timber.

"To this day I'm not sure what I saw," Richard said. "They were about three feet off the ground. I thought at the time it might be a couple of deer or two men without shirts. One of the scenarios I was running through my mind was that Kymberly might be camped out in the woods with someone."

Richard triple-timed it on the ATV, speeding around blown-down trees and knocking over brush. He'd gotten a kick of adrenaline and was eager to find whatever it was that had caught his eye.

When he got to the area where the white flashes had been, they were gone. But it wasn't his nature to give up. He was in the hunt now, like a bloodhound with its nose held aloft, testing the wind for a fresh scent. He scanned back and forth, twisting his head and neck all around, continually sweeping the terrain in a three-sixty for any kind of movement, an unusual color, something out of place, a foreign object, anything at all.

And then he saw it.

The prize lay crumpled on the ground about fifty yards away and partially obscured by knee-high brush. It was a burgundy—or garnet—colored cloth. Richard drove up to it and saw three small leaves lying on top of a hooded sweatshirt turned wrong-side out. He noted the lack of any other windblown forest litter or fine particle debris on the garment. His pulse quickened. Instinct told him it hadn't been there long. He called in the GPS coordinates to Lieutenant Allen. The time was 4:45 p.m.

The ATV was in neutral, the engine chugging away at an idle. Above the motor noise he heard an audible sound—possibly a voice.

"At first, I couldn't get a good course on it or tell for sure what it was because it was so weak," Richard said. "So I shut my bike off to listen."

Kymberly Meredith had been missing for six days when Warden Rich Wilcox found her lying in this spot, on the edge of a dried pond in a remote wilderness area, 2009.

"Please help me," called out the plaintive and frail voice of a young woman. "Don't leave me. Please don't leave me. I'm paralyzed. I can't move my legs."

"I assured her I wasn't going to leave her," Richard said. "As I got closer I saw her hand sticking up above the marsh grass at the edge of a dry pond. When I first got to her I was shocked. Shocked she was still alive. There were thousands and thousands of festering bug bites and sores all over her body. And she'd been cut and bleeding from crawling through the saw palmettos and briars. Her mouth and nose caked solid with black mud. Her eye sockets were sunken and gray. Her body was so emaciated it reminded me of photographs I'd seen of prisoners of war at Auschwitz. Most of her clothing was gone, so I took off my uniform shirt and wrapped it around her. She reminded me of my sister, and I didn't want the media to photograph her like that.

"I gave her a bottle of water, and she gagged. I told her to sip a little at a time. Then she grabbed my hand and begged me not to leave her. I assured her help was coming."

The lieutenant arrived a few minutes later with a team of six rescue personnel riding in the back of his state four-wheel-drive F-150 pickup. While first responders prepared Kymberly for a backboard extraction, Ben hacked a path through head-high palmettos with a machete to maneuver his truck down to the pond's edge.

Ten minutes later Kymberly was strapped to a stretcher riding in the bed of Ben's patrol truck as it raced down old logging roads with the rescuers hanging on. To shorten the ride, the lieutenant ran over a scraggly barbed-wire fence and met the ambulance on the road shoulder of Highway 26.

Kymberly was transported to Shands Hospital in Gainesville, where she stayed for ten days while being treated for extreme dehydration and severe sunburn.

Postscript

I was retired two years as a lieutenant in this region when I arranged a reunion five weeks after Kymberly's ordeal with Richard, Ben, and Kymberly at Barbara Meredith's hair salon in Keystone Heights—a tiny town located on a flat, sandy ridge seven miles north of Melrose.

We arrived promptly at ten in the morning, the appointed time for our meeting. This was an opportunity for closure, one last time to reconnect, for both the wardens and the mother and daughter.

Kymberly wore a burgundy FSU Seminole T-shirt and comfortable black shorts. She seemed embarrassed, tentative at first, by the attention we brought. Her bright and sunny attitude belied the only physical reminders of her ordeal, the tan elastic bandages wrapped from ankle to knee around both legs, where she was still being treated for sunburn. She told the wardens that she drank marsh water to survive and covered herself with mud for protection from the sun. She dreamed she had eaten leaves but wasn't sure if she had or not . . . and that was about all the young woman from Melrose could recall. Parts of her story would be forever missing: big gaps, huge chunks of time

Kymberly Meredith and Warden Rich Wilcox, ten weeks after the rescue, 2009.

when delirium likely wiped out—and mercifully so—specific recall of the painful ordeal she'd suffered through.

As they parted, Barbara gave Richard a tearful hug, telling him, "You've saved my daughter's life. Hopefully, God will return the favor."

16

THE CRITTER CATCHER

If one were to fly fifteen miles northwest of Orlando and then drop a giant lawn dart, it would hit smack dab in the middle of Florida's most polluted water body, Lake Apopka. Contaminated decades ago from agricultural back-pumping and sewage runoff, the once trophy largemouth bass fishery and home to twenty-one thriving fish camps now struggles to survive. Understandably, the lake's toxic waters also have been designated "off-limits" for the legal harvest of alligators.

Alligators are tough prehistoric predators. They continue to flourish in Lake Apopka as they have in one form or another on earth for 37 million years, seemingly content to swim through the lake's pea-green waters while gorging on tons of hapless gizzard shad. Wherever populations of any species that have a marketable value (think fine leather belts, boots, shoes, wallets, and food products) are left to grow unchecked, black-market poachers pay close attention. And so do the game wardens.

So it is here, in the region of Lake County, home to more than a thousand inland freshwater lakes and the heart of Florida's citrus belt, that our story begins.

On Patrol

Ten o'clock on a hot and humid night, September 15, 2011. Warden David Straub, with one arm draped out the open driver's window, casually nodded his cleanly shaven head to the slow beat of an outlaw country music ballad blaring from the dash radio of his plain-painted, unmarked patrol truck. Big knobby off-road tires rumbled against smooth asphalt pavement as he idled toward the entrance of the Montverde Boat Ramp on Lake Apopka. The sounds blended together to make the perfect tonal mix of "redneck out for a drive." At least that was the impression he hoped to send to anyone suspicious enough to give his state ride a hard look.

The headlamp beams lit up a green metal sign with plain white lettering that informed those towing boats to continue straight ahead. Instead, David swung smoothly to the right, making a deliberate pass by the entrance so he could look down a long shallow slope to the water's edge. Under the glow of a pale moon sat a darkened airboat, its stern backed up to the shore, with two vague figures moving around it. David never touched the brakes, but cruised into a subdivision of neatly aligned tract homes. Ahead, sodium vapor lamps cast a pinkish glow along paved streets fronted by concrete driveways and manicured lawns.

David rolled the window up and turned down the music. "Not sure who we've got down there," he said to his partner, Reserve Warden John Parrish. "But they could be some players. Let's make a loop through the subdivision, and we'll hide the truck in the orange grove a quarter mile up from the ramp."

"Sounds good," John said. "I'm ready to catch somebody."

As they completed the circuit through the housing development, David reached down to a row of switches on the radio console. He toggled off the brake lights and then cut the headlights. The truck became a dark shadow as it rolled across the boat ramp access road and into the grove. David carefully nosed the Dodge 2500 pickup ahead. Stiff, thorny branches scraped against the cab, while clumps of unripened fleshy fruit bumped against the windshield until they were hidden well out of sight from any passersby. While neither man was thinking about it at the time, they'd parked on top of a relic sand dune ridge that formed part of Sugarloaf Mountain to the northwest. At an elevation of 312 feet, it was the highest point in peninsular Florida and an iconic Sunshine State landmark.

David and John opened their doors to the scent of tart green orange juice—leaked from the raw hanging fruit split open by the windshield wiper blades when they'd passed underneath. They slid out of their seats and onto the ground. Each man slowly pressed his door shut until the latch caught with a metallic click. A truck door slamming on a still night can be heard for a long way.

"We'll have to be careful how we step," David said, surveying long, clean rows of freshly plowed dirt between the trees, which gave off a thick smell of moist earth. "It looks like the grove owner just had the weeds knocked down with a harrow. Let's stick to the edges of the trees where there's still grass growing."

"Right behind you," John said.

David listened to the scrunch of John's steps and thought he could not have asked for a better backup. The forty-eight-year-old reserve warden stood six foot one and weighed in at a meaty 230 pounds. In 2004 he'd done a tour with the U.S. Navy Seabees in Iraq as a builder and as part of a security force for the Marine Corps. While John was low-key in temperament, he could get switched on when the call for action came.

They'd only walked a few paces when David paused. "Listen," he said, cocking his head to one side.

"Sounds like they're getting on it," John replied, as the airboat went full throttle with a thunderous roar.

They padded through the grove, hiking downhill, while they tracked the airboat's progress by the noise as it powered north along the lake's western shoreline. The lawmen stopped where the grove terminated near the shoreline and about a football-field length away from the boat ramp. In front of them lay a sandy, two-rut track that ringed the grove's outer fringe. It served as an unimproved maintenance road for citrus workers.

David put a pair of 7-power binoculars to his eyes, gently fingering the focus dial. Chrome trim glinted from a parked Chevy pickup truck. Homemade guide-on boat trailer stanchions constructed from white PVC pipe emitted a pearly glow. He lowered the optics and turned toward John. "Wait here while I get the tag numbers off that truck and trailer."

He returned in a few minutes, having already run the tags from a palm-sized handheld radio he carried in a nylon belt holster.

"The truck comes back to 'Bobby-Ray Dicks,'" David said.

"Isn't he the critter catcher?" John asked.

"The one and only. He'll sell anything that walks, crawls, swims, or flies: green frogs, snakes, lizards, snapping turtles, flying squirrels. He didn't make the hour-and-a-half drive from where he lives over on the west coast to stick some frogs. Bobby-Ray will be catching gator hatchlings tonight, and we're going to have to be on our best game to catch him."

"How do you think he'll get them out?"

"He'll drop them off at a predetermined pickup spot somewhere along the shoreline, or he'll take them out right here. If he takes the gators out at this ramp, he'll arrange for a pickup man to meet him. There's no way he would risk carrying them out by himself. He's way too sharp for that."

"Didn't you tell me a year or so ago that he tested you, kind of like he was trying to get a sense of your abilities as a game warden?" John asked.

"Yeah," David said. "I was patrolling in my airboat one day on the Withlacoochee River, and of all things I see Bobby-Ray standing on the bank. He waves me over. I ask him what he was doing there, and he said he was the caretaker for a twenty-acre tract of land. Then he told me he wanted to show me a cave he found. So I went on this two-hour hike with him. All the time I felt like he was sizing me up.

"He quizzed me about everything—plants, snails, limpkins, lizards, squirrels, what made that trail and what made this kind of track. I played to his ego and downplayed what I knew. But his woods knowledge was off-the-charts crazy, a lot better than mine. Bobby-Ray was marking in his mind: Does this guy know what he's doing? Can I cut corners? Or do I have to go the extra mile not to get caught? I knew when I left him that day we would play hell catching this son-of-a-gun."

"What about the cave?"

"So finally we came up on this cave that was cut into a lime-rock formation along the bank. I guess an underground stream had flowed out of it at one time. We had to squat down and duck-walk through it. We went around a few bends, and it began to get dark. I turned on my flashlight, but I had to get out of there. I'm bad claustrophobic."

As David stood there in the dark talking to John, one thing that niggled in the back of his mind were the choices in remote landings where sacks of contraband hatchlings could be stashed for later pickup. He made some quick calculations and figured Dicks wouldn't spend the extra twenty bucks in gas or the time it would take to send a pickup vehicle all the way around to the far side of the lake on the eastern shore. (At 30,671 acres in size, with a shoreline length of forty miles, Lake Apopka is the fourth-largest lake in Florida.) That only left one likely spot, other than the Montverde Ramp.

David depressed the mic button on his handheld and directed another warden to the Apopka-Beauclair Canal at the north end of the lake. He explained how to find a well-trodden footpath that led across a berm and down to the shoreline, where the warden could hide behind a clump of cattails and watch for the airboat. It would be the logical spot to conceal sacks of baby alligators for retrieval later.

At the moment, there wasn't much the men could do except settle into the all too familiar routine of a tedious stakeout, as they monitored the airboat's progress by the sweep of a headlamp beam and the growl of its engine. They knew it would be several hours before Bobby-Ray came back to the ramp.

Warden David Straub

David Straub, thirty-nine, thinks of himself as a big-game hunter. He unabashedly admits to being hooked on collecting trophies, though not in the traditional sense of a hunter on safari in Africa. The trophies he seeks are those of a determined conservation lawman who has dedicated an eleven-year career to chasing and catching professional wildlife crooks up and down the state. Undeniably, some of the culprits are known in certain regions of Florida as the best of the best: hard-bitten characters who employ deception, wit, guile, and old-fashioned woodsmanship skills in an attempt to outfox game officers.

"What motivates me," he explained during an interview, "is the mental chess, the cat-and-mouse game. It intrigues me. I've worked in thirteen different counties, including one three-year stint as an undercover officer. Whenever I arrived in a new county, I'd check out the players. Once I notched their ear [a figurative reference to the process of catching a wild hog alive, slicing off the testicles, and then cutting a triangle of the ear flap out with a pocketknife to mark it], I was ready to move on to the next challenge."

David enjoyed an advantage over wardens in uniform patrol because he is a member of the elite Resource Protection Unit (RPU). The RPU is a specialized division of seasoned officers who typically patrol in plainclothes and occasionally conduct short-term covert operations that target major wildlife violators.

The ability to blend in, to become a chameleon, is one key to the unit's success. On most days, David can be found wearing a worn camouflaged ball cap with a Wildlife Turkey Federation patch sewn above the bill, a plain black T-shirt, faded camouflaged hunting pants, and knee-high snake boots. A short-barreled .40-caliber Glock pistol, pepper spray, and handcuff case are concealed beneath his T-shirt, which hangs loosely below the belt. He carries it all on a rugged six-foot-one frame honed through grueling aerobic workouts. At the time, he was recovering from a shoulder injury he'd received while training for a Tough Mudder competition, a brutal cross-country obstacle course.

His philosophy about the job reflects a maturity not found in most rookie wardens. He calculates his moves against certain outlaws months, even years, in advance. "If a younger officer," he says, "happened to check a notorious individual, their first approach would be to write them up for any chicken-crap violation they could find, like coming into a boat ramp with a torn lifejacket on board. My approach is different. I like to see what makes the guy tick. I want to get into their head rather than write a fifty-dollar citation that's going nowhere. That's why I went on that hike with Bobby-Ray along the bank of the Withlacoochee River."

The Airboat

Bobby-Ray held the rudder stick, his foot pressed lightly against the throttle pedal as he and his buddy idled down the shoreline of Lake Apopka. The bright spotlight strapped to his forehead cast a pure white flood beam against the slick surface and into the water-anchored cattails and dollar bonnet pads. Pairs of pearl-sized pinkish-orange eyes reflected back at him. Dozens of them. With a practiced hand, Bobby-Ray leaned over the side with a pair of extended metal snake tongs and snatched up a baby alligator, dropping it into a cooler held open by his friend, who quickly slammed the lid shut. This time of year newly hatched gators floated together in pods, swimming aimlessly about in the water, oblivious to predators—either man or natural.

It was close to midnight when Bobby-Ray sensed something wasn't right. Maybe it was his imagination. Maybe it was intuition. Maybe it was just nerves. But he felt a sudden and inexplicable urge to shut the engine down. They needed to take a look-and-listen break.

"Why are you shutting down?" his partner asked, concern edging into his voice.

"Something's not right," Dicks replied. "I can feel it."

"Did you see anything?"

"No. Just be still and listen."

Then they felt a wake gently lap against the side of the airboat. It barely rocked the hull.

"I knew it," Dicks said. "We ain't alone." Then he toggled off the headlamp and scanned the horizon for the silhouette of an unlit vessel.

"You want me to dump the hatchlings?" his buddy asked, nervously clutching the cooler.

"Hell, no! They're worth good money, and I got bills to pay. We're going to sit here for a while and see if we hear another boat get up."

Twenty minutes passed and nothing. Not a sound. Not another boat wake. Not even a ripple.

"Okay, maybe it wasn't anything, but I think we need to get off the lake," Dicks said. "Go ahead and sack up the hatchlings while I call my old lady. She'll make the pickup."

Bobby-Ray's "old lady" was actually his fiancée, a thirty-some-year-old brunette with hair chopped off at the collar. She stood barely five four and had the forearms of a rodeo barrel racer. She owned a pack of pit bull dogs that she ran through the woods with to hunt wild boar. Alone. The hogs were often caught alive and the testicles cut off before releasing them back into the wild to fatten. She carried a .44 Magnum revolver in an underarm carry holster and a long-handled sheath knife for backup. She was the kind of backwoods gal who could hold her own in a mud-wrestling contest.

The phone call to Bobby-Ray's fiancée was brief. "I got something for you to pick up," Dicks told her. "Call me when you get to the Montverde Boat Ramp, and make sure the backseat floorboard is cleared out."

The Wardens, 4:00 a.m.

"They're easing back to us," David said, while he watched the airboat's red and green bowlights go from barely discernible pinpricks to clear, golf ball–sized glares. Then the boat started idling in lazy circles.

"Looks like they're waiting for someone," John said.

"Yeah, the pickup man will be here shortly," David said. "I want you to stay here. I'm going to slip up closer to the ramp so I can see what's going on. You need to come running when you hear me identify myself."

"Got it."

Out of habit, David carefully stepped from one patch of tall grass to the next, wherever he could find a clump untouched by the tractor plow. He stopped by the second row of orange trees in from the boat ramp, a distance of about thirty yards.

Headlamp beams broke over the hill and headed straight down the ramp. Tires hissed on blacktop as a Ford F-150 pickup wheeled around and backed up to the waterline. The high beams flipped on, shining straight up the hill.

The windows were rolled down. David could see the head-and-shoulders silhouette of the driver talking into a cell phone. He strained to hear the conversation but couldn't make out a single word over the running engine.

The Airboat

Bobby-Ray's fiancée made the call. "I'm here."

"Okay, I need for you to walk out the grove for tire tracks," Dicks said, talking into his cell phone while he eyed the bright-red taillights of her truck a half mile away. "See if there's anything fresh across the dew. If you see something that don't sit right with you, anything at all, call me back and let me know. I'll dump everything."

"Okay."

His fiancée stepped out and quietly shut the door. She left a three-month-old infant (fathered by Bobby-Ray) strapped to a baby carrier in the backseat of the extended-cab four-door pickup. She hurriedly walked toward the maintenance road that skirted along the edge of the grove. She had to pee. Bad.

Warden David Straub

David saw her crouched over, coming toward him in the moonlight, shining the ground with a flashlight just like a game warden would. She had one hand cupped over the lens, panning for tracks. David had performed the same exact maneuver hundreds of times himself. Instead of being the predators, David and John had now become the prey. Both men were worried they'd be discovered. She could track like an Indian.

David quietly eased around behind a thickly limbed orange tree that stood at the end of the second row. He awkwardly climbed up into the dense branches, clinging there like an oversized monkey. Waiting. He prayed she wouldn't take it into her mind to walk around to the backside of the tree.

She stopped on the opposite side of the orange tree. David kept his

Warden David Straub mimics how Bobby-Ray Dicks's girlfriend cupped her hand over a flashlight to shield the glow, 2012. She followed this orange-grove service road looking for game-warden tire tracks. Straub was hidden inside an orange tree as she walked by.

breath shallow and quiet. He wrapped both arms around the upper trunk; the balls of his feet rested precariously on the lower branches.

There was about a foot or two of bare trunk beneath the lowest limbs. If one foot slipped off its perch she might spot it.

Inside the orange tree it was dark. In the lunar glow outside it was near daylight. The pickup gal was shielded from David's view by an outward wall of dense foliage. Then he heard a zipper being undone. The awkward rustle of clothes pulled down. A few moments later a steady stream let loose.

Finished, she picked up the flashlight. Holding it low to the ground she methodically swept the beam slowly from side to side, a technique that would reveal shadows in the faintest of foot tracks or tire-tread patterns. Her steps made a soft scrunch in the fine-powdered dirt. She continued down the grove maintenance road for a hundred yards, turned around, and made a beeline back to the truck.

David stepped down from the tree and peeked around one side. He saw her put a cell phone to her ear. He couldn't make out the words but knew it was fixing to "go down."

The Airboat

Bobby-Ray flicked his cell phone open.

"I walked them out. The tire tracks are old," his fiancée said. "Nobody's here."

"I'm headin' in," he said, shutting the phone with one hand and stuffing it into his pants pocket.

He fired up the airboat and mashed the throttle; the wind tugged at his cheeks while a six-cylinder Lycoming aircraft engine roared in the cage behind him. When Dicks made the commitment to move, he liked to move fast.

Warden David Straub

David watched as Dicks drove the hull up into tall marsh grass beside the ramp. He leapt from the bow before it slid to a full stop. David had never seen anyone move so fast in his life. Dicks carried a bulging white mesh dive sack in each hand. Scooting around the truck's rear bumper, he came abreast of the driver's side rear door and yanked it open. He tossed the two bulging sacks of squirming, grunting baby alligators on the floor beneath the baby's seat.

His fiancée sat behind the steering wheel, staring out the front windshield, one hand on the shifter ready to drop it into drive. The engine was idling.

David barreled downhill at a dead run, chest thrust outward, arms pumping furiously, letting the declining slope of the boat ramp aid his acceleration. He met Dicks at the door and yelled, "Game warden!" He briefly illuminated himself with a flashlight to show a leather badge holder hanging from a dog-tag chain across his chest. Bobby-Ray slammed the truck's body with the palm of his hand, shouting, "Go! Go! Go!" The truck didn't budge. His fiancée was no dummy. She had enough sense to know when it was time to call it quits.

Dicks was really agitated and stepped to the back of the truck. He reached down for something in the bed. His hands were not visible.

Warden David Straub points to a patch of weeds next to the Montverde Boat Ramp, 2012. This is where Bobby-Ray Dicks beached his airboat on the night Straub caught him with 260 alligator hatchlings.

In the blink of an eye the situation had become a "No Shit!" drill. In a blur David drew the Glock and held it by his side. "Bobby-Ray, it's Dave. I'm going to hurt you if you don't show me your hands." What David couldn't see was a lead pipe resting in the truck's bed, only inches away from Dicks's fingertips.

Bobby-Ray went limp. The message had finally sunk in. "Man, you got me" he said, in a somber tone. "You got me." He staggered away from the truck.

Bobby-Ray's thoughts suddenly turned inward. "I got lazy," he said feebly. "I knew you all had a boat out there."

"Dave, you got everything okay?" John huffed, as he suddenly emerged from the gloom.

"Everything's fine. How about cuffing Bobby-Ray for me and then secure his partner who's still in the airboat? Keep him down there while I talk to Bobby-Ray for a minute."

"I'll take care of it."

The infant continued to sleep soundly, oblivious to the excitement going on around her. David reached under the baby carrier and retrieved the squirming sacks. He picked one up in each hand and hefted them. Each bag felt like it weighed a good twenty pounds. "My goodness, Bobby-Ray. How many you got here?"

"Two hundred and fifty to three hundred," Dicks answered. "We had a bad night. Normally we do a lot better. (Both bags together would later total 260 hatchlings.) So what are you charging me with?"

"Well, I could charge you with each hatchling. But I'm not that hard to get along with. I'll do you one felony count for all the gators.

"Listen, Bobby-Ray, I know you've got a prior felony conviction, but I know a fellow who might help you out a little if you'd be willing to talk to him."

"Who's that?"

"He's my captain, Gregg Eason. I'm not promising you he'd lighten your load, but it might be worth a conversation."

"Alright, I'll do it."

"His sail was furled," David later recalled. "He knew when he went into that interview room he was there to play ball."

The Interview

That morning, 9:00 a.m., Lake County Jail. Bobby-Ray sits in a metal folding chair backed into the corner of a cramped interview room. Beside him is a small rectangular table constructed of white molded plastic and metal legs. The table is spare except for a video camera set up on a tripod. The camera angle catches Bobby-Ray in profile. A small red LCD light blinks to indicate that it is on.

Fluorescent ceiling lights accentuate the bland surroundings and give Bobby-Ray's skin a pale, unhealthy appearance. It doesn't help that he hasn't changed his clothes since he was arrested the night before. He wears camouflaged jeans and an untucked, dingy gray T-shirt with what looks like a soaked-in stain across the left shoulder. He has a full head of close-cropped dark hair that is tussled and a scraggly three-day-old growth of beard. Overall, his appearance is grimy, like a skinny automotive mechanic who's just spent eight hours turning a wrench on a sweltering hot summer day.

The video shows what looks like a huge gap where his front teeth should have been. For some reason the angle of the light and the camera position does not reveal that his two front teeth are actually three-quarters rotted, pencil-like stubs.

Bobby-Ray crosses his arms and slouches down into the chair. Bored. Beneath tired eyelids, dark-brown pupils swivel attentively between Capt. Gregg Eason and Lt. Don McMillen, who sit an arm's length away. Don's left forearm occasionally flicks into view as he adjusts a yellow legal pad where he jots down notes.

Bobby-Ray's state of mind is similar to that of many suspects about to be interviewed: *I know what I know, but I don't want you to know what I know, except to give you enough to appear cooperative.* He also knows the drill and does not offer unsolicited comments. He only speaks when spoken to.

The two investigators often work as a pair. They are dressed similarly: casual pressed slacks, crisp long-sleeve shirts and tie, with empty holsters that normally hold a short-barreled Glock (firearms are not permitted inside the jail). Clipped next to the belt buckle is a star-shaped, shiny brass badge stamped with the words "Florida Fish and Wildlife Conservation Commission."

At fifty-nine years old, Don has a healthy shock of thick blond hair fringed with gray and bright blue, engaging eyes that retain a hint of his teenage youth working as a beach lifeguard before he entered the University of Florida, where he received a bachelor of science degree in wildlife management. Gregg, forty-three, wears his dark hair short, in a military flattop. With an erect posture and squared-off shoulders, he carries himself with quiet confidence and calm authority, no doubt a reflection of his four-year stint in the U.S. Marine Corps.

The two men are similar in that they use a methodical thought process to uncover the criminal element. But internally they use a different method. Gregg wants to tackle any problem head-on and see it through to its completion immediately. He's incisive, quick, and mentally agile. He usually doesn't think about an interview much beyond the interview itself. Donnie is more reflective, patient, and analytical. He can put a project down and pick it back up again days later with no lapse in interest or continuity. Combined, the two lawmen have forty-seven years of experience in conservation law enforcement. Dicks doesn't know it yet, but he is about to go up against two formidable opponents. Gregg and Don specialize in interviews of wildlife crime suspects.

The voices of the two investigators come across on the audio. Their diction is calm, friendly, but not overly so. They show neither interest nor lack of interest in Bobby-Ray.

They introduce themselves and walk Dicks through the preliminaries, which consist of reading him his Miranda warnings and swearing him in under oath. They explain the penalty for lying and that the reason they are conducting this interview is to collect information on the unlawful taking of hatchling alligators.

Gregg will take the lead in asking questions. Don will take notes and step out occasionally to make phone calls to verify if what Bobby-Ray tells them is true.

In the beginning, Gregg tells Dicks, "Tell it to me like I never heard the story before." That's because Gregg and Don never had heard the story before. David Straub had already gone to bed, and the only briefing the two investigators had received was a five-minute phone call from another officer in charge of securing Bobby-Ray's truck and airboat inside the FWC evidence compound in Ocala. They had no clue about Bobby-Ray's background or what he may be involved in.

This would be a learn-as-you-go interview. Everything Gregg was taking in he was having to process in his head, and at the same time formulate questions to keep Dicks talking.

Twelve minutes into the recording it begins to get interesting, " . . . went three or four miles and then it got spooky," Dicks said, "and we shut off to listen for awhile."

"You mean you got boogered?" Gregg asked.

"I got scared about what I was doing," Dicks said.

"So you thought someone might be watching you?"

"Yeah. We about quit and threw everything back. But I didn't and went about doing what I was doing. We went down a little more and heard a boat, stopped, and seen the waves off the boat. Never did see the boat. But the waves was there."

"You never did see the boat?"

"There was a boat out there."

"You're correct there was," Gregg said.

Bobby-Ray is leaning with his back against the wall, fingers interlaced behind his head. His eyes widen, while a look of astonishment spreads across his face. *He was right!*

By design, Gregg has just validated Dicks's observations. He is playing into his paranoia: *How did I get caught?* It is also a subtle way of acknowledging that Gregg realizes how in tune Dicks is with his environment.

Gregg boosted Dicks's ego with a bluff. As far as Gregg knew, there was not another boat on Lake Apopka that night. But the mental sleight of hand also serves another purpose. He wants to convince Dicks that they know every move he has made over the last few months.

"What time was that?" Gregg asked, curious about when Dicks felt the wake.

"Never look at a clock," Dicks said.

"You basically go off the clock in your head."

"It was morning time."

The interview grinds ahead as they discuss trivial matters until Gregg gets into the touchy area of how many hatchlings Bobby-Ray deals in. The ultimate goal is to learn the identity of the buyer(s).

"Here is one of those truth-or-consequences questions," Gregg said, in a well-modulated voice that rarely changes tempo or pace except for dramatic emphasis. There is a certain comfort in listening to him speak. Having polished his craft from hundreds of face-to-face interviews with wildlife crooks, the captain knows a thing or two about delivery. Gregg watches Dicks keenly. "How many alligators have you caught in the last twelve months? About? More than a hundred? More than five hundred? Less than a thousand? Two thousand? You've caught a lot, right?"

Bobby-Ray sits very still—attentive. Arms crossed. He is processing, trying to decide what he will say next and how much it will affect him. So far he's bought into everything Gregg has been selling him.

"I've been known to—," Dicks answered.

"Trying to establish the honesty level here," cut in Gregg.

"I couldn't give you a number."

"I would say it's safe to say it was over a thousand, wouldn't you? And that's being conservative."

Bobby-Ray hesitates. He draws a deep breath. Gregg senses he needs more oxygen to his brain to process what he's going to say. Will he lie or will he tell the truth? It is obvious this is a sensitive area for him.

Bobby-Ray exhales. "Yes sir, I'd probably say it was over a thousand."

"You're good. I want you to know that. It's not everybody that can go out and catch alligators like you do. Not everybody can catch snakes and critters like you do."

Bobby-Ray's thoughts suddenly turn inward. He's trying to figure out where he went wrong. The mind of a suspect under arrest tends to wander.

"Who was it that put you all onto me?" Dicks asks. "What did I do wrong to mess up?"

"That probably wouldn't be appropriate for me to say," Gregg answers. "But I can tell you this . . . there's a big picture we're looking at."

"Yes, sir."

"It has different strings, different runners on it. And you're one of the main parts of that. You're just a part of the investigation." Gregg has just hammered home the point that Dicks is a spoke on a wheel and not the axle. He is beginning to believe he has been caught up in the web of a big undercover operation.

"If I tell you all the numbers will it hurt me?" Dicks asks.

"Honesty is the best policy," Gregg answers.

"I probably caught close to ten thousand."

"What did you get paid last year per hatchling? I know how much they were sold for last year retail. I just want to know how much you were selling them for wholesale."

"Eight dollars apiece." Bobby-Ray took the bait.

"What's the most you ever got paid at one time?"

"Best was cash, ten thousand dollars . . ."

This is an important revelation, one that establishes Bobby-Ray as a major wildlife trafficker in juvenile crocodilians, with an annual income of eighty thousand dollars. Gregg begins to explore who the other players are in direct competition with him. Dicks does not give him a name but tells him there is only one other group in the state that is a large-volume dealer in black-market gator hatchlings. In fact, he tells the captain that Lake Apopka had already been picked over by someone else. That was one reason he didn't come to the ramp with more hatchlings. He confidently states that he catches, on average, seven thousand gator hatchlings each year from Lake Apopka.

Gregg is curious how Bobby-Ray views himself in comparison to his competition. "In the big scheme of things, who's the big fish?" Gregg asks.

"You got him," Bobby-Ray boasts.

The mental map in Gregg's head is beginning to take shape. Piece by piece, he has carefully extracted nuggets of information from Bobby-Ray. The puzzle pieces begin to fit together. It is time to find out who Bobby-Ray sells to. Gregg suggests that some alligator farms are known to buy unpermitted alligator hatchlings under the table.

"Like I said earlier, I'm not going to tell you any names," Dicks emphasizes.

"Maybe we can work it out where you don't have to tell us a name," Gregg says. "Maybe we already know."

Bobby-Ray shrugs his shoulders, a silent cue that this is a possibility. The criminal creed of "there's no honor among thieves" apparently carries over into the illegal wildlife trade as well.

"What did you do to get rid of ten thousand alligators? Gregg asks. "You don't have to tell me names. Tell me what you did."

"Delivered them to different buyers," Dicks answers.

"How many buyers?"

"Depends on demand."

Don steps out of the room to get a list of all legitimate/permitted gator farms in the state of Florida. There are ten major ones that control hatchling and egg production. They are known within FWC as the "Golden Ten."

The conversation narrows to who exactly Bobby-Ray is selling to. Gregg revisits an earlier question with Bobby-Ray: "You didn't answer my question earlier. It's not that you weren't trying to, we just got sidetracked. Roughly, of the seventeen thousand hatchlings you said you caught over the last two years, what percentage went to the pet industry and what percentage went to alligator farms?"

"Don't know where they send them. They could go either way." A few minutes later Dicks admits to delivering directly to a "farm" within an "hour's" drive of his home, where they are raised for the "hides."

"[That leaves a] big question hanging out there," Gregg says. "Would you be willing to sell to your two buyers for us?"

"Sorry, I can't. The way I look at it, I hadn't done wrong to nobody. Whatever I took out of the river was wild. I feel like I had every right to it. I don't feel like I'm stealing from a soul."

"In your mind, if it's a wild animal it doesn't bother you to do it?"

"Well, in a way, yes. In a way, no. I don't much like breaking the law. But there's nothing you can do that you can't break a law."

Don returns with the list. He turns to Gregg, "Are we at the point where we can throw a name out?"

"He knows we're going to ask him at some point," Gregg answers.

Don holds up an unlined sheet of paper with several names printed in blue ink for Dicks to see. It partially blocks the camera lens. He places his fingertip next to the first name.

"Do you know him?" Don asks.

Bobby-Ray scrunches his face up, puzzled. He leans in closer. His face is less than a foot from the notepad. He has a hard time reading what Don has hastily scribbled. Finally, he shakes his head, no.

Don points to another name. No luck there either.

When he points to the third name, Dicks laughs and says, "You all know the answer to that. Let's put it this way, if you ever do a count there, he's going to lose a lot of paper.[1] He used to be a shyster son-of-a-bitch." Bingo! Gregg and Don have a winner. The name is of a permitted alligator farm in Florida. But not the one Bobby-Ray sells to.

Dicks will not give up the name of his primary buyer. He will only

---

1 That is, if FWC investigators were to conduct an audit, it would reveal the gator farm was allegedly cooking the books.

reveal, in a roundabout fashion, what county the business is located in.

Gregg asks Bobby-Ray if he has anything more he would like to say, or would he like to wrap it up.

"I want to wrap it up," Dicks says.

Dicks asks about his bond. Gregg tells him he hasn't seen the booking report yet. He also tells him he will likely have problems with a bang stick and ammunition found during an inventory of his truck. Bobby-Ray can possess neither since he is a convicted felon. (He will later be charged with possession of ammunition and a firearm by a convicted felon, a third-degree felony.)

Don stands up and turns toward the door, as if to leave. Then, in an artfully executed theatrical move reminiscent of many courtroom television dramas, he appears to change his mind, and turns back to face Bobby-Ray. He causally throws out the name of a gator farm located near Florida's central-east coast. "How long have you been dealing with him?" he asks. For a moment the question hangs lightly in the air, like a delicate feather caught in a gentle updraft. It seems so benign, an innocent afterthought.

"About three or four years," Bobby-Ray says, off the cuff, and without a clue he has just nailed the coffin shut on one of his alleged buyers.

Gregg and Don can finally leave. They got what they came for.

Postscript

The outcome in court fell frustratingly short of what the wardens would like to have seen for a sentence. Dicks was put on probation and paid fines and court costs of $877 for the felony charges of unlawful alligator possession and possession of a firearm/ammunition by a convicted felon.

During a recorded interview, Captain Eason summed up his thoughts on the outcome: "More so than ever in my career, the court system is so jammed, the resource violations do not typically get the glamour and attention they deserve. I was not surprised by the seeming lack of penalty or punishment in this case. Like I told Straub, 'It does not diminish the catch. This is a fabulous example of using good old-fashioned game-warden skills to sit and wait and figure out what's going on and not give up. For many officers, a case like this would be the highlight of their career.'

"Someone like Bobby-Ray Dicks does not stop violating conservation laws. He will not stop. He will get caught again."

★

In what began as a seemingly unrelated case in 2012, FWC Investigator Steve Wayne initiated an investigation into an unlicensed central Florida reptile dealer. Over the next two years, he intercepted fifty-four illegal shipments containing one or more of the following species: alligators, caimans, crocodiles, Nile monitor lizards, green anacondas, and red-eared sliders. The dealer and his partner were selling reptiles over the Internet and by telephone orders. They bilked shipping companies of mailing fees in excess of $1 million by using unmarked boxes with fictitious return addresses for multiple shipping companies. Wayne partnered with the United States Fish and Wildlife Service and the United States Secret Service to bring the case to completion. It was, according to one national commercial shipping firm, the "largest fraud case" in the history of that company. The two suspects were charged with more than two hundred state wildlife violations and federal felony violations for the Lacey Act (false labeling), Lacey Act (wildlife trafficking), bank fraud, mail fraud, aggravated identify theft, and conspiracy.

In an interesting twist of happenstance, one of the two targets in this case happened to be the man Bobby-Ray Dicks unwittingly gave to Capt. Gregg Eason and Lt. Don McMillen during the interview.

In early 2016, FWC announced that Steve Wayne received the prestigious award for 2016 Investigator of the Year.

17

SHOT ALL TO HELL

On the hot and humid evening of July 15, 2009, Christopher Eddy and his girlfriend headed out for a secluded place to get away. Eddy knew of just the spot where they could be alone in a remote patch of Brevard County scrubland—fifteen miles west of the Kennedy Space Center. It was an area well away from the prying eyes of nosy tourists and alert homeowners, like out at the end of Satellite Boulevard, where the smooth dirt stops and the county motor-graders have to turn around. Marginal land gouged out with drainage canals and covered in tangled brush. Bug-infested, crawling with snakes, prone to sporadic flooding—the kind of place where if the ground shook and the leaves fell from an earth-rattling explosion no one would notice.

The couple's backcountry jaunt was intended to be a fun time for Eddy, and an occasion for him to pursue his favorite, albeit extremely dangerous, hobby. Police reports would later show that he was darn good at it, too. Christopher Eddy was a bomb maker. He loved to blow things up.

Up to this point, the twenty-three-year-old Eddy had moved through life like an errant pinball that had somehow managed to make it around all the hard obstacles without getting nicked. But his luck was about to run out. Ditto for a forty-three-year-old lawman named Vann Streety, a ten-year veteran game warden who happened to be on routine patrol that day.

The warden's world was about to become a living nightmare.

★

Eddy stood five nine, had dark close-cropped hair, a narrow face, and a lean, wiry frame that tipped the scales at 170. But his eyes, his most disturbing feature, were like black pits, empty and hollow, so intense they made you want to look away.

The young man grasped the steering wheel of a silver 2006 Kia sport-utility vehicle as it bumped along on an uneven sandy track that wove through a desolate tract of land—a half mile before it would dump out into the north end of Satellite Boulevard. Beside him sat his girlfriend, Tammie Temple, who was thirty-seven and slender with waist-length dark-brown hair. The two had known each other for four years and had been living together for the past four months. She was the breadwinner. He hadn't hit a lick at work in two years.

Back in the rented apartment he shared with Temple and her ten-year-old son was a selection of bomb-making materials that would have made a terrorist proud: TAPT, used in suicide attacks and extremely volatile; nitroglycerine, a component of dynamite; another explosive similar to what the Al-Qaeda shoe bomber used; and gun cotton, a component of modern smokeless gunpowder.

In everyday conversation, Eddy came across as coarse and not particularly literate. But ask him to explain complex chemicals used to make explosives and how they interacted, and you'd think you were listening to a lecture from a trained chemist. The Internet had been his teacher since he was thirteen, and he'd been a devout student.

So far, Eddy's day had gone pretty well. He'd driven out with his girlfriend to a section of remote land beyond Satellite Boulevard and blown up some TAPT, because he knew it was "getting old and becoming unstable."

Awash in happy thoughts of a successful detonation, he peered out through the windshield and beyond the hood and saw a disturbing sight, a shiny silver F-150 pickup nosing toward him in the distance.

On top of the cab was a slender emergency blue light bar covered in clear Plexiglas. Stuck to the side door panels were green, white, and black decals that read, "Florida Fish and Wildlife Conservation Commission."

Eddy had just smoked a joint. He had an outstanding traffic warrant. All of little consequence, really; at the most, a lawman might lock him up for a night in jail. But Eddy didn't see it that way. Cops continually harassed him with these piddling tickets. Why couldn't they just leave him the hell alone? He had no money. He had no job. How was he supposed to come up with the money to pay the fines? It wasn't his fault.

It also wasn't his fault when the fly-by-night gold-mining operation in Colorado went bust after one month, or when his boss at the underground cable company "let him go." It wasn't his fault when he decided to opt out of the U.S. Coast Guard after only two months. Nor was it his fault that his girlfriend continually badgered him about money and pressured him to find a job.

One day Eddy finally caved and told Temple he'd found employment as a security guard. He lied. He solved the problem of a paycheck by hocking his dad's guns. Inside his head, the pressure was building. He did not like being told what to do, and he'd about had enough.

All Christopher Eddy ever wanted out of life was the freedom to tinker with his bombs and blow them up. And any authority figure that got in his way would have hell to pay.

Earlier that day, Warden Vann Streety took his meal break at home. His mother was visiting and had cooked a wonderful dinner of homemade spaghetti, served with a fresh Caesar salad and a basket of piping-hot garlic bread. Seated around the table were his three children: two-year-old twins, a boy and girl; and his four-year-old son, a kindergartner. He was a single dad and appreciated it whenever his mom could spare the time to take care of the kids. Talk quickly turned to church and where his mother had sung lately. She was a

Warden Vann Streety (now a lieutenant) in uniform, 2011.

classically trained opera singer and donated her time and talents to local churches in her hometown of Palatka, in northeast Florida.

Vann sang, too. In high school, he was the drum major for the marching band and also played the trumpet. He was on the soccer team and ran cross-country, mostly 5K races. Before joining FWC in 1998, he spent ten years working as an emergency medical technician running ambulance calls for Tallahassee Memorial Hospital.

Vann was "vertically challenged" as he jokingly liked to refer to his five-foot-six stature. He had a tight, trim build; jet-black hair; blue eyes, alert and penetrating; and precise, energetic movements. He spoke the same way he moved—in crisp, clean sentences, carefully drawing each word from a deep-well vocabulary.

Put Vann in cowboy boots, dark jeans, a tight-fitting T-shirt, and a rodeo belt buckle, and he could easily double as a Nashville country-music star. He had that kind of look.

Vann had been a member of the elite FWC Special Operations Group teams (FWC's version of a rural SWAT team) on September 28, 2006, when the cop killer Angelo Freeland went to ground in an area of dense, junglelike terrain east of Lakeland in central Florida. Freeland had killed a Polk County K-9 deputy and his dog, wounded another deputy, and got into a shootout with two Lakeland police officers.

The following day Vann was one of two hundred special weapons and tactics team members who walked shoulder to shoulder searching three hundred acres of shallow ponds, scrub oak thickets, and old-growth tree hammocks for Freeland. Around ten in the morning Vann found Freeland hiding under a fallen oak tree tented in matted vines. The man who had become the target of the biggest manhunt in Polk County history lay in total darkness, hidden beneath tangled mats of bright-green leafy vegetation that blocked all sunlight from penetrating below. Vann used his weapon's mounted light to illuminate Freeland's face and head. The black beard and scraggly dreadlocks helped confirm who he was.

Vann screamed, "Let me see your hands! Let me see your hands!"

Hearing the shouts, fellow officers swarmed to his position and joined in issuing shouted commands to reveal his hands.

Freeland's hands were covered by what looked like a blanket. He pulled his left hand out, fingers spread as wide as they could be, shaking. But his right hand remained hidden by the cloth. FWC Lt. Roger Brutus darted in and snatched it away. Freeland brandished a silver-colored .45-caliber pistol (taken from the slain deputy) in his right hand.

Officers who had a clean shot acted from firearms training classes and the gut instinct to survive. FWC Officer Rob Miller fired the first round from a Marine Magnum .870 12-gauge pump shotgun. A millisecond later Vann emptied five rounds into him with a .223 Bushmaster semiautomatic rifle.

By now a barrage of gunfire had erupted, some weapons cycling on full auto. Bullets flew everywhere, kicking up dust, shredding vines, knocking chunks of bark from the trunk of the fallen oak. In the span of three to four seconds, nine officers—including four FWC SOG Team members—fired eighty-nine rounds at Freeland. When his body arrived at the morgue it was little more than diced mincemeat. To the considerable credit and skill of the medical examiner, he was able to count sixty-eight distinct bullet holes, one shot under his left eye, eleven to his torso, and fifty-six in his legs and arms.

"He wasn't running anywhere," Vann later told a *Lakeland Ledger* reporter during an interview. "The only thing he had to do was to shoot or give up. And he was not giving up."

On June 14, 2007, the *Ledger* wrote, "In a press conference today, Polk Sheriff Grady Judd said Freeland served as an assassin. . . . Officials suspect him of killing up to fifteen people in Latin America for not paying their drug debts. They are unsure if he killed anyone in Florida, but are still investigating that angle.

"Freeland was 'pure evil in the flesh,'" Judd said.

★

Vann glanced at his watch, pushed away from the dinner table, and whisked everyone outside in time to watch the space shuttle *Endeavour* launch. Afterward, he kissed his children and his mom good-bye and climbed into his state ride, a silver F-150 four-wheel-drive pickup. He carefully fitted an electronic earbud—wired to his shoulder mic—into his left ear. He pressed the talk button and told dispatch he was "Ten-eight [in-service]."

His first order of business was to follow up on a tip about a man living on a canal in a nearby trailer park who was illegally feeding alligators. Upon arriving home from work, the homeowner would habitually feed the gators by tossing them rolled-up bread balls. Vann set up on the culprit, but he was a no-show. Instead, a neighbor showed up with a rod and reel and repeatedly cast at a gator trying to snag it. Vann let him go with a warning.

After working the complaint, Vann wondered, "Well, what else am I going to do this evening?" He shuffled through a mental Rolodex of likely spots to patrol and decided on an undeveloped tract of land north of Satellite Boulevard. The area had become known to law enforcement for a seemingly endless list of violations: littering, trespass, marijuana growing, deer poaching, and no fishing license were just a few of the potential cases that might come out of this kind of dystopian no-man's land. It was an area more suitable for the backdrop to a Mad Max movie than a nature park, given the heaps of loose trash, piles of building debris, old tires, and broken appliances discarded at random up and down the road.

As Vann approached the north end of Satellite, he pulled off onto the shoulder and parked. Ahead was the turnoff for a two-rut track—in some places no more than a pig trail—that swept northeast through the woods for about four miles until it came to a dead end. He disembarked from his patrol truck and crept up to the corner, took his binoculars, and focused them down the road. The woods trail was sandy and dry with dips and swales and humps that weaved unevenly through the vacant land. Nearly impenetrable walls of brush and scrub pushed in from both sides.

About a half mile away was a white pickup parked crossways in the road. A man was outside the truck, bent over, picking up spent bullet casings. The yellow license tag told Vann it was a county employee. Vann recognized him and decided to say hello.

The warden clambered back into the F-150 and turned onto the woods track. He steered through the humps and dips and pulled up next to the county truck. He asked the man if he'd heard any gunshots or seen anyone. He told Vann, no. Right about then, Vann saw a patch of silver paint and part of a lit car headlamp coming his way. Then it dropped out of sight as the driver wheeled through a dry washout and came back into view again as it crested higher ground. Vann could clearly see both headlights shining. The car looked like a Kia SUV.

Vann bid farewell to the county employee, who climbed into his pickup and headed out to Satellite. Vann steered his state ride in the opposite direction toward the Kia.

Even in a desolate area like this, the rights of private property owners have to be upheld. Vann had received complaints of deer poaching, littering, and trespass from several landowners who owned five- and ten-acre parcels of property fronting the sandy woods track. The warden decided to stop the car and question the driver about his motives for being out there.

Any cop will tell you that a head-to-head traffic stop is the least preferred and one of the most dangerous. But game wardens do it all the time. They have no choice. You can't pick and choose how to stop a vehicle in the woods because they can suddenly appear from anywhere—a side road, from behind, or in front. You have to learn to work with the situation as it unfolds.

Vann toggled the emergency blue lights on and parked his F-150 so it was diagonally blocking the road. The Kia came to a stop in the middle of the road, just a few yards away. A young man in his twenties, clean-shaven, sat behind the steering wheel. In the passenger seat sat a woman, a little older, with long brown hair.

The time was 8:03 p.m. The sun hung low in the western horizon while tall trees cast long, dark shadows across the sandy track. But there was still plenty of ambient light left to see by.

Vann walked toward the Kia, eyes on the driver, assessing his next move should the driver suddenly hit the gas. "He's in a two-wheel-drive," Vann recalled, "a compact SUV with street tires. Even if he came at me, he would have to spin the tires, and that would give me time to take evasive action. I'm thinking of all this as I'm approaching him."

Vann stood behind the Kia's doorpost to address the driver. "Hi, my name is Officer Vann Streety with FWC."

"Why did you stop me?" the driver answered, clearly agitated. "This is a violation of my rights. You have no right to stop me."

"Time out, let's start over," Vann said, as he calmly repeated the introduction. He explained there had been complaints from property owners of trespass and asked the driver what he was doing out there.

"I own property out here," the driver said.

"Then you should understand what I'm doing. I'm looking into incidents of illegal hunting and dumping."

"Yeah, I know people dump all kinds of stuff on my property."

"Well, fine. You should understand then that I'm working for you."

"Oh, you still don't have any right to stop me," the driver insisted. "This is a violation of my rights."

"May I see your driver's license, please?" Reluctantly, the driver dug out a laminated Florida driver's license and handed it over to Vann.

Vann tucked his head slightly and spoke into the shoulder mic. He asked for a warrant check using brief number codes. Because of the earbud, only Vann could hear the dispatcher's response.

By now Christopher Eddy was bouncing up and down in the seat, mouthing off. Then he leaned forward.

Vann caught the movement. "Do me a favor and keep both hands on the steering wheel," ordered Vann, whose vision had now become laser focused.

"This is bullshit. You have no right to stop me."

Vann got a whiff of burnt marijuana. There is no other smell like it. He leaned into the open window and asked, "Ma'am what is your name?"

She froze, staring straight out through the windshield as if she was in a catatonic trance.

"What is your name?"

She turned her head and gazed at Vann with a cold, blank stare. "Tammie," she answered, and slowly returned her attention to the examination of some random object in the far distance.

"This was a huge red flag for me," Vann said. "She was scared to death and as nervous as a long-tailed cat in a room full of rocking chairs."

Vann ordered Eddy out of the vehicle and had him step back to the rear of the Kia. He jumped out barefoot, wearing a white T-shirt emblazoned with the image of Jesus and brown surf shorts. "Where is the dope I smell on you and in your car?" Vann asked.

"I don't smoke that crap," Eddy said, while nervously pacing back and forth and gesturing wildly with both arms.

Dispatch informed Vann that Eddy had an outstanding warrant for a misdemeanor traffic violation.

"You have an outstanding warrant," Vann told him. "Turn around and interlace your fingers behind your head. You're under arrest."

Eddy only partially complied. Then he bolted toward the front of the Kia. When he reached the driver's door, he grabbed the handle and began to pull it open.

Vann followed as he drew an expandable baton with his left hand and struck Eddy across the upper right arm with a stinging blow. Unfazed, Eddy swung the door wide and reached down toward the inside door pocket.

Vann saw the partially exposed grip of a stainless-steel semiautomatic pistol. He dropped the baton and shoved his right hand straight down on top of his duty holster. During firearms qualifications on the three-yard line, Vann can draw, fire, and hit a man-sized target in .98 seconds with a 9mm Glock 17. But Eddy didn't have to undo two retention snaps on a holster. He didn't have to rock it back to release it. He only had to pick up an unsecured firearm with the grip already up, ready to meet the palm of his hand.

Eddy beat Vann to the draw. He wielded a ten-shot .45 Astra A100 semiautomatic pistol. A frightening weapon, it can turn an armadillo inside out. The nearly half-inch-diameter bullet can bore a massive wound channel through human flesh and vital organs.

Eddy's eyes zeroed in on Vann's gun hand. He shot from the hip, gunslinger style. The bullet nearly sliced Vann's right hand in half, fracturing a knuckle and breaking four metacarpal bones before it exited and struck the top of his service pistol, disabling it. The gunshot wound left Vann's shooting hand grossly disfigured and worthless. He was now living every lawman's worst nightmare. The bad guy had the advantage.

"I didn't know he'd hit my hand," Vann recalled. "There was only time for one thought, 'Oh, shit, there's a gun.' Give me half a second more and I would have had my gun out putting lead downrange. I've done it a thousand times before."

After Eddy popped off the first round he ran away from Vann and took cover behind the patrol truck, on the driver's side.

Vann began moving too. He ended up on the opposite side of the F-150 from Eddy. The two men were separated by only thirty feet. A toddler could have easily tossed a rubber ball that distance, underhand.

"I'm trying to get my gun out, and I don't know why I can't," Vann said. "I didn't know I'd been hit. I'm thinking, 'Why the hell can't I get my gun out?' All I was doing—with my hand gimped up—was pushing down on the weapon. It felt like I had a death grip on the gun and me yanking and pulling. The damn thing just wouldn't come out of the holster. That's what my brain was telling me I was doing. I could not close my fingers, and I didn't know it."

Eddy looked Vann square in the eye and raised the gun. Vann stared straight down the muzzle. It looked huge.

"Aw, shit!" Vann thought, as he squatted in the middle of the road. He was in the open and couldn't return fire. He and Eddy were separated by the front tires, the engine block, and hood of the F-150.

Eddy tracked Vann with the .45's barrel as he dropped below the hood.

Bang!

The second round punched straight through the sheet metal of the patrol truck's hood, bounced off the top cover of the fuel injector, slammed into the underside of the hood and stopped.

"When he fired that round, I was in a squatting position," Vann said. "The realization had sunk home big time: I'm in a gunfight. I've been shot at twice. I can't get my gun out, and I don't know why. I'm getting my ass handed to me. I've got to go!"

Just like a wounded deer, Vann followed the path of least resistance. He pounded south down the hard-packed sand track. Dense walls of subtropical growth crowded in from both sides: gnarly trees, scrub brush, tangled vines, and native palms forced Vann to stay in the open. He'd just stepped into hell's shooting gallery.

Vann had to put space between him and the threat. It was the only chance he had of surviving. If he stopped, he died.

Bang!

"That one's in my vest," Vann told himself and continued to haul ass. It felt like he'd been hit in the back by a lumberjack swinging a twelve-pound sledgehammer.

Bang!

"That's another one in my vest," Vann thought. It was becoming an uncomfortable mantra.

Maybe it was luck, maybe divine guidance, when Vann Streety's badge, along with a commemorative challenge coin (not shown), stopped a .45-caliber bullet, 2009.

Incredibly, both rounds were separated by only two inches and landed dead center above his lower spine. Unfortunately for Vann, Eddy happened to be a crack shot with a .45. Given the display of marksmanship so far, how much longer could the warden's luck hold out?

Bang!

The fifth round hit a leather wallet in his right hip pocket, where there happened to be a silver-dollar-sized commemorative coin and his badge. The bullet struck them dead on, expending all of its energy upon impact.

Bang!

The sixth round hit an all-metal, multipurpose Gerber tool attached to Vann's gun belt. It ricocheted off and embedded two to three inches deep in the soft flesh of his hip.

Vann was still running all-out—in a race for his life—driven by an incredible adrenaline dump. He became top-heavy and pitched forward. "I caught myself with both hands," Vann recalled. "My feet kept turning over, and I bounced right back up into a running position."

But no matter how fast he ran or how hard he tried to tap into the stamina and speed he once had as a skinny high school teenager running 5K cross-country meets, he could never beat a 230-grain copper-jacketed bullet traveling at almost nine hundred feet per second. From forty yards away, the bullet would impact on target in about one-tenth of a second—in the blink of an eye.

Bang!

If the sand in an hourglass represented how much luck Vann had left in his life, there would be one teaspoon left. "I remember seeing the shirtsleeve on my left arm puff out," Vann said. "There was a little noise like air escaping. I didn't feel anything. There was very little bleeding."

Thanks to Eddy, Vann now had a new joint. The bullet shattered the upper humerus on impact. With each stride, the arm beneath the break swung manically out of control. It slapped him in the face like a flaccid slab of bacon before wrapping around the back of his head. Then it would flop down and fly up again. Up. *Slap*. Down. Up. *Slap*. Down. "I knew that wasn't good," Vann said, during a moment of understated reflection. "But at least the shooting had stopped."

Up to this point, Vann never once looked behind. "I felt if I had looked back," Vann explained, "I just knew I would get tackled. I didn't know if Eddy was shooting from a stationary position or running and gunning right behind me down the road."

Vann sneaked a peek over one shoulder and saw his patrol truck and the Kia, maybe fifty to seventy-five yards away. But he did not see the shooter.

Time to reassess. He asked himself, "Where is my gun?" For the first time he looked down at his right hand. "Oh, shit!" Now he knew why he couldn't get his gun out. His right hand was all gimped up and bleeding. He couldn't make a fist. He peered up into the sky, asking, "God, what do I do now? Nobody knows I'm in this."

Instinctively, he reached for the shoulder mic to key it up. All he ended up doing was pawing it with his worthless right hand. "Aw, crap," he thought. "How am I going to solve the problem?" Vann looked down and wiggled the fingers in his left hand. He still had full articulation of them. He scooped up the left hand and forearm with his right arm, and folded it in, bending it at the left elbow. Now he could lay his left hand on top of his left shoulder where the mic was clipped. He squeezed the talk button.

Gasping, exhausted, and out of breath, Vann issued a desperate call for help. (What follows is a partial transcript of that radio call.)

VANN: I need a medical helicopter. I've been shot multiple times. 520 and Satellite Road. I'm at the north end of Satellite Road. I'm at what they call the shooting range [a wide spot in the woods road where target shooting takes place]. Both of my arms are just about inoperable. I need a medical helicopter now! Do you copy?

DISPATCH: We have multiple units ten-fifty-one [en route].

VANN: How about a helicopter?

DISPATCH: Medical helicopter ten-fifty-one.

VANN: Ten-four. When the suspect returns I'm not going to be able to fight back. My arms and hands are disabled. Get here fast!

After the call, Vann edged to the east side of the road. Underneath a Brazilian pepper tree grown over the dirt track he found partial concealment. "I was looking at my weapon," Vann said, "and felt my left hand coming around behind my back, like we're trained to do when the right arm becomes immobilized. We're trained to come behind with the left hand, grab the gun belt, and tug it until the holster is close enough for the weapon to be drawn. I'm watching the weapon, and all the time my brain is telling me my left arm is doing everything it's supposed to do. But it wasn't doing anything. It was like the ghost itching someone has six months after an amputation. So I abandoned the idea of drawing my duty sidearm."

Vann needed a gun. He lunged forward on his left leg, knee bent, left foot flat on the ground, his right knee planted firmly in the dirt behind. Using his good right arm, he worked it up underneath his functioning left hand. He leaned forward, manually grabbed the pants cuff of his left leg, and slid it up until an ankle holster was exposed. Using the one good arm, he placed his one good hand on the grip of his backup pistol, a 9mm Kahr. The fingers and palm of his left hand wrapped around the gun. He pulled that hand up and back by raising his right forearm. He had drawn the weapon. He was finally armed. Vann knew the fight was not over. Eddy's escape route led right past him.

Vann stole a glance down the road. No movement. He believed Eddy would continue to stalk him. The armament remaining in his patrol truck could start a small war. He was very concerned. If Eddy got his hands on the M-4 assault rifle with a thirty-round magazine filled with .223-caliber ammo, it could be all over for him. The ballistic vest he wore would not stop a round from a high-powered rifle.

"I am dead," Vann said, "if he comes at me with that gun. And just briefly I pictured my uniformed body lying on that dirt road. The picture in my mind came from what I've seen in the past: traumatic gunshot wounds to the head with half of the skull missing, the hair all matted with blood and the brain exposed and covered in dirt. I momentarily transposed myself with one of those unfortunate victims. I told myself, 'Absolutely fricking not. I am not going to be found like that.' I decided I had to get the hell out of there. I took off running again. I glanced over my shoulder just to check, and here he comes."

The Kia bounced slowly closer. The daytime headlamps remained on. In the waning daylight they shined a little less brightly than at night.

Vann was exhausted. The adrenaline, the injuries, and the shock had taken a toll. "I made a conscious decision right then," Vann said. "If he was going to try to kill me today, he was going to have to follow me into the woods to do it. So I made a hard left and dove into the brush."

Vann lowered his head and shoulders like a running back and plowed ahead. But Vann wasn't in the NFL. He didn't weigh 240 pounds. In comparison, he was a lightweight at 145 and lacked the heft and brawn to bulldoze. And he'd lost the use of the two most important appendages needed to break a trail. He made it about fifteen feet and fell face first. His feet tangled in vines. He couldn't free himself because his one good hand still clutched the backup pistol. He heard the Kia's engine approaching. He rolled onto his back, brought the gun to his chest and propped his left hand up with his good arm so he could shoot down his back trail. The working arm subbed as a sandbag—a brace to support his gun hand and fire his weapon from. Elevation and horizontal sight shifts could be made by adjusting the position of the right forearm.

This was Vann's Alamo. His back was against the wall. With three kids at home who needed a dad, he mentally prepared to defend this position lying flat on his back and fight to the death. Within the next second or two he expected to be fully engaged in an all-out gun battle with Eddy.

To see Vann, all Eddy had to do was turn his head and look to the left—out the driver's window—as he passed by the warden's entry point into the woods.

The metallic hiss of a four-cylinder car engine became increasingly louder. Vann tilted his head up. He watched a patch of silver emerge through the tall grass and weeds beyond his feet. The SUV's front bumper . . . door panel . . . rear bumper . . . crawled through his limited field of vision and stopped one car length away from where Vann had stepped into the woods. The rear bumper was barely visible through the undergrowth.

Christopher Eddy couldn't be sure exactly where Vann ducked into the woods. He'd prepared for a shootout though. Earlier, he re-loaded the pistol with a fresh magazine holding nine live rounds of .45 ammo. Thankfully, Eddy wasn't an expert woodsman who knew how to track. If he had been, it would have been a simple effort to fol-low Vann's boot prints or look for the small drops of bright-red blood soaked into white sand. Any Cub Scout could have done it.

One thought weighed heavily on Vann as he eyed the SUV: "Will Eddy stay in the Kia or get out and actively hunt for me on foot?"

The question was answered when Eddy stuck the big semiauto outside the driver's window and blindly fired. A barrage of gunfire erupted as bumblebee-sized slugs ripped through the bushes near Vann. (An investigation would later establish he'd fired ten rounds.)

Inside the Kia, Tammie Temple screamed at Eddy, "What are you doing? What are you doing?"

"I'm sorry," Eddy told her.

Then the Kia sped away.

Vann watched. He listened. He waited. His breathing was ragged, but he did his best to still it. In spite of everything he'd gone through, he still felt in total control. After a couple of minutes he stood up and crept out to the edge of the road. He looked south toward the intersection of Satellite and Cherven, which was several hundred yards away. The Kia was stopped at the intersection. Vann speculated that Eddy was trying to figure out which way to go. Then it turned left onto Cherven and disappeared out of sight.

"At this point," Vann recalled, "I don't know definitively if Eddy was gone for good or wouldn't come back to look for me. But I decided to step back into the open and risk running for my patrol truck, which was roughly the length of a football field away. The exertion put my pulse off the charts—maybe two hundred beats per minute. It felt like a sledgehammer beating against the inside of my chest. Then I became concerned about the brachial artery in my left arm. Did it sustain major damage from the bullet? If it did, and as fast as my heart was pumping, I could have bled out. I needed to put a tourniquet on it."

Vann staggered up to his patrol truck. His breathing labored. It was the most grueling hundred-yard sprint he'd ever run in his life. The total time elapsed from when he first stopped Eddy was maybe seven to eight minutes.

Vann thought about what to use for a tourniquet. He wanted to remove his gun belt to get to his regular belt and use it. But that was impossible. He had no fully functioning upper appendages. Then he considered using his mic cord, but that wouldn't work for the same reason. "The tourniquet would have to be tied high," Vann explained, "just below the head of the humerus, up under the armpit. I abandoned that idea. If you can't tie a tourniquet, direct pressure is the next best thing. So I leaned in through the open door of my patrol truck and pushed my upper left arm and body against the side of the seat. I still had my backup weapon clutched to my chest."

Then dispatch called to check on Vann. The dispatcher was new. Instead of reassuring him that help was on the way, she kept asking if he was 10–4.

"Every time she called," Vann said, "I had to answer as I'm leaning in. The seat's right in front of me and I have the mobile mic [for the truck radio] lying there. I have to release pressure, lay the weapon down, grab the mic, talk, put the mic down, grab the gun, and apply pressure again. That's when you can hear the anxiety in my voice. After doing this for five or six times, I'm like 'Holy crap,' someone please just drive down Satellite and find me!'"

A Brevard County sheriff's deputy rolled up on the scene first. He jumped out with an AR15 semiautomatic rifle ready to rock and roll.

"The threat's gone," Vann told him. He followed up with a quick explanation of his background as an EMT.

"What do you need for me to do?" asked the deputy, who would not normally defer to anyone but made an exception in Vann's case because of his experience as an emergency first responder.

"A tourniquet. Now!" Vann said. "Get your first-aid kit out of the trunk and come over here with it. We'll figure out something."

They made a tourniquet from a bandage. The deputy wrapped it around Vann's upper left arm and cinched it down tight. "It hurt like hell," Vann remembered.

The deputy checked Vann's wrist for a pulse and couldn't find one. He asked Vann, "Now what do you need?"

"I need to lie down," Vann said. "I'm about to pass out."

An FHP trooper arrived a few minutes later. He and the deputy loaded Vann into the bed of the F-150 pickup and drove him about two hundred yards to the intersection of Cherven Road and Satellite Boulevard, where an ambulance shuttled him to a temporary command post and improvised heliport at a Chevron Service Station a few miles down the road. The welcoming thrum of a life-flight chopper could be heard coming Vann's way.

Indeed, Warden Vann Streety was shot all to hell. But he would eventually recover and return to work.

Friday, July 17, 6:15 p.m.

After forty-six hours on the run, Christopher Eddy was bug-bitten, hungry, with no mobile communication device and only eighty-five cents in coins left in his pockets. He wore a filthy white T-shirt and knee-length board shorts. His hair was disheveled and a shadow of unruly stubble sprouted from his chin.

He'd tried to steal a car from Juan Ponce de Leon Landing, a small county park in Melbourne Beach, when an armed homeowner approached him. Eddy ran away yelling, "I'm homeless. I'm homeless." Local law enforcement cordoned off the area. Cops take care of their own, regardless of the color of the uniform or agency mission. Eddy was going down, one way or the other.

Eddy made a wise choice when he surrendered to a Brevard County sheriff's deputy who found him hiding in the sand dunes. Inside a small box buried in the sand was the .45 Eddy used to shoot Vann. Deputies would recover it later.

Orlando Channel 2 News rolled up on the scene. As the event was captured on film, the sheriff's deputy—dressed in a sharply creased, dark-green uniform—can be seen escorting a handcuffed Eddy by the elbow. They push through pockets and drifts of soft, sugary sand and emerge from a gap between palmetto-covered dunes.

Eddy and his law enforcement escort made a beeline for the nearest squad car. The camera and sound continue to roll.

"Why did I shoot the person?" Eddy repeated, after being asked the question by the local television reporter.

The deputy, who was about to stuff Eddy inside the green-and-white, likely sensed a confession in the offing. What a wonderful opportunity to let the prisoner speak without the worry of legal technicalities like the Miranda warning. Anything Eddy said to the press could be used later in court against him. The deputy braced Eddy against the back door of the squad car and allowed him to answer the question.

"Because I felt my freedom was being violated," Eddy replied, while glaring back at the camera. "If I wanted to kill him, I could have, but I shot him in the vest on purpose."

Even if the viewers of the eleven o'clock nightly news had never heard those words spoken, Eddy's eyes told it all. They were dark and vacant, void of any remorse. In a few hours detectives would be equally astounded by his unfiltered comments.

Later that evening Special Agent (SA) David M. Lee of the Florida Department of Law Enforcement and Lt. Todd Goodyear of the Brevard County Sheriff's Office conducted an interview with Eddy. Eddy was not shy about offering up information as to why he shot Vann and about his unusual hobby of building bombs.

The investigators told Eddy that the sheriff's department bomb squad detonated his bomb-making materials out in the street in front of the apartment he and Temple shared. The chemicals, along with a shrapnel bomb, were so volatile that a remote-controlled robot was used to remove them. SA Lee was standing at the end of the street when it went off.

MR. EDDY: Oh my God, did they set everything off at one time?
SA LEE: I felt the shock wave.
MR. EDDY: That stuff's awesome . . .

Later in the interview Eddy offered up these personal insights into his abilities to handle firearms and explosives.

MR. EDDY: Blow any damn thing up I wanted to, shoot up anybody. I ain't going to miss. I could have robbed anybody, blown up—could have done all that stuff and had you guys absolutely out there going haywire over somebody. But me . . . I'm not violent. . . . I don't like violence.

The discussion drifted back to the topic of why he shot Vann Streety.

MR. EDDY: Yeah, I shot him [Vann Streety], but I mean he had a vest on. . . . If I wanted to, I could have popped him in the head and killed him, but that was not my intention. . . . Y'all go [get] one of them psychiatrists that show you the things that [where they] really know how to get inside people's head and stuff and you can find out that I'm a good person.

Right.

The Aftermath

Vann spent fourteen months recuperating from the gunshot wounds before returning to his regular patrol beat. He had one operation to surgically implant a titanium rod into his upper left arm to replace the shattered humerus. He had two reconstructive surgeries on his right hand so he could eventually use it for something other than a gnarled club. Today, that hand is strong, but he still has trouble fully closing it around a narrow object like the handle of a hammer.

Fellow FWC officers, family, friends, and neighbors chipped in personal time to cook meals, clean house, and transport his children to and from school for the month or so he was unable to drive. Veritable shifts of help were scheduled 24/7 so he would not undergo the burden of raising three children under the age of five alone while hindered by a lengthy physical rehabilitation. "What this meant to me," Vann explained, "was that I didn't have to do this by myself. I had a vast network of friends and family that selflessly gave everything: emotional, physical, and monetary support. It meant being able to recuperate without having to worry about everyday life things."

Two-and-a-half years later, Vann would face yet another hurdle—the trial of Christopher Eddy. What he found most unsettling was being tried like the suspect in a crime. "The defense," Vann recalled, "tried to paint me as someone I knew I wasn't: an overbearing, overzealous rogue cop who would violate people's rights and make bad arrests. That assertion was baseless. Anybody who knew me, or had been checked by me or worked with me in the past would know that was not the kind of person I was. They even pulled my personnel file searching for complaints. But there were no complaints. My file was clean.

"By this time I'd forgiven Eddy for what he did and was at peace with letting the court system and God have the final say on what would happen to him."

Eddy's defense was based on Florida's "stand your ground" law, which generally means someone has a right to use force in self-defense without an obligation to retreat first. They argued that Van's initial traffic stop of Eddy was illegal. They argued that Eddy was illegally detained. And that Vann abused his authority when he attempted to arrest Eddy for the outstanding warrant and later struck him with the baton when Eddy resisted.

In Vann's opinion, it was an outrageous and desperate argument to begin with. The jury agreed. On October 14, 2011, Eddy was convicted for six counts of attempted first-degree felony murder of a law enforcement officer and for six counts of aggravated battery of a law enforcement officer. On January 5, 2012, Circuit Judge Morgan Reinman sentenced Eddy to five life sentences to be served consecutively.

One would think, given the ample time provided for sober reflection during the twenty-nine months Eddy sat in a jail cell awaiting trial, his subsequent conviction, and a harsh but fair sentence meted out by the judge, that a moral window would have opened within his soul. Surely he would have come to regret the decision to shoot Warden Vann Streety multiple times.

One would be wrong.

After having been sentenced to the five life terms, and as Eddy left the courtroom that day on his way down the elevator, an officer asked him if he had any regrets.

"Fuck, no," he snarled.

Christopher Eddy is in a better place, and so are we, the good citizens and visitors of Florida, who will be forever shielded from a happenstance meeting with someone who is, in every sense of the words, "a ticking time bomb!"

Author's Note

Tammie Temple lied when interviewed by police. She intentionally misdirected them by saying Eddy had thrown the .45 Astra pistol into the woods before they fled from the woods north of Satellite Boulevard. She also failed to tell them of another young man who became an accomplice by picking Eddy up and bringing him a fresh change of clothes. During a second interview, Temple admitted to the lies. She was arrested and later convicted for being as "accessory after fact of first-degree felony murder." On February 19, 2010, she was sentenced to two years in prison. The male accomplice received the same punishment.

ACKNOWLEDGMENTS

This book could never have reached fruition without the kind help and patient tutelage of a great many folks.

Many thanks to Jack Owen and Jerry Teske of the Putnam Writers Group. After all these years I like think of us as writer battle buddies. Through the ups and downs of hundreds of intense manuscript critiques, we have somehow managed to survive intact, but more importantly, we have kept our good humor and friendship steadfast. And to my longtime friend Chris Christian, an outdoor/freelance writer who is responsible for kick-starting my writing career and admonishing me to never forget "Joe Six-Pack," the typical reader of everything outdoors. Thank you for graciously chewing through every word of the raw manuscript and for offering helpful comments.

To the dedicated wardens and other primary characters in these stories who spent countless hours patiently talking with me on the phone or in person: I can't tell you enough how much I appreciate your help with this project and taking the time to make sure I got the facts right. A heartfelt thanks goes out to, Gray Leonhard, Jeff Hahr, Paul Hoover, Donnie Hudson, Robby Holland, Mike Thomas, George Pottorf, Lance Ham, Ken Pickles, David Straub, John Parrish, Gregg Eason, Don McMillen, Vann Streety, Rich Wilcox, Scott Peterson, Larry Jernstedt, Eric Meade, Steve Stafford, Judge Clements, Richard Rossi, Beverly Raposa, Ron Infantino, Dwain Mobley, Matt Tyre, Randy Bowlin, Bill Head, Ben Allen, Lorri Binford, Curtis Lucas, Steve Wayne, and Curtis Brown.

A special thanks to the notorious outlaw Roger Gunter for once again sharing his stories and giving me a glimpse into the wild life of a serial poacher.

A special note of gratitude goes out to journalist Laura Neme, Ph.D, author of *Animal Investigators* and a contributor to *National Geographic*, and to business owner and outdoorsman James T. "Tom" Mastin. Both took on the enormous job of peer review for the University Press of Florida. They spent countless hours reading the manuscript and then offered insightful comments that helped fashion it into the finished product it is today.

The staff at UPF deserves a special round of applause; professional, efficient, and inspiring are the first adjectives that come to mind when thinking of them. Thanks to my editor, Sian Hunter, who has a fine eye and a deft hand for manuscript critique, and to all the unnamed staff I will likely never hear of, but who toil daily behind the scenes.

Finally, to the inspiration of my wonderful son, Jason, and Karen, my lovely bride of forty years.

INDEX

BOB H. LEE is a former lieutenant and thirty-year veteran of the Florida Fish and Wildlife Conservation Commission (FWC). During his career, he caught hundreds of poachers in the act and through complex wildlife investigations. Prior to his retirement in 2007, he taught man-tracking classes through the FWC Law Enforcement Academy. He also writes freelance articles for law enforcement and outdoor magazines. He lives with his wife, Karen, on eighteen acres next to a secluded lake in south Putnam County. This is his second book.

Connect online: www.bobhlee.com